CURRENT LEGAL PRO

Volume 48
PART I: Annual Review

CURRENT LEGAL PROBLEMS 1995

Volume 48

Part I: Annual Review

Edited by

ANDREW LEWIS

with the assistance of

Jane Holder

On behalf of the Faculty of Laws
University College London

OXFORD UNIVERSITY PRESS
1995

Oxford University Press, Walton Street, Oxford OX2 6DP
Oxford New York
Athens Auckland Bangkok Bombay
Calcutta Cape Town Dar es Salaam Delhi
Florence Hong Kong Istanbul Karachi
Kuala Lumpur Madras Madrid Melbourne
Mexico City Nairobi Paris Singapore
Taipei Tokyo Toronto
and associated companies in
Berlin Ibadan

Oxford is a trade mark of Oxford University Press

Published in the United States
by Oxford University Press Inc., New York

British Library Cataloguing in Publication Data
Data available

Library of Congress Cataloging in Publication Data
Data available
ISBN 0–19–826041–5

1 3 5 7 9 10 8 6 4 2

Typeset by Cambrian Typesetters Frimley, Surrey
Printed in Great Britain
on acid-free paper by
Biddles Ltd., Guildford and King's Lynn

CONTENTS

TABLE OF CASES

Table of Cases

TABLE OF LEGISLATION

European Community Treaty as Amended by the Maastricht Treaty

Treaty on European Union – Maastricht 1992   *151–159*

Table of Legislation

TABLE OF INTERNATIONAL TREATIES AND CONVENTIONS

INTRODUCTION

This, the fourth *Current Legal Problems Annual Review* to be produced by the Faculty of Laws, University College London, is also the first to appear under my editorship, assisted by Jane Holder. The first three volumes of the *Review* were ably edited by my predecessor Ben Pettet to whom is due all credit for having established and maintained the project first conceived by the former Head of the Department at UCL, Professor Bob Hepple. The patterns so established have considerably eased the tasks of their successors. As on previous occasions the *Review* forms Part I of the 1995 *Current Legal Problems* volume, the second part of which, containing the texts of the 1994/5 Current Legal Problems Lecture series, will appear later in the year under the editorship of Professor Michael Freeman.

The established pattern of the *Review* is to provide analysis of some sophistication of developments in six identified key areas: Contract, Tort, Property law, Criminal law, the law of the European Union and Public law. There is some degree of artificiality in the selection of topics, exemplified in this volume by the difficulty encountered by the contributors in Contract and Tort in keeping out of each other's areas. It is also necessarily the case that many significant developments in key areas of the law, for example in Family law and Company law, are not reflected in this volume. Nevertheless the selection is not arbitrary. The essence of this publication is to provide a degree of analysis going beyond the case note which seeks to identify developments in terms of legal principle (and assuredly to criticise where this task has not successfully been carried through in the hurly-burly of forensic life).

I have already referred to the fact that the authors of the reviews of *Contract* and *Tort* both initially identified a number of decisions on concurrent liability and negligent misrepresentation as falling within the scope of their concern.[1] These are here treated in the *Tort* review section but will require careful consideration by those

---

[1] Amongst others *Henderson* v *Merret Syndicates Ltd* [1994] 3 WLR 761; *Spring* v *Guardian Assurance plc* [1994] 3 WLR 354 and *McCullagh* v *Lane Fox* [1994] 08 EG 118.

whose primary interests may lie in the sphere of contract. Within
Property law some rather metaphysical questions about the nature
of both legal and equitable property interests form the main focus
of attention. The cases show the courts, not unnaturally, to be
adept at the manipulation of such issues though the political
question whether such matters are not better treated on general
principle by the Law Commission and eventually Parliament is an
important one: certainly the review underlines that there is a most
pressing need for this sort of intervention in the case of leasehold
tenants' continuing liability. The *Criminal Law* review surveys a
wide range of issues largely concerned with violence to the person
but concludes with an examination of a robust judgment on
children's liability by the not inaptly named Laws J which
demonstrates that the common law retains a vigour and capacity
for principled development in the hands of judges which a perusal
of decisions of the highest courts might on occasion lead one to
doubt.

As with tort and contract the spheres of Public law and European
Union law (now here so identified following the coming into force
of the Maastricht treaty) are not always easy to keep distinct. The
authors of both review sections deal in particular with developments relating to the direct applicability of Union law by national
courts. Whereas the authors of the *Public Law* review rightly see
the decision in the *Equal Opportunities Commission* case[2] as
establishing a significant gain for the review of state action,
including national legislation, which transgresses community law,
the review of EU law itself draws attention to a degree of caution in
the most recent European Court decisions which may presage a
withdrawal from the position thought to have been established in
Factortame and *Emmott*.[3] As the authors of the review conclude it
is indeed to be hoped that this apparent conservatism is to be
explained as a move towards a more politically effective enforcement of Union citizens' rights along the lines of *Francovich*.[4]

This does not exhaust the area of overlap between the subject-
matter of these reviews. The envisaged changes to criminal
procedure now contained in the Criminal Justice and Public Order

[2] [1994] 1 All ER 910.
[3] Case C-213/89 *R* v *Secretary of State for Transport, ex p Factortame* [1990]
ECR I-2433; Case C-208/90 *Emmott* [1991] ECR I-4869.
[4] Joined Cases C-6 & 9/90 *Francovich* and *Bonifaci* [1991] ECR I-5357.

Act, encapsulated in the abolition of the 'right to silence', are the subject of sustained criticism on constitutional principle in the concluding section of the Public law review. Earlier surveys of this question in the pages of *Current Legal Problems* have, as here, been uniformly hostile to the type of change proposed.[5] It will be to be seen whether any effective political pressure can be exerted to minimise the impact of provisions which may prove not merely to be ineffective but also an embarrassment.

Andrew Lewis

University College London
October 1994

---

[5] See D. Galligan, 'The Right to Silence Reconsidered' (1988) 41 *CLP* 69; I. H. Dennis, 'Reconstructing the Law of Criminal Evidence' (1989) 42 *CLP* 21; A. Lewis, 'Bentham's View of the Right to Silence' (1990) 43 *CLP* 135.)

CONTRACT

Stephen A Smith

There have been a number of significant developments in contract law during the past twelve months, albeit across a relatively small range of topics. The most important developments are in the law on undue influence. In *Barclays Bank v O'Brien*,[1] the House of Lord's introduced a new framework for determining when a surety may have a security set aside because of the undue influence of a third party, while in *CIBC Mortgages plc v Pitt*[2] the same court rewrote the law on the need to prove manifest disadvantage in cases of actual undue influence. A third decision on undue influence, *Cheese v Thomas*,[3] focused on remedial issues, but the Court of Appeal's novel decision to 'split the losses' raises fundamental questions about what it means to be 'unduly influenced'.

As in last year's *Annual Review*, remedies—and in particular the compensation principle and its relationship to equitable relief—are the subject of two important decisions. The judgments in *Ruxley Electronics Ltd v Forsyth*[4]—where damages were awarded for cost of repair rather than diminution in value—and *Jaggard v Sawyer*[5]—where damages were awarded for 'lost opportunity to bargain'—show that the judiciary is still experiencing real difficulties in this, admittedly complex, area of the law.

Developments in the two other topics considered in this year's *Review* are less significant. Under the heading of 'unfair contract terms', we check on the government's progress in responding to the EEC Directive on Unfair Contract Terms[6] and consider briefly the Privy Council's interpretation, in *Boustany v Pigott*[7] of the common law's approach to 'unconscionable' contracts. Finally, in Part IV, we look at the Court of Appeal's refusal in *Re Selectmove*[8]

---

[1] [1993] 4 All ER 417.   [2] [1993] 4 All ER 433.
[3] [1994] 1 WLR 129.
[4] [1994] 1 WLR 650. In the discussion of *Ruxley*, The *'Rozel'* [1994] 2 Lloyd's LR 161 is also considered briefly.
[5] Unreported, Court of Appeal, 7 August, 1994.
[6] Directive 93/13 EEC (OJ 1993 L 95/29).   [7] (1993) 42 WLR.
[8] [1994] *The Times*, 13 January.

to extend the reasoning of *Williams* v *Roffey Bros*[9] to cases involving part payment of a debt.

The reader should be aware that the past year has also seen an unusually large number of decisions dealing with the interrelationship between tort and contract, as this applies both to liability and measure of damages.[10] These decisions are discussed in the Tort section of the *Review*.

I. Undue Influence

Two important issues in the law of undue influence have been considered, not always in a consistent fashion, in a number of Court of Appeal decisions over the last decade. The first is whether it is necessary to prove that a contract was manifestly disadvantageous in order to have it set aside for undue influence. The second is whether and in what circumstance a bank is entitled to enforce against a wife a securety on her husband's debt, where that security was improperly obtained by the husband's undue influence or misrepresentation. Lord Browne-Wilkinson's judgments in *Barclays Bank* v *O'Brien*[11] and *CIBC Mortgages plc* v *Pitt*[12] are to be welcomed for the impressive way they approach—and resolve— each of these issues.

O'Brien and *Pitt* were separate appeals, but the judgments were delivered together and are best read in tandem. In *O'Brien*, the defendant wife had charged her share in the matrimonial home in order to secure an overdraft facility for her husband's company. In *Pitt*, the wife's share in the matrimonial home was used to secure a loan, the stated purpose of which was to pay off a first mortgage and purchase a second home. In reality the husband used the loan to buy shares on the stock market. In both *O'Brien* and *Pitt* the husbands had acted improperly in gaining their wives' cooperation. In *O'Brien*, the husband misrepresented the amount of the guarantee, while in *Pitt* the husband subjected his wife to undue influence. In neither case was the wife advised by the bank to

---

[9] [1990] 1 All ER 512.

[10] *Henderson* v *Merret Syndicates Ltd* [1994] 3 WLR 761; *Spring* v *Guardian Assurance Plc* [1994] 3 WLR 354; *Marc Rich & Co AG* v *Bishop Rock Marine Co Ltd* [1994] 1 WLR 1071; *The Pioneer Container* [1994] 2 ALL ER 250; *William Sindall Plc* v *Cambridgeshire County Council* [1994] 1 WLR 1016; *McCullagh* v *Lane Fox* [1994] 08 EG 118.   [12] [1993] 4 All ER 433.

[11] [1993] 4 All ER 417.

receive independent legal advice, nor did she receive such advice, and in each case the wife did not fully understand the documents which she signed. Finally, subsequent events in each case turned out such that the banks called in the guarantees.

The House of Lords set aside the guarantee in *O'Brien*, but not in *Pitt*. Lord Browne-Wilkinson's judgments establish two important propositions. The first, enunciated in *Pitt*, concerned the need to prove that the impugned transaction is manifestly disadvantageous in cases of actual undue influence. In *Bank of Credit and Commerce International SA* v *Aboody*,[13] the Court of Appeal held that manifest disadvantage must be shown in order to succeed on a claim of either presumed or actual undue influence. This ruling presented a problem for Mrs Pitt because the Court of Appeal (though not the trial judge) found that the mortgage in *Pitt* was not manifestly disadvantageous. Mrs Pitt had no chance of succeeding against the bank because she could not even establish the minimum requirement of showing that she had been unduly influenced.

Lord Browne-Wilkinson might have challenged the finding that the transaction was not manifestly disadvantageous, but instead he took the bolder step of overruling the decision in *Aboody*. He held that in a case of *actual* undue influence, that is, where there is direct evidence of undue influence (as in *Pitt*), no further evidence is required in order to support a claim of undue influence. The requirements for succeeding in a case of *presumed* undue influence were left unchanged.

This ruling eliminates one of the more obvious anomalies in the law of contract. Lord Browne-Wilkinson said that undue influence was 'a species of fraud'.[14] It might be more correct to describe undue influence as a species of duress,[15] but whatever the exact formulation, it seems clear that the problem with a contract tainted by undue influence is that one of the parties has not truly consented. As such, direct proof that a party has been unduly influenced should be sufficient in itself to set aside a contract—just as evidence of duress or fraud are sufficient grounds to set aside a contract. Cases of presumed undue influence are different. Here the court does not have direct evidence of undue influence; all it has is evidence of a relationship in which there is a high risk that one of

---

[13] [1990] 1 QB 923.   [14] [1993] 4 All ER 433, 439.
[15] This description may not be entirely accurate in cases of presumed undue influence: see the discussion of *Cheese* v *Thomas* which follows.

the parties may be unduly influenced. In these situations, a contract should not be set aside without further evidence that the risk has materialized. Manifest disadvantage provides that evidence.

Lord Browne-Wilkinson did not discuss what sort of direct evidence needs to be shown in order to succeed on a plea of actual undue influence, nor did he say anything about the meaning of 'manifest disadvantage'. Yet it seems likely that we may see changes in both of these areas as a result of *Pitt*. So long as manifest disadvantage was required for both actual and presumed undue influence cases, the precise definition of 'actual undue influence' did not matter that much. The relationship in question typically also fell into a category in which a presumption of undue influence could be raised. But after *Pitt*, the distinction between the categories becomes important. Now, once actual undue influence has been established, the case is over. The likely result of this difference will be that judges will in future be more hesitant than at present to categorize cases as falling into the category of actual undue influence.

As for 'manifest disadvantage', the test as presently understood appears to be one of substantive fairness. Are the goods or services exchanged of equal value? If the point of the requirement of manifest disadvantage is to provide evidence of lack of consent, as *Pitt* suggests, this definition may be too narrow. That a contract is unfair is a good indication that the worse-off party did not genuinely consent, but so too is evidence that a contract is imprudent. For example, elderly people do not usually put the entirety of their life savings into high-risk investments. We should be suspicious when we see such an imprudent transaction. Yet in most cases such a contract is entirely fair. The facts of *Pitt* are similar to this example. Assuming that the wife would have shared in the gains that her husband made on the stock market, the contract was not disadvantageous, though it may have been imprudent. This distinction between unfairness and imprudence may explain why the trial judge and the Court of Appeal in *Pitt* disagreed on whether the contract was manifestly disadvantageous.

Pitt might support an even more radical reinterpretation of 'manifest disadvantage'. Why not apply a straightforwardly subjective test: Is it likely that *this* plaintiff would have genuinely consented to *this* contract? Such a test would be difficult to apply in practice, but if manifest disadvantage is meant to provide evidence of undue influence, then in theory at least this is the test courts should be applying.

The second proposition established by Lord Browne-Wilkinson dealt with the issue of whether and in what circumstances a wife can avoid a guarantee on the grounds that she was subject to her husband's undue influence or misrepresentation. This issue was the focus of the *O'Brien* judgment. Lord Browne-Wilkinson began by stating that in general a guarantee procured by the improper behaviour of a third party can be set aside in three situations: (a) the third party was acting as the creditor's agent; (b) the creditor had actual notice of the impropriety; or (c) the creditor had constructive notice of the impropriety *and* took insufficient steps to ensure that the guarantor entered the transaction freely and with sufficient information. The agency route has been applied to some husband-wife cases in the past, but Lord Browne-Wilkinson held, rightly in my view, that it is a 'very rare occurance' in which a true agency relationship can be established. Actual notice may occasionally be established, but in *O'Brien* and *Pitt*, as in most cases of this type, the bank had no actual knowledge of the husband's impropriety.

This leaves constructive notice. A creditor is normally taken to have constructive notice, Lord Browne-Wilkinson said, if the relationship between the guarantor and the principle debtor falls into either of two categories. Following *Aboody*, Lord Browne-Wilkinson labelled these categories 2A and 2B (category 1 cases are cases of actual notice). Category 2A comprises a specified group of relationships, such as, for example, solicitor/client and doctor/patient. A presumption of undue influence is raised in these cases because a high risk of undue influence is inherent in the relationship. Since the early part of this century it has been held that the marital relationship does not fall into this category.[16]

In category 2B cases, the creditor has knowledge of a de facto relationship of trust and confidence between the guarantor and beneficiary such that there is a real risk of undue influence or other impropriety. Knowledge of prior undue influence between the parties, for example, would typically put a creditor on notice in this way. In some cases involving husbands and wives, creditors might

---

[16] *Howes v Bishop* [1909] 2 KB 390; *Bank of Montreal v Stuart* [1911] AC 120.

have such knowledge, but this is not the norm and could not be shown in either *O'Brien* or *Pitt*.

None of the established categories in which relief might be given, then, appeared to be available to Mrs Pitt or Mrs O'Brien. In the Court of Appeal decision in *O'Brien*, Scott LJ's response to this result was to hold that the defendant could rely upon the 'special protection' which equity had long afforded 'married women who provide security for their husband's debts'.[17] Lord Browne-Wilkinson rejected this approach. Instead, he introduced a third category of constructive notice. In addition to 2A and 2B situations, a creditor will be put on constructive notice, Lord Browne-Wilkinson held, if two conditions are met: (1) the guarantor is cohabiting with the principal debtor; and (2) the transaction is on its face not to the financial advantage of the guarantor. Lord Browne-Wilkinson added later that other relationships, for example between a son and an elderly parent,[18] might in appropriate circumstances also satisfy the first requirement. Where a creditor is put on constructive notice in this way, the guarantee can be enforced only if the creditor has taken reasonable steps to ensure that the guarantor is making a free, informed decision. In the normal case this requirement is satisfied if creditors insist that 'the wife attend a private meeting (in the absence of the husband) with a representative of the creditor at which she is told of the extent of her liability as surety, warned of the risk she is running and urged to take independent legal advice.'[19] In 'exceptional' cases, where the creditor has knowledge of facts 'which render the likelihood of undue influence not only possible but probable', the creditor should go further and insist that the wife is separately advised.

Applying these requirements to the facts of the two cases, Mrs O'Brien's defence succeeded, but Mrs Pitt's did not. The difference between the cases was that in *Pitt* the transaction was not *on its face* disadvantageous to the wife. Although the husband used the loan to gamble on the stock market, its stated purpose was to pay off a mortgage and buy a second house.

Perhaps the best way of analysing Lord Browne-Wilkinson's reasoning is by considering three possible objections. The first objection is that he misunderstood constructive notice. Lord

[17] [1992] 3 WLR 593, 610.
[18] See eg *Avon Finance Co Ltd* v *Bridger* [1985] 2 All ER 281.
[19] [1993] 4 All ER 417, 429, 430.

Browne-Wilkinson says that it is 'the proper application of the doctrine of notice which provides the key to finding a principled basis for the law',[20] yet the doctrine of notice is meant to apply to situations in which the party put on notice could, through reasonable steps, have become aware that an earlier transaction was tainted by impropriety. In *O'Brien* and *Pitt* there was only one transaction and, more importantly, it is hard to see what 'reasonable inquiries' the banks might have taken to learn of the husband's improprieties. For the requirement of reasonable inquiries, Lord Browne-Wilkinson has substituted the requirement to take reasonable steps to ensure the promisor is making a free, informed choice.[21]

Lord Browne-Wilkinson's understanding of the doctrine of notice does not conform to the conventional meaning. Nevertheless, his underlying argument is clear enough and, it is submitted, entirely sound. Where circumstances are such that a reasonable creditor would be aware that there is a high risk of a surety having been unduly influenced or otherwise wronged, there is a duty to take reasonable precautions to guard against this possibility occurring. What the creditor has 'notice' of is not an actual impropriety, but the likelihood of an impropriety.

The second possible objection is to Lord Browne-Wilkinson's view of what is required, in cases like *O'Brien* and *Pitt*, for creditors to be put on notice. It is difficult to speak authoritatively on this issue without a good grasp of the empirical data on which it largely turns, but on first impressions, at least, Lord Browne-Wilkinson appears to have adopted a reasonable midway position. Scott LJ's invocation of a 'special equity' in favour of wives has the effect of placing the marital relationship into the 2A category in all but name. Aside from the inconsistency which it introduces into the law, this approach overestimates the percentage of women who, in this day and age, need special protection. To take the opposite approach and conclude that creditors should be put on constructive notice only where they have actual knowledge of a relationship of trust and confidence seems equally extreme. Whatever we might wish were the case, there is, in 1994, a greater risk of undue influence in marital relationships than in ordinary commercial

---

[20] Ibid 428.
[21] This issue is discussed in more detail in a paper presented by John Mee at the contract/restitution section of 1994 SPTL Conference.

dealings. Lord Browne-Wilkinson's third category of constructive notice falls nicely in between these two approaches. The requirement of 'disadvantageous on its face' picks out those transactions involving husbands and wives in which a creditor ought to realize there is a special or additional risk that one of the parties may have treated the other improperly. Giving the same protection to cohabitees and other people in analogous situations is, needless to say, appropriate.

The third possible objection to Lord Browne-Wilkinson's judgment focuses upon the content of the creditor's duty to inform and advise. As with the previous objection, this might come from either of two directions. First, it may be said that while explaining the nature of a transaction and advising or even insisting on independent legal advice can be helpful in a case, like *O'Brien*, where the impropriety in question is misrepresentation, in the more common case of undue influence the efficacy of these precautions is questionable. The point is a good one, but, unfortunately, the only effective way of ensuring that someone subject to undue influence genuinely consents is to remove the source of undue influence. This is not a job that the law, or at least the law of contract, is capable of achieving.

From the other direction, creditors might also object to Lord Browne-Wilkinson's formulation of the duty to inform and advise. It is not the content of the duty which is, or at least should be, objectionable—the 'normal' steps are already part of the banking code of practice—but the difficulty of telling when more than the norm is required. Lord Browne-Wilkinson appears to envisage something like a sliding scale: the greater the likelihood of the guarantor being subject to undue influence, etc., the greater the creditor's duty to take precautionary steps. This principle is fine in theory, but may be difficult to apply in practice. We will undoubtedly see litigation in the future on this issue.

Before leaving *O'Brien,* a problem with the remedy should be noted. In the last two sentences of his judgment, Lord Browne-Wilkinson dismissed the appeal and stated that the wife was entitled 'to set aside the legal charge on the matrimonial home'.[22] This is odd because in the Court of Appeal only a part of the mortgage was set aside. The husband's misrepresentation had taken

---

[22] [1993] 4 All ER 417, 432.

the form of saying that the mortgage was for £60,000 rather than £135,000. The Court of Appeal held that the wife was therefore liable for the risk she had knowingly undertook, that is, for £60,000. Lord Browne-Wilkinson said nothing about this issue and it is unclear if he actually intended to set aside the whole mortgage. But if he did, this seems wrong. A single impropriety may taint a whole transaction, but here it was not the bank, but the husband that committed the impropriety. The bank (merely) failed to take certain positive steps. In these circumstances, the bank should be penalized only to the extent that taking those steps might have made a difference.[23]

The judgments in *O'Brien* and *Pitt* settle controversies in the law of undue influence law over which the Court of Appeal has been battling for years. Yet as the decision in *Cheese* v *Thomas*[24] shows, the ability of the Court of Appeal to discover new and interesting issues in this area of the law continues unabated. The plaintiff in *Cheese*, an 85 year old man, had entered into an agreement with his nephew, the defendant, whereby the plaintiff would provide £43,000 towards the purchase price of a house and the defendant would provide the remaining £40,000. The title of the house would be in the defendant's name, but the plaintiff would be allowed to live rent-free in the house until he died. The defendant did not keep up his mortgage payments and the plaintiff became worried and brought an action to rescind the agreement.

The case raised two issues. First, should the agreement be set aside for undue influence? Second, if the agreement is set aside, on what terms should it be set aside? The second issue was important because the house had fallen in value by nearly £30,000 by the date of trial. The defendant argued that if the agreement was set aside, the £30,000 loss should be shared between the parties.

On the first issue, Sir Donald Nicholls VC agreed with the trial judge that the agreement should be set aside for undue influence. A '2B' presumption of undue influence was raised by the close relationship of the parties, the greater business experience of the nephew, and evidence of prior undue influence. As for manifest

---

[23] Shortly after the decisions in *O'Brien* and *Pitt*, the Court of Session in Scotland, in a case similar to *O'Brien*, *Mumford* v *Bank of Scotland* (August 4, 1994, Court of Session), confirmed that the law of Scotland has no doctrine of constructive notice. Lord Johnston held that only actual notice of impropriety would serve to put creditors on notice.   [24] [1994] 1 WLR 129.

disadvantage, this was established by three features of the transaction: (1) the plaintiff had parted with all his capital; (2) the plaintiff was committed to living in the house even if he chose or needed to move later on; and (3) the plaintiff had no protection in the event that the defendant failed to keep up his mortgage payments.

This analysis of manifest disadvantage is interesting in light of our discussion of *Pitt*. It is not obvious that the transaction was, strictly speaking, disadvantageous—or at least not 'manifestly' disadvantageous. Had the arrangement worked out, the plaintiff would have been able to live for the rest of his life in a house far better than one he would have been able to afford on his own. From this perspective, the transaction is better characterized as a gamble that did not pay off. It was clearly an imprudent gamble—and as such provided good evidence that the plaintiff had been subject to undue influence—but it was not manifestly disadvantageous. Sir Donald Nicholls VC may have been aware that he was interpreting the requirement of manifest disadvantage loosely. Rather than simply saying that the transaction was manifestly disadvantageous, he said instead that it was 'properly described as' manifestly disadvantageous.

The most interesting and important part of Sir Donald Nicholls VC's judgment concerns the terms on which the contract should be set aside. The Vice-Chancellor said that while normally the loss consequent to a contract set aside by undue influence fell entirely on the defendant, on the special facts of this case 'justice requires that each party should be returned as near to his original position as possible'.[25] More specifically, each party should share the loss from the fall in value of the house in proportion to their contribution towards the purchase price of the house. The special facts which justified this novel remedy were: (1) the transaction was properly characterized as a joint venture; and (2) the defendant was not guilty of any improper behaviour.

Each of these assertions is questionable. The characterization of the transaction as a joint venture, though not implausible, is far from inevitable. The plaintiff did not receive a proprietary interest in the house, he merely had the right to reside in it during his lifetime. Seen in this light, it is just as accurate to describe the

[25] [1994] 1 WLR 136.

relationship as that of lessor/lessee. The plaintiff paid a sum of money in return for which he was given the right to live in the house until he died.

The claim that the nephew was blameless is even more dubious, but it does, at least, raise some interesting and important questions about what it means to be 'unduly influenced'. At first blush, it might seem that undue influence must always involve some sort of wrongdoing. If someone has *unduly* influenced someone else, then it appears to follow from the word 'undue' that there has been wrongdoing. This conclusion is also consistent with Lord Browne-Wilkinson's view that undue influence is a species of fraud (or, as I suggested, duress). But we need to be careful here. Cases of *actual* undue influence must, I think, always involve some sort of wrongdoing. The evidence that supports a claim of actual undue influence is evidence of one person exerting undue pressure upon another person. In some cases of presumed undue influence, however, the situation might be different. It is possible, I think, to be unduly influenced by another person without the other person actually doing anything. If I am infatuated with someone I may agree blindly to whatever that individual suggests. This is not to say that 'passive influencers' are always blameless. Just as the bank in *O'Brien* had a duty to take precautions because of the evident risk of undue influence, so too an individual who 'passively' influences another person should take precautions if the risk of undue influence is evident. It is only where a reasonable person would have been unaware of the undue influence that she was exerting that no blame at all should be attached.

The nephew in *Cheese* does not fit into this last category. He may not have been, in the words of Sir Donald Nicholls VC, 'morally reprehensible', but he was, at a minimum, negligent. In light of the circumstances and in particular the fact that he had previously unduly influenced his uncle, the defendant should have been aware of the risk of undue influence and taken steps to reduce this risk.

II. Remedies

Ruxley Electronics Ltd v *Forsyth*[26] raises a classic question in the law of contract, that of the appropriate measure of relief for breach

---

[26] [1994] 1 WLR 650.

of contract in cases where the cost of performance or repair is greater than the diminution in value resulting from the breach. In *Tito* v *Waddell (No 2)*,[27] Megarry VC held that a mining company that had failed in its obligation to replant worked land was not required to pay for the cost of replanting. Instead, the company need only pay a sum—much smaller—sufficient to compensate the plaintiffs for the change in the market value of their land. In *Radford* v *De Froberville*,[28] by contrast, Oliver J held that a defendant who had breached an obligation to build a boundary wall on the plaintiff's property must pay for the cost of building the wall, irrespective of whether the wall would increase the value of the property. It is this second approach which the Court of Appeal in *Ruxley* followed.

The plaintiff contractor had built a swimming pool for the defendant for a fee of £31,000. Unfortunately, the pool was only 6' deep rather than 7'6" as specified in the contract. The breach had no effect on the market value of the defendant's property, but as it would be necessary to rebuild the entire pool in order to achieve the correct depth, the cost of repair was £21,560. At trial, the judge awarded the defendant £2,500 for loss of amenity. The defendant appealed.

The Court of Appeal (Dillon LJ dissenting) allowed the appeal, awarding the defendant the full cost of repair. Staughton LJ, who delivered the main judgment, held that damages in cases like *Ruxley* should be calculated on the same basis that damages are calculated in 'normal' damages claims. The defendant should be awarded the sum necessary to put him in the same position he would have been in if the contract had been performed. This is the cost of repair because only this sum allows the plaintiff to get exactly what he bargained for. Cost of repair is usually equivalent to diminution in value, but where there is a difference it is the former amount which should be awarded.

Aside from these general propositions, Staughton LJ offered little positive argument in support of his conclusion. Instead he focused on two requirements which allegedly must be met before cost of repair can be awarded. First, it is often said that the plaintiff must show that he intends to use the money to carry out the repairs.[29]

---

[27] [1977] Ch 106.   [28] [1978] 1 All ER 33.
[29] See eg *Radford*; *Imodco Ltd* v *Wimpey Major Projects Ltd and Taylor Woodrow International Ltd* (1987) 40 BLR 1.

The plaintiff in *Ruxley* was in fact prepared to give an undertaking to carry out the repair, but Staughton LJ said the undertaking was irrelevant. Whatever past decisions may suggest—and Staughton LJ thought the authorities went both ways on this issue—it should not matter what the plaintiff intends to do with the money and, in particular, whether he intends to use it for repair. As Staughton LJ rightly point outs, nowhere else in the law do the courts show a concern over what plaintiffs intend do with their damages.

The second requirement which allegedly must be met before cost of repair can be awarded is that it must be 'reasonable for the plaintiff to require the work to be done'.[30] Staughton LJ did not dispute this requirement, but held that it was met on the facts of the case. His explanation is unusual. Reasonableness, he said, is essentially a question of mitigation. It is reasonable for the work to be done unless the plaintiff can purchase an equivalent substitute for a lesser sum. In this case, buying a substitute would have meant buying a new house so it was reasonable to have the work done.

This unusual interpretation of reasonableness could lead to severe results. If the pool in *Ruxley* was only one inch below the correct depth, it would still have been 'reasonable' to rebuild it according to Staughton LJ's test. It does not matter how trivial the breach is. Stated differently, the possibility of the promisee making a windfall gain is irrelevant. The difficulty of estimating the promisee's loss is also irrelevant on Staughton LJ's approach. Even if the court can accurately assess the promisee's loss—for example if Mr Ruxley wanted the pool for commercial purposes—and even if the loss is very small, cost of repair may still be awarded.

To see if there is an alternative way of deciding cases like *Ruxley* we need to step back for a moment and consider some of the underlying issues. What makes *Ruxley* so hard to decide is that all possible measures of damages are unsatisfactory in some way. Diminution in value is unsatisfactory because the promisee may be undercompensated. Mr Forsyth cared whether his pool was 6' or 7' deep, even though potential purchasers of his house might not. Cost of repair is unsatisfactory because it may overcompensate the promisee. It is possible that the repair of Mr Forsyth's pool was worth £21,560 to him, but it seems unlikely. A third possibility,

---

[30] See eg *Radford*; *Imodco*.

adopted by the trial judge, is to try and place a monetary value on
the loss in enjoyment that the plaintiff would suffer as a result of
the defect, that is, to try and estimate his 'loss of amenity'. The
difficulty with such an approach is that the court lacked reliable
evidence on which to make this estimate. The depth of the pool was
a matter of personal preference.

The 'personal' nature of Mr Forsyth's loss is the key to
understanding *Ruxley*. If his loss was not 'personal' the case would
be easy to decide. *The 'Rozel'*,[31] a shipping case decided shortly
after *Ruxley*, illustrates this point. The owners of the Rozel sued a
charterparty for failing to return the vessel in the condition
stipulated in the contract. Because of a repair to the generator the
ship was not, as required, in the same 'classification' group that it
was in at the start of the contract. The cost of new repairs necessary
to put the vessel back into the original classification was £87,000.
The change in classification did not, however, affect the value of the
vessel.

Philips J held that diminution in value was the appropriate
measure of damage. He rightly distinguished *Ruxley* on the ground
that it involved 'personal preferences'. Where the purpose of a
contract is commercial, the promisee can only recover for breaches
which have commercial implications. This must be right. Prima
facie the aim of contract damages is to compensate, so far as money
is able, for loss resulting from breach of contract. That loss is
normally equivalent to the change in market value of the promisee's
'property' (broadly understood) caused by the breach. The amount
often coincides with the cost of repair, but the latter amount is
irrelevant strictly speaking. The relevant issue is the extent of the
promisee's loss, not the cost of completing the contract.

This picture get complicated when, as in *Ruxley,* changes in
market value do not provide an accurate gauge of the promisee's
loss. This usually happens in non-commercial transactions, but not
always. In *Sky Petroleum Ltd* v *VIP Petroleum Ltd*,[32] for example,
a wildly fluctuating oil market made it impossible to assess with
any confidence the promisee's loss. How should the courts should
approach cases like *Ruxley* where change in market value is a poor
guide. Mention of *Sky Petroleum* raises a possibility not considered

---

[31] [1994] 2 Lloyd's LR 161.   [32] [1974] 1 WLR 576.

by counsel or the court in *Ruxley*: an award of specific performance. In cases in which it is difficult to assess losses accurately—
typically cases involving 'unique' goods *(Sky Petroleum* being the
exception)—specific performance is the normal remedy. Would
specific performance work in *Ruxley*?

One possible objection is that specific performance would be
wasteful. The court is ordering a repair which, it seems likely, costs
more than its value to the beneficiary. But there is no reason to
assume that wasteful performance will actually occur. In all
probability the parties will come to an agreement whereby, for the
payment of a sum less than £21,560, the defendant agrees to waive
his rights to specific performance. If performance really is wasteful,
it will be in both parties interest to reach such a settlement. To be
sure, the Mr Forsyth will almost certainly end up being over-
compensated to some degree. But the extent of overcompensation
will be less than that resulting from awarding the full cost of repair.
The alternative, awarding diminution in value, ensures that Mr
Forsyth will be undercompensated. Given the choice of over-
compensating the innocent party, Mr Forsyth, or the contractor,
the former is preferable.

This is not to suggest that in every case where there is some
difficulty in assessing damages the courts should grant specific
performance. The risk of wasteful performance and overcompensation should be taken into account. Whether specific
performance should be ordered in any particular case depends,
first, on exactly how difficult it is to assess damages. Second, the
amount of damages is important. If damages are likely to be very
small in relative terms, then, even if we cannot estimate the loss
exactly, it is better to take an educated guess than to risk wasteful
performance and overcompensation.

Applying these considerations to *Ruxley*, the best solution
appears to be the one adopted by the trial judge. He assessed the
defendant's 'loss of amenity', that is, his real loss, at £2,500. This
amount is no doubt a very rough approximation, but given the high
cost of repair, a rough approximation is preferable to an order of
specific performance. If this solution is not taken, specific performance is the next best option. The two possibilities considered by the
court—diminution in (market) value and cost of repair—are the
least desirable options.

The interrelationship between equitable relief and damages was also important in the other significant—and difficult—case dealing with remedies, *Jaggard* v *Sawyer*.[33] The parties in *Jaggard* owned adjacent houses on a private road. Ten residents in total lived on the road, each of whom had agreed to various covenants restricting development. The defendant acquired a property backing on to his lot upon which he built a second house. Access was by a driveway off the private road. It was accepted by all parties that these actions constituted a trespass and a breach of covenant. Prior to the commencement of construction, the plaintiff notified the defendant that the defendant would be committing a trespass and breach of contract if he carried through with his plans and the plaintiff indicated she would seek an interlocutory injunction if the defendant persisted. The defendant went ahead and built the second house. The plaintiff did not request an interlocutory injunction, but waited until the house was nearly complete before seeking an injunction to tear down the house. The defendant argued that damages should be awarded in lieu of an injunction. By the date of the appeal, the house was fully built and let to a third party.

Bingham MR and Millett LJ held, on similar grounds, that the plaintiff should be awarded damages in lieu of an injunction. The amount of damages—£6,250—was based on the sum that a reasonable plaintiff would have demanded an order to relax the convenant.

My comments focus primarily on the second issue, that of the measure of damages. The authority to award damages in lieu of an injunction has existed since Lord Cairns' Act 1858 and the considerations determining its exercise were not in dispute in the appeal.[34] Millett LJ's judgment contains most of the discussion concerning the measure of damages. In fixing damages at the sum that a reasonable plaintiff would have accepted in compensation for relaxing his rights, he closely followed *Wrotham Part Estate Co Ltd* v *Parkside Homes*.[35] In that case, Brightman J awarded damages for the breach of a non-development covenant on the basis

---

[33] Unreported, Court of Appeal, 7 August, 1994.
[34] *Shelfer* v *London Electric Lighting Company* [1895] 1 Ch 287 lists four factors which support an award of damages: (1) the injury to the plaintiff is small; (2) the injury to the plaintiff can be estimated in money; (3) the injury can be compensated adequately by money; and (4) it would not be oppressive to grant an injunction.
[35] [1974] 1 WLR 798.

of a 'reasonable' hypothetical bargain between the plaintiff and the defendant. There was, however, one significant question mark over *Wrotham Park*—the Court of Appeal's decision in *Surrey County Council v Bredero Homes Ltd*,[36] discussed in last year's *Review*. *Bredero* also involved the breach of a covenant restricting development, but this time the Court of Appeal awarded damages on the standard basis of diminution in value. As the breach had not caused the plaintiffs any loss, the court awarded only nominal damages. *Bredero* appears to conflict with *Wrotham Park*. The bulk of Millett LJ's judgment is devoted to proving that there is no conflict between those cases and, furthermore, that *Wrotham Park*, not *Bredero*, provides the correct precedent for *Jaggard*.

Millett LJ's reasoning is not always easy to follow, but if I have understood him correctly it runs as follows. The availability of damages under Lord Cairns' Act depends upon whether it is possible, at least in theory, for the court to award an injunction. It is not necessary that the plaintiff actually request an injunction, but because damages are given in lieu of an injunction, an injunction must at least be possible. This requirement alone distinguishes *Bredero* from both *Wrotham Park* and *Jaggard*. In *Bredero*, it was impossible to grant an injunction because the houses had been sold on to third parties. In *Wrotham Park* and *Jaggard* by contrast, an injunction was in theory still available.

Where damages are not available under Lord Cairns' Act, as in *Bredero*, they must be sought at common law. When assessing damages at common law, the theoretical availability of an injunction figures again. The extent to which the plaintiff's property (or whatever) has been diminished in value depends in part on his right to an injunction. If the plaintiff has the right to an injunction, then his property is worth more because he can sell his right to parties who wish to infringe it. Thus, for the same reason that damages in *Bredero* could not be awarded under Lord Cairns' Act—it was impossible even in theory to award an injunction—the measure of damages at common law was zero.[37]

---

[36] [1993] 3 All ER 705.
[37] Staughton LJ did not consider what would have happened if the breach in *Bredero* had also caused the plaintiff direct harm (aside from the loss of opportunity to bargain), but presumably common law damages would still be available under this head.

Where an injunction is available, damages will again be the same under Lord Cairns' Act and common law, at least in the standard case. Under both Lord Cairns' Act and the common law, damages are measured by diminution in value. Under each heading the theoretical availability of an injunction must again be taken into account and in each case the plaintiff's loss is measured by how much he could have received in a hypothetical 'reasonable' bargain to relax the covenant.[38] It is for this reason that in *Wrotham Park* 'the measure of damages at common law and under the Act was the same'.[39]

At this point, a further complication must be introduced. Early in his judgment, Millett LJ stated that damages under Lord Cairns' Act will 'inevitably extend beyond the damages to which the plaintiff may be entitled at law'.[40] Damages at common law were for past wrongs, he said, while damages in substitution for an injunction 'relate to the future, not the past'. It is hard to reconcile these statements with the statement that in *Wrotham Park* 'the measure of damages at common law and under the Act was the same'. A partial reconciliation, however, may be found in a distinction that Millett LJ later drew between cases involving a 'single past breach' and cases involving 'future and continuing breaches'. Millett LJ said that in cases involving single past breaches, like *Wrotham Park*, damages at common law and under the Act were the same. But in cases where damages are claimed in 'respect of future trespasses or continuing breaches of covenant' damages at common law and under the Act will differ. This is because the common law cannot award damages for future wrongs. The result is that damages at common law and under the Act are *sometimes* the same.

This distinction between past and future breaches introduces a number of new problems. Millett LJ said that *Jaggard* was a case of future and continuing breaches, yet it is not clear how it differs from *Wrotham Park* in this respect. To be sure, the physical existence of the defendant's house in *Jaggard* would continue to

---

[38] It was for this reason, Millett LJ suggested, that Megarry J in *Wroth* v *Tyler* (1974) Ch 30 and Lord Wilberforce in *Johnson* v *Agnew* [1980] AC 367 thought damages under Lord Cairns' Act and at common law were the same. As I discuss above, Millett LJ went on to question this view.

[39] Unreported, Court of Appeal, 7 August, 1994, transcript page 18.

[40] Ibid. 2.

conflict with the non-development covenant, but the same was true of the development in *Wrotham Park*. The house in *Jaggard* was not fully completed at the date of trial, but this seems a slim basis on which to vary an award of damages. The other difference between *Jaggard* and *Wrotham Park* is that in the former the plaintiffs were also claiming for trespass. Yet in all material respects the trespass action and the breach of covenant action were identical. The harm was the same in each case. The oddest thing about Millett LJ's distinction between past and future breaches, however, is that he proceeded to completely ignore the distinction when it came to fixing damages. Adopting his framework, the difference between past and future breaches should have lead to different awards in *Wrotham Park* and *Jaggard*, yet the same measure of damages was applied in each case.

The judgment appears to contain at least two other internal inconsistencies. First, if the availability of an injunction at *the date of trial* is the crucial factor in assessing damages, then the 'hypothetical bargain' should be situated at that time and not, as was done, at the time just prior to breach. The difference is no mere technicality. At the date of trial in *Jaggard*, the offending house was nearly completed. The defendant would undoubtedly have been willing to pay far more at that point to have an injunction waived than he would have been willing to pay before he had started building. In addition, if the later date is used, then the plaintiff should also receive additional damages for any harm caused by the breach up to the date of trial.

Second, damages should be based upon the amount that the actual parties would have settled for and not the amount that a 'reasonable' plaintiff would have demanded (or, as in *Wrotham Park*, the amount of a reasonable bargain). If, as Millett LJ stated, the court's aim is to compensate the plaintiff, then the court should try to compensate *the* plaintiff, not some hypothetical plaintiff. That a hypothetical 'reasonable' bargain may undercompensate the plaintiff is demonstrated by the decision in *Wrotham Park*. The evidence in *Wrotham Park* suggested that the plaintiff placed an extremely high, if not infinite, value on the covenant, yet he was awarded only a fraction of the profit which the defendant made from the breach.

Notwithstanding these inconsistencies, the basic ratio of *Jaggard* is clear enough. In cases where it is theoretically possible to award an injunction, and an injunction is refused, damages should be awarded for the plaintiff's lost opportunity to negotiate a relaxation of its rights. This is an odd proposition. Both the availability and measure of damages depends on the theoretical availability of a different remedy, a remedy which, moreover, the court is unwilling to grant. The proposition could also lead to radical changes in the law if we took it seriously. Millett LJ's reasoning ought to apply equally well to specific performance. Should courts be able to grant damages for lost opportunity to bargain in lieu of specific performance? Specific performance is 'theoretically' possible for most breaches of contracts. Finally, the ratio of *Jaggard* leads to prima facie unjust results. If a plaintiff waits one day too long, and an injunction ceases to be possible, then damages are not just reduced they are eliminated altogether.

These and other difficulties with the judgment all stem, I suggest, from a misunderstanding about the nature of contractual obligation.[41] Millett LJ's approach assumes that contractual rights are a type of property rights. If you want to break a contract you must get permission of the promisee, just as if you want to take someone's property you must get her permission. Everything that we know about contract remedies is inconsistent with this picture. We are, in general, perfectly free to break contracts so long as we are willing to compensate promisees for their losses. If Millett LJ is right then every time we breach a contract, or at a minimum every time we intentionally breach a contract, we should have to pay promisees for their lost opportunities to waive their rights.

It is submitted that we should approach *Jaggard* in the same way that we approach any other case of breach of contract. I outlined this approach in the discussion of *Ruxley*; indeed the two cases raise very similar issues in this regard. The first question to ask is has breach caused any loss, present or future, to the promisee? This question alone dispenses of *Bredero*. In *Bredero* the breach of the convenant did not cause the promisee—a city council—any loss. The same was true in The '*Rozel*' case. The breach in *Jaggard*, however, did lead to a real loss. If the breach does cause a loss, the next question is whether we can estimate the loss. Where it is not possible to estimate the loss, the normal route is to order an

---

[41] My comments are restricted to the breach of covenant claim. It is possible that different considerations apply to trespass.

injunction or specific performance. In *Jaggard* it would have been difficult to estimate the loss accurately. As in *Ruxley*, the breach related to a matter of personal preference. Prime facie, then, an injunction should have been granted. There is an exception to the above rule, however, which is that if it is clear that, whatever the exact figure of loss may be, it is small in comparison to the cost of performance, then an attempt should be made to estimate the loss, however approximate the result. It was this approach, I suggested, that was most appropriate in *Ruxley* and the same is probably true of *Jaggard*. The relevant evidence is unavailable, but it seems likely that the plaintiffs loss would be relatively low in comparison to the value of the defendant's house.[42]

III. Unfair Contract Terms

The EEC Directive on Unfair Contract Terms[43] comes into effect on January 31st, 1994. The Directive was discussed in last year's *Review*, but at that time no information was available on the crucial issue of how the government proposed to bring UK law into line with Directive. The Department of Trade and Industry has since published two consultation documents setting out successive draft proposals.[44] The final form of the government's response is still under consideration, but as comments on the second consultation document are not due until November 14, 1994, major changes to the current proposals seem unlikely.

The government has taken a minimalist approach. It is intended that the Directive be implemented through regulations, introduced under section 2(2) of the European Communities Act 1972, which reproduce almost verbatim the substantive tests of the Directive. The only innovation, if it may be called that, concerns enforcement mechanisms—an area in which the Directive, in particular Article

---

[42] The use of a suitably framed 'hypothetical bargain' may be a useful heuristic device when trying to assess losses. Asking what *this* plaintiff would have accepted in compensation is a not unreasonable method of determining the value she placed on performance. But we should be clear that the hypothetical bargain is only a device; we are not actually trying to compensate the plaintiff for lost opportunity to bargain.

[43] Directive 93/13 EEC (OJ 1993 L 95/29).

[44] Both consultation documents are entitled 'Implementation of the EC Directive on Unfair Terms in Consumer Contracts (93/13/EEC)'. The first was issued in October 1993 and the second in September 1994.

7, more or less forces governments to introduce independent proposals.

The final version of the regulations is likely to introduce at least a few new wrinkles, so I shall say little about the details of the proposed regulations. Two general observations, however, can safely be made. First, and perhaps most importantly, the government's proposed route makes no attempt to sort out the mess which is bound to result from the overlapping jurisdictions of the Directive and the Unfair Contract Terms Act 1977. Exclusion clauses are covered by both the Directive and the Act yet, as the authors of the second (but not the first) Consultation Document acknowledge, the standards of review under each document differ. The only way to avoid the above problems would appear to be through the introduction, via primary legislation, of a single overarching scheme dealing with unfair contract terms. Framing such legislation is a difficult task, so it is perhaps not surprising that, at least at this stage, the government has adopted the regulatory route. It can only be hoped that this is a temporary measure. In the meantime, anyone trying to work out consumer protection law in the UK will have a difficult job.[45] The Act and the Directive are confusing enough on their own; the combination could prove a nightmare. This is particularly regrettable in an area like consumer protection where there is an obvious need for clear, accessible, law.

Second, because the regulations repeat almost verbatim the terms of the Directive, they also reproduce nearly all of the inconsistencies and unclarities which exist in the Directive. As discussed in last year's *Review*, there are at least five major respects in which the Directive is unclear: (1) the basic meaning of 'unfairness' and in particular the relevance, respectively, of substantive unfairness and procedural unfairness in assessing validity; (2) the breadth of the exclusion from review of terms specifying price and terms defining the 'main subject matter of the contract'; (3) the relevance of unclear wording to validity; (4) the significance of parts of a contract being individually negotiated; and (5) the weight to be given to the annexed list of terms 'which may be regarded as unfair'. To be sure, the government must implement the Directive:

---

[45] It is possible that the complexity of the law will itself leave the UK in breach of the EC obligations: see Case 167/73 *French Merchant Seaman* [1974] ECR 359 and 372.

it cannot invent its own scheme. But the Directive clearly envisages that member states should have some latitude in how the Directive is implemented. It appears that in the UK, at least, that latitude will be exercised entirely by the judiciary.

Finally, a few words should be said about the recommendations, introduced in the second consultation paper, in respect of enforcement mechanisms—bearing in mind that more changes in this area may be expected. Article 7 of the Directive sets out three main requirements: (1) 'that effective means exist to prevent the continued use of unfair terms in contracts'; (2) that such means allow for representative actions by 'persons or organisations, having a legitimate interest in protecting consumers . . . to prevent the continued use of such terms'; and (3) that remedies be available which may be 'directed jointly or severally against a number of sellers or suppliers'. The authors of the second consultation paper appear to have realized that doing nothing (as suggested in the first paper) would probably leave the government in breach of these requirements. Their proposal is that, in addition to bringing actions before the courts, individuals be allowed to bring complaints about unfair terms before the Director General of Fair Trading. The Director has a duty to consider the complaint and, if 'he considers it appropriate to do so', may seek an injunction against the use of an unfair contract term. The same regulation further provides that any injunction granted may relate not only to a particular contract but to similar terms used or recommended for use elsewhere. This response may still leave the government in breach of its obligations, in particular the obligation to allow representative actions by 'persons of organisations having a legitimate interest in protecting consumers', but it undoubtedly introduces significant changes into UK law.

The EEC Directive has a much wider scope than the Unfair Contract Terms Act 1977, but there remain a considerable number of contracts which are only subject to review for 'unfairness' under common law rules. The exact scope and basis of such review has never been very clear and it is suggested that the Privy Council's decision in *Boustany* v *Pigott*,[46] though undoubtedly reaching the correct result, does little to alter this situation.

The appellant Boustany had secured a commercial tenancy from

---

[46] (1993) 42 WLR.

the respondent at a price of approximately 1/6 the market value and for period of up to 20 years. The respondent was 71 years old and though of apparently sound mind, had not been in control of her affairs for many years. The lease was obtained after the appellant 'lavished flattery and attention' on the respondent and during a time when the respondent's nephew, who normally managed her properties, was—to the knowledge of the appellant— out of the country. The solicitor used by the appellant to prepare the lease was not the respondent's family solicitor. The solicitor did point out the disadvantageous nature of the lease to the respondent, but this warning had no effect. The respondent later died and her representative sought to have the lease set aside as an unconscionable bargain.

Given these facts, it is not surprising that Lord Templeman agreed with both the trial judge and the Court of Appeal that the lease should be set aside. The ratio of his decision, however, is unclear. Lord Templeman began by noting the trial judge's finding that the three requirements of *Fry* v *Lane*[47] were satisfied in this case: (1) the sale was at considerable undervalue; (2) the respondent did not have independent advice; and (3) the respondent, though not strictly 'poor and ignorant', was in an analogous position. But then, rather than commenting on these findings—or even saying whether they mattered at all—Lord Templeman turned immediately to what he said was the real issue in the case, that of whether the appellant's behaviour was unconscionable. Lord Templeman did emphasize that the existence of unconscionable terms or of a stronger bargaining position were not enough in themselves to have a contract set aside, but other than this he said nothing more about the law. As for the appellant's behaviour, Lord Templeman quickly concluded that in view of the history of the transaction, the appellant had acted unconscionably. The appellant had 'prevailed upon Miss Pigott to agree to grant a lease on terms which they knew they could not extract from Mr George Pigott [the nephew], or anyone else'.

It is evident that Lord Templeman was prepared to grant relief in situations which do not precisely meet the *Fry* v *Lane* requirements. The requirement of 'poor and ignorant' was not strictly satisfied nor, perhaps, was the requirement of no independent advice. This

---

[47] (1888) 40 Ch D 312.

much is good. The difficulty with the judgment is that the relevance of the *Fry* v *Lane* requirements, however loosely they are interpreted, is left up in the air. At its broadest, Lord Templeman's judgement suggests that courts need merely look for a combination of unconscionable terms and unconscionable conduct (and, perhaps, unequal bargaining positions). This sounds very much like Lord Denning's 'inequality of bargaining power' doctrine from *Lloyds Bank* v *Bundy Ltd*,[48] though it seems unlikely that Lord Templeman intended to reintroduce such a broad power in so unassuming a fashion. The narrower interpretation of the judgment is that in order to prove unconscionability, the claimant must not only satisfy the *Fry* v *Lane* requirements (understood broadly), but must *also* prove that the defendant acted unconscionably. This result would be odd because, as the trial judge noted, satisfying the three requirements of *Fry* v *Lane* is meant to support an inference of unconscionable conduct. Nothing more should be needed. In the end, I think that Lord Templeman intended something in between these two interpretations, but exactly what remains a mystery.

One other feature of Lord Templeman's judgment is worth highlighting in view of our earlier discussion of the meaning of 'manifest disadvantage' in undue influence cases. I suggested then that, in light of its evidentiary function, the test of manifest disadvantage in undue influence cases should be satisfied by contracts which were 'imprudent' even if they were not actually unfair. On whatever interpretation we take of Lord Templeman's judgment, he clearly does not see this argument as applying to cases like *Boustany*. Lord Templeman held that in order for the respondent in *Boustany* to succeed, the court needed to find actual evidence of unconscionable conduct. He was not satisfied with drawing an inference of unconscionability by virtue of the *Fry* v *Lane* requirements being satisfied. It follows, therefore, that the need to prove manifest disadvantage in *Boustany* was not based on the inference of unconscionable conduct that might be drawn from such a finding. Substantive unfairness was significant in and of itself. It further follows that if, for example, the appellant in *Boustany* had persuaded the respondent to invest all her savings in a high risk joint venture, the contract would have been valid.

---

[48] [1974] 3 All ER 757.

IV. Consideration

In the landmark 1990 decision of *Williams* v *Roffey Bros*,[49] the Court of Appeal held that a promise to perform an existing contractual obligation may amount to good consideration, provided the promisee receives a practical benefit. The decision set the stage for a number of possible major developments in the law of contract. The elimination of the requirement of consideration, the expansion of estoppel, and the development of a mature doctrine of economic duress are perhaps the most obvious possibilities. For this reason, the judiciary's response to *Roffey Bros* has been eagerly awaited. Few cases of any significance have yet reached even the Court of Appeal. If the decision in *Re Selectmove*[50] is any indication, we shall need to wait until cases move to the very top of the court hierarchy before a significant response is seen.

The appellant company in *Selectmove* was in arrears to Inland Revenue for unpaid tax and National Insurance Contributions. During a meeting with a representative of Inland Revenue, Selectmove proposed a scheme whereby it would pay off the arrears at £1,000 month and make future payments on time, in return for which Inland Revenue would drop its demand for payment of the entire debt. The representative replied that he would speak to his superiors and would let Selectmove know if the scheme was unacceptable. The representative did not get back to Selectmove. The company proceeded to make payments in accordance with the new agreement, but eventually failed to make certain of these payments on time. Inland Revenue demanded the entire sum owing and eventually brought the present action to wind up the company. In response to the demand for winding up, Selectmove replied that it had a good faith dispute, based primarily on the new agreement but also on estoppel, with Inland Revenue.

Gibson LJ rejected Selectmove's claims and held that the full sum was due. There was some discussion in Gibson LJ's judgment about whether the representative of Inland Revenue had authority to conclude an agreement. I shall ignore this issue, but another peripheral issue deserves a brief mention. Inland Revenue argued that their representative could not have accepted the company's proposed scheme, because an offer cannot be accepted by silence

---

[49] [1990] 1 All ER 512.   [50] [1994] *The Times*, 13 January.

'save in the most exceptional circumstances'.[51] Gibson LJ found it unnecessary to decide this issue, but he indicated that in principle he thought *Selectmove* was just such an exceptional case. What made *Selectmove* different was that it was the offeree himself who had said that the offer was to be taken as accepted unless the offeree replied. This makes sense. The only difficulty is that of the timeframe. If, as in *Selectmove*, no cut-off date for a reply is specified, when does acceptance take place? Implying a 'reasonable' period may not be satisfactory in the context of offer and acceptance. A few minutes one way or the other can make all the difference.

The main issue in *Selectmove* was whether the new agreement between Inland Revenue and Selectmove was invalid for lack of consideration. In *Foakes* v *Beer*[52] it was held that part payment of a debt does not constitute consideration. Selectmove argued that, in light of the decision in *Roffey Bros*, the principle of *Foakes* v *Beer* should no longer be considered good law. Gibson LJ indicated considerable sympathy for this view. He cited Lord Blackburn's 'powerful' opposition to the rule on part payment in *Foakes* v *Beer* itself and noted that part payment cases appeared to fit within the principle of *Roffey Bros*. A creditor, Gibson LJ said, would 'no doubt always see a practical benefit' in cases of part payment. Nevertheless, Gibson LJ held that he was bound firmly by the precedent of *Foakes* v *Beer*. *Foakes* v *Beer* had not been overruled. If this was to happen, 'it must be by the House of Lords or, perhaps even more appropriately, by Parliament after consideration by the Law Commission'.

Gibson LJ's position cannot be faulted in terms of strict precedent. Nevertheless, a bolder court might have taken a less deferential stance. *Foakes* v *Beer* has long been subject to criticism. Indeed, Lord Blackburn himself only accepted the principle because he felt bound by the precedent of *Pinnel's Case*.[53] *Roffey Bros* provides a good example of how a court can avoid precedent when it has a mind to. The Court in *Roffey Bros* said that they were not overruling *Stilck* v *Myrick*,[54] but it seems plain that their judgment did exactly that. Admittedly, *Stilck* is an ambiguous decision and

---

[51]   *Allied Marine Ltd* v *Vale do Rio Doce SA* [1985] 1 WLR 925, 937.
[52]   (1884) 9 App Cas 605.
[53]   (1602) 5 Co Rep 117a; 77 ER 237.
[54]   (1809) 2 Camp 317; 6 Esp 129.

easier to distinguish than *Foakes* v *Beer*. On the other hand, the court in *Roffey Bros* did not have the advantage of the precedent which they created. As it is, the law is left in an inconsistent state. Whether or not the performance of an existing legal obligation amounts to good consideration depends on the nature of the obligation.

A second argument put forward by Selectmove was that Inland Revenue was estopped from going back on its undertaking to not demand payment of the entire sum owing. Estoppel has never been accepted as a means of getting around *Foakes* v *Beer*, although for a court interested in doing so there is much to recommend this route. The end result is the same as extending the principle of *Roffey Bros* to such cases. In *Roffey Bros* itself, Russell and Glidewell LJJ said that they would have liked to hear an argument based on estoppel. And an estoppel argument is easier to make in part payment cases. In *Roffey Bros* the defendants would have needed to use estoppel as a sword; in *Selectmove* estoppel would have functioned as it normally does, as a shield. As for *Foakes* v *Beer*, though the effect of allowing estoppel would be to overrule it, the case did not deal directly with estoppel so it is not an insurmountable barrier. The view that estoppel is only suspensory and cannot extinguish rights is a problem for part payment cases,[55] but this is a relatively minor obstacle.

Gibson LJ did not discuss any of these issues. Instead, he dismissed the estoppel claim quickly on the grounds that the representative lacked authority and that, the company having failed to keep its promise to make timely payments, it would not be inequitable to demand full payment. The reasoning cannot be faulted, though it would have been nice to see a short discussion, even if only in obiter, on the merits of extending estoppel to cases of part payment.

[55] G.Treitel, *The Law of Contract*[8], London, 1991, 121–123.

TORT

Richard O'Dair and Roger Halson[1]

The year under review has been both exciting and unsettling for tort lawyers as the Courts have considered a number of issues of great importance. Confining ourselves for the moment to the House of Lords, there have been decisions on concurrent liability,[2] employers liability for references,[3] strict liability for environmental damage[4] and the assessment of damages for personal injuries.[5] The judgments under review can profitably be considered from a variety of perspectives. Those interested in judicial reasoning will be struck by the increasing influence of academic literature on the decisions of the superior courts. Moreover one issue which pervades many though not all of the decisions is the difficulty which the Courts have recently experienced in understanding the interrelationship between tort law and other areas of the law particularly contract. More generally, it is salutary for tort lawyers to consider Professor Birks' comment that

it ought to be possible to take any legal subject and to cut away its detail so as to reveal the skeleton of principle which holds it together. If there is a subject for which that task seems impossible, the probability is that it is so disorganized that it should properly be described as unintelligible.[6]

One is left at the end of the period under review with the impression that whilst some progress has been made in relation to tort much remains to be done. Too many decisions seem still to be made without any attempt to relate them to coherent general principles with a consequent growth in inconsistency and anomaly.

---

[1] The introduction and sections I–V and VII–IX were first written by Richard O'Dair and section VI by Roger Halson. Each has read and commented upon the sections written by the other.

[2] *Henderson v Merret Syndicates Ltd* [1994] 3 WLR 761.

[3] *Spring v Guardian Assurance Plc* [1994] 3 WLR 354.

[4] *Cambridge Water Co v Eastern Counties Leather Plc* [1994] 2 WLR 53.

[5] *Hunt v Severs* [1994] 2 WLR 602.

[6] P. B. H. Birks, *An Introduction to the Law of Restitution* (Oxford, 1986), 1.

I Concurrent Liability in Contract and Tort

In *Henderson* v *Merrett Syndicates Ltd*,[7] the House of Lords was forced to confront questions about the interrelationship of and borderline between contract and tort which have long been the subject of debate amongst academics. The plaintiffs were Lloyd's names who had suffered huge losses on the insurance market. The names were required by the rules of the market to employ a members' agent to advise them inter alia as to their choice of syndicate. In some cases the members' agents undertook personally the management of the syndicates, in which case the names were known as direct names. In others, members' agents employed for this purpose managing agents to whom they delegated their power to enter into contracts of insurance on behalf of the names but who had no contract with the names. In this case, the plaintiffs were known as indirect names. In these proceedings the names sought redress for the allegedly negligent manner in which the loss making syndicates were managed. Among the issues before the House of Lords were the questions (i) whether direct names who were admittedly owed a contractual duty of care were also owed a duty of care in tort and (ii) whether indirect names were owed a duty of care in tort by the managing agents to whom their members' agents had delegated the management function.

The House of Lords was unanimous in deciding both issues in favour of the names. In the case of direct names, the defendants' argument was that even if in the absence of a contract the facts would have been such as to support the existence of a duty of care in tort, once the parties took the further step of entering into a contract then their respective rights and remedies should be confined to those afforded by the law of contract.[8] They therefore sought to overturn the acceptance by Oliver J in *Midland Bank Trust Co Ltd* v *Hett, Stubbs & Kemp*[9] of the principle of concurrent liability.

This argument was perceived by Lord Goff[10] as based on the view that the role of the law of tort was merely to fill the gaps left by the law of contract and was in this sense subordinate. With this

---

[7] [1994] 3 WLR 761.   [8] Ibid 773C-E.   [9] [1979] Ch 384.
[10] With whom Lords Nolan, Keith and Mustill concurred. Lord Browne-Wilkinson delivered a short concurring judgment.

premise, he was unable to agree. In a passage of outstanding importance, Lord Goff stated that

[the defendants'] approach involves regarding the law of tort as supplementary to the law of contract, i.e as providing for a tortious liability where there is no contract. Yet the law of tort is the general law, out of which the parties can, if they wish, contract.[11]

Accordingly the correct approach was to analyze whether the facts were such as to support the existence of a duty of care and then to ask whether the terms of the parties' contractual arrangements were such as to exclude that duty. On the facts of this case, the relevant duty of care was based on the principle established by *Hedley Byrne* v *Heller*[12]. This principle was not confined to the giving of information or advice nor to acts rather than omissions but was such that a duty of care was owed by all those possessed of special skill or knowledge who voluntarily agreed to exercise care in the application of that skill or knowledge for the benefit of another.[13]

Turning to the effect on this prima facie duty of the fact that the direct names had entered into a contract with those managing the syndicates, Lord Goff refused to regard the making of a contract as per se sufficient to exclude the duty of care in tort. Whether or not the speeches in *Hedley Byrne* could be read as confining the principle to situations where the parties were not in a contractual relationship[14] was not decisive. Logic demanded that the plaintiffs' rights should not be diminished because they had agreed to pay the defendant for his help and assistance. Any other result would have the unacceptable result that a medical patient would lose the benefit of a tortious duty of care when he agreed to be treated privately.

Turning to the case of the indirect names, Lord Goff applied the same premise. Accordingly, the starting point was that the managing agents had voluntarily undertaken a responsibility to the indirect names to exercise care and skill in performance of their management functions. Then and only then was it appropriate to consider the impact of the contractual chain between the plaintiffs and the defendants. As to this, there was nothing in the relevant

---

[11] [1994] 3 WLR 787H. [12] [1964] AC 465.
[13] [1994] 3 WLR 775H–777C.
[14] For a vigorous argument to this effect, see J. M. Kaye, 'The Liability of Solicitors in Tort', (1984) 100 *LQR* 680.

contracts of agency and subagency to exclude the duty in tort. Moreover there was no reason in principle why the defendants should not simultaneously have assumed responsibility under the *Hedley Byrne* principle both to the members' agents and to the indirect names.[15]

Despite its alleged foundation in logic, Lord Goff's reasoning is in fact at best incomplete and at worst wrong. As to its being incomplete, it is true that if the facts would otherwise support the existence of a duty of care, the mere making of a contract cannot itself be seen as evidence of evidence of an implied term by which the plaintiff genuinely, if tacitly, agrees to forego his remedies in tort. It does not follow however that the plaintiff should always be allowed to bring a claim in tort so as to avoid aspects of the law of contract which are unfavourable to him. In particular, the alternative claim should not be allowed if the policy underlying the relevant rule of contract law is thereby subverted. In this case the names wished to claim in tort so as to take advantage of the fact that the provisions of the Latent Damage Act only apply to claims in tort. This however required the Court to examine just why Parliament had chosen to exclude claims for breach of a contractual duty of care from the 1986 Act. If the exclusion were found to be based on a coherent policy which would be subverted by the alternative claim in tort that claim should not have been permitted. The point can by clarified by considering another possible motivation for a plaintiff's opting for a claim in tort, namely the fact that the principles governing remoteness of damage are more favourable to plaintiffs in tort than they are in contract; unless the plaintiff can rely on the second limb of *Hadley v Baxendale*, the contractual claim requires a higher degree of forseeability than the claim in tort.[16] If this difference is justified on the grounds that parties to a contractual relationship can if they so wish extend the defendant's liability by making known precisely what damage will be caused by breach (thus taking advantage of the second limb of the rule in *Hedley v Baxendale*[17]), then the same policy should apply whether the claim is framed in contract or tort. For this

---

[15] [1994] 3 WLR 789G–H.
[16] See the analysis in *The Heron II* [1969] 1 AC 350 of the relationship between *Hedley v Baxendale* (1854) 9 Ex 341 (contract) and *The Wagon Mound (No.1)* [1961] AC 388 (tort).
[17] Cf Lord Reid in *The Heron II* [1969] AC 350, 385–386.

reason, it is a pity that the rationale of the relevant provisions of the Latent Damage Act was not explored in more depth. Similarly, it is worrying that the reasoning in *Henderson* seems to give plaintiffs an unfettered right to sue in tort regardless of the issue before the Court.

Assuming, however, that further investigation of the Latent Damage Act would not have revealed policy reasons sufficient to justify excluding the claim in tort, there remain doubts about the correctness of the ultimate decision, all of which centre on Lord Goff's analysis and application of the *Hedley Byrne* principle.

We can begin by noticing that if the defendants in *Henderson* had been asked to manufacture machinery which had later proved defective thus causing the plaintiff economic loss, the defendants would not have been liable in tort. The *Hedley Byrne* principle has never been regarded as extending so as to impose a duty on those who cause economic loss by their careless construction of property.[18] It is difficult to view as rationally defensible a principle which says that there may be liability in tort in respect of a voluntary undertaking to provide a service except where the service consists in the construction of property, where the liability can only be in contract.

Next, we should note some of the uncertainties to which the decision gives rise. *Henderson* has very significant implications for the way judges respond to a claim by one contracting party that the other is liable for economic loss caused by breach of a tortious duty of care. In a number of recent cases, courts have responded by considering whether it is possible to imply into the contract a term containing the alleged duty. If not, it has been said to be inappropriate to undermine this decision by finding that a duty was owed in tort.[19] Following *Henderson*, the correct approach must be to begin by asking if there is a duty of care in tort. Nor will this be easy where the alleged liability is based on *Hedley Byrne*, for Lord Goff is quite clear that the liability is based upon a voluntary assumption of responsibility.[20] This concept has been said by a number of judges, particularly in cases like *Smith* v *Bush*[21] where

---

[18] *Nitrigin Eireann Teoranta* v *Inco Alloys Ltd* [1992] 1 All ER 854, QBD May J.
[19] Eg *Reid* v *Rush and Tomkins Group Plc* [1990] 1 WLR 912; *National Bank of Greece SA* v *Pinios Shipping (No.1)* [1989] 3 WLR 185, CA and *Bank of Nova Scotia* v *Hellenic War Risk Association (Bermuda) Ltd* [1990] 1 QB 818.
[20] [1994] 3 WLR 776D–F.   [21] [1991] 1 AC 831.

plaintiffs have relied on information supplied under a contract to which they were strangers, to be an unhelpful[22] or indeed to be little more than a verbal formula used to express a conclusion reached upon other grounds.[23] If so, it gives insufficient guidance as to when a duty will in fact be owed. Lord Goff's response was to state that the voluntary assumption of responsibility was based upon an objective principle.[24] Thus the existence of the duty in tort can it seems be ascertained only by applying the objective principle of agreement developed in the context of the contractual doctrines of offer and acceptance. This would seem to be a recipe for confusion.

Particularly puzzling and productive of uncertainty is Lord Goff's treatment of the argument by the defendants that the duty of care was excluded in the case of the indirect names by the absence of a direct contractual relationship, the parties having contracted with a members' agent. This argument was moreover strengthened by Lord Goff's own finding[25] that their members' agents were contractually liable for any negligence by the managing agents to whom they had delegated the functions. Thus, the plaintiffs had arguably entered into contractual arrangements designed to give them an adequate remedy (for breach of contract against the members' agents) even in the absence of a claim in tort against the managing agents. Yet Lord Goff held these arrangements insufficient to exclude the claim in tort. We are told that the case is highly exceptional and that it would be different in the case of a claim in tort for economic loss brought by a building owner against a subcontractor chosen by the owner but employed by the main contractor.[26] Similarly we must assume that Lord Goff's own decision in *Muirhead* v *I.T.S.*[27] that the ultimate user of a defective product has no claim in tort in respect of economic loss caused by product defects is distinguishable. Yet the distinction between these various cases is never identified let alone justified. One distinguishing feature of *Henderson* might be said to be that the defendants, though not employed by the plaintiffs were nevertheless their agents for the purpose of entering into contracts of insurance. Yet this cannot itself be the distinguishing feature because we are told

---

[22] [1991] 1 AC 864–865 Lord Griffiths.
[23] *Caparo Industries Plc* v *Dickman* [1990] 2 AC 605, 607 Lord Oliver.
[24] [1994] 3 WLR 776G.   [25] [1994] 3 WLR 791F–G, 797H.
[26] Ibid 790D–G.   [27] [1986] QB 507.

that subagents generally do *not* owe their principals a duty in tort.[28] The unexplained difference in treatment between apparently similar cases is difficult to defend.

Part of the explanation for these difficulties is surely that liability under *Hedley Byrne* is more appropriately classified as contractual than tortious. The argument for this view is that central to liability under *Hedley Byrne* is the defendant's undertaking to do something for the plaintiff and then either not doing it at all or doing it badly thus causing damage. As Lord Devlin pointed out in *Hedley Byrne*, this would be regarded as sufficient to create a contract in a system unencumbered by the doctrine of consideration.[29] In other words, *Hedley Byrne* has only been regarded as an example of liability in tort in order to avoid confronting directly the argument that in modern times the presence of consideration is not the sole ground which will justify the enforcement of a promise.[30] On this view consideration might be regarded as merely one indication that the promise was made with sufficiently serious intent to justify its enforcement.[31] However this issue has not been confronted directly. Instead, in the words of Professor Markesinis, the rigidities of the common-law of contract have led to an expansion of the law of tort.[32]

If the argument that *Hedley Byrne* is in fact an example of contractual liability is accepted, then of course the actual decision in *Henderson* is wrong. Whether it is the giving of consideration or the plaintiff's injurious reliance which justifies the enforcement of the promise, there is only one promise and the liability is contractual. Therefore the applicable limitation provision must be that governing contractual claims. In addition, reclassification of the liability as contractual would resolve most of the anomalies and inconsistencies described above. Thus for example whether the defendant agrees to provide the plaintiff with pure services or services consisting in the construction of property, the defendant's liability would equally be contractual, the enforcement of the defendant's promise being justified either because of the defendant's injurious reliance (*Hedley Byrne*) or because of the giving of

---

[28] [1994] 3 WLR 790D–E.   [29] [1964] AC 526, 529.
[30] P. S. Atiyah, *Essays on Contract* (Oxford, 1986), chapters 2 and 8.
[31] Lon Fuller, 'Consideration and Form' (1941) 41 *Columbia LR* 799.
[32] B. S. Markesinis, 'An expanding Tort Law—The Price of a Rigid Contract Law', (1987) 103 *LQR* 354.

consideration. Moreover, on this view, Lord Goff's willingness to test for a voluntary assumption of responsibility by applying the objective test for offer and acceptance becomes explicable. The test is used because the liability in question is contractual. Reconciling the different examples of chains of contracts remains difficult however. One suspects that had the liability in question been perceived as contractual Lord Goff would have been reluctant to find that the defendants entered into an informal *Hedley Byrne* type contract in the face of the surrounding networks of more formal contractual arrangements. If so the case would be a good example of how an inappropriate conceptual categorization of a plaintiff's claim can lead to the wrong result.

II Negligent Misrepresentation: Employers References

The issue in *Henderson* was the relationship between contractual and tortious liabilities. In *Spring v Guardian Assurance*[33] the liability of an employer to a former employee in respect of a careless reference turned in part on the relationship between the tort of negligence and the torts of defamation/malicious falsehood.

The plaintiff had been an employee of an estate agency known as Corinium and an agent for the sale of insurance policies issued by Corinium's parent company Guardian Assurance. The plaintiff was dismissed by Corinium which suspected he was in any case about to join a rival company. Not surprisingly, he then sought to do just that, but prospective employers were bound by the rules of Lautro[34] to seek and Guardian Assurance were bound to give a reference as to his character. The reference described him as dishonest and lacking in integrity thus effectively ending his career in life insurance. The trial judge found that this was untrue but resulted not from malice but from a failure properly to investigate the facts. The plaintiff sued Corinium and Guardian Assurance alleging inter alia liability in the torts of negligence, defamation and malicious falsehood. The claims based on malicious falsehood and defamation were doomed by the judges finding that the statements

[33] [1994] 3 WLR 354.
[34] The Life Assurance and Unit Trust Regulatory Organisation, the self regulatory body to which the Secretary of State for Trade and Industry and the Securities and Investment Board have delegated the powers conferred by the Financial Services Act 1986 to regulate the life insurance industry.

were made without malice. As to defamation, liability is strict but employers references are subject to qualified privilege,[35] so that mere negligence is insufficient to attract liability.[36] Malicious falsehood requires proof of malice by the plaintiff.

On appeal to the House of Lords, the question was whether the defendants could nevertheless be liable in negligence. It being accepted by all but one[37] of their Lordships that the relationship between an employer and his former employee was one of sufficient proximity[38] the defendants advanced two reasons why they should not be held liable. The first was that a decision in favour of the employee would undermine the torts of defamation and malicious falsehood each of which requires the plaintiff to prove malice.[39] Since this represented a careful balancing of the interests of the employee and the need to encourage frankness in the giving of reference this would be contrary to principle. The second argument was that this was one of those rare cases in which a court would refuse to recognize a duty of care because the consequence of such recognition would be contrary to the public interest.[40] A majority[41] of the House of Lords refused to accept either argument and accordingly found for the plaintiff. Lord Keith's point that the public's need for protection from untrustworthy sellers of financial products is such that their former employers must be encouraged to convey the merest suspicion of dishonesty is striking. Nevertheless, the decision is on balance to be welcomed. However their Lordships response to the defendants' arguments is disappointing.

---

[35] *Jackson* v *Hopperton* (1864) 16 CB (NS) 829; *Phelps* v *Kemsley* (1942) LT 18.

[36] See generally *Horrocks* v *Lowe* [1975] AC 135, 149 Lord Diplock.

[37] Lord Keith (359D); Lord Lowry (375H); Lord Slynn (384D–H) and Lord Woolf (391C). Lord Goff concurred in the result for different reasons: prefiguring in this respect the views he was to express in *Henderson* as to the ambit of liability under *Hedley Byrne*, Lord Goff held that regardless of the terms of the contract of employment the employers had voluntarily assumed a responsibility for ensuring that any reference provided would be compiled with reasonable care.

[38] Or between a principal and his former agent: their Lordships thought that there was no relevant distinction for the purposes of the issue before them and hence no separate reference will be made in the text to the position of agents.

[39] For opposing views on this case see A. Demopoulos, 'Misleading References and Qualified Privilege' (1988) 104 *LQR* 191; T. Weir, 'The Case of the Careless Referee' [1993] *CLJ* 376 and P. S. C. Lewis (1988) 17 *ILJ* 109.

[40] For an incisive critique of the decision of the Court of Appeal on this point see T. Allen, 'Liability for References: *Spring* v *Guardian Assurance*', (1994) 57 *MLR* 111.

[41] Lord Lowry, Slynn and Woolf. Lord Goff dissented as to the reasoning and Lord Keith as to the result.

As to the first, their Lordships gave a number of reasons why their finding for the plaintiff did not undermine the law of defamation and malicious falsehood. It was said (i) that defamation and malicious falsehood do not involve the concept of a duty of care;[42] (ii) that an action for defamation is founded upon the inaccurate terms of the reference whereas the claim in negligence is based on the lack of care of the author;[43] (iii) that the tort of negligence unlike the other torts involves proof of facts sufficient to constitute proximity;[44] (iv) that the law on qualified privilege was settled before the generalization of the tort of negligence by *Donoghue* v *Stevenson*; and (v) that defamation and malicious falsehood protect the plaintiff's interest in reputation rather than his employment prospects.[45] Points (i) and (ii) can be dismissed as mere semantics. Point (iii) ignores the fact that employers references are a well established example of the defence of qualified privilege: see *Stuart* v *Bell*.[46] It follows that when subsumed under the label of defamation all the facts upon which the plaintiff relied in *Spring* had been authoritatively held not to entitle him to the remedy claimed. This result should not automatically be altered by a relabelling of the facts as negligence. Point (iv) ignores the fact that the tort of defamation has not developed in ignorance of the possibility of making liability in effect depend on negligence by allowing such a plea to defeat qualified privilege[47] but has rather chosen to reject such a course for clear and well-defined reasons of public policy. It therefore follows that the defence of qualified privilege should not lightly be made redundant by the tort of negligence. Point (v) merely distinguishes the tort of defamation from that of malicious falsehood, the function of which is precisely to protect trading interests against the harm which can occur when false but not defamatory statements are made to third parties.[48] However, since malicious falsehood like defamation depends on proof of malice, the alleged distinction merely shows that the claim in negligence is subverting malicious falsehood rather than defamation without showing why this is not equally undesirable. Ultimately the House of Lords failed to answer the defendants' argument that

---

[42] 384B–C Lord Slynn.   [43] 395G Lord Woolf.
[44] 375E–H Lord Lowry.
[45] 399A–B Lord Woolf; 384C–D Lord Slynn.
[46] [1891] 2 QB 341 CA.   [47] See *Horrocks* v *Lowe*, supra note 36.
[48] *Salmond & Heuston on the Law of Torts*, 20th ed. by R. F. H. Heuston and R. A. Buckley (London, 1992), 393.

the facts on which the plaintiff relied in *Spring* would be insufficient to justify an award of damages when labelled defamation or malicious falsehood because of the alleged public interest in encouraging uninhibited references and that the mere evocation of the label negligence should not lead to a different result. The conceptual categories used to organize and map out the law of tort are merely tools to be used in reaching desirable results, the ultimate question in every case being whether the plaintiff has alleged facts sufficient to justify the remedy sought.[49] In *Spring*, the House of Lords were being asked to change the law and it was important that this be acknowledged.

As to the exclusion of a duty of care on the grounds of public policy, their Lordships treatment of the defendants' argument was again disappointing. Prima facie the potential adverse consequences of the imposition of a duty to employees are, firstly, that employers might refuse to give references thus harming the very group (employees) that the imposition of the duty is intended to assist or, secondly, the giving of excessively favourable references thus harming prospective employers and their customers. The defendants seem to have relied on both possibilities. With the exception of Lord Woolf, to whose judgment we shall return, the response of the judges who found for the plaintiff is typified by Lord Slynn who stated that he could not believe that

employers will refuse to give references or will give such bland or adulatory ones as is forecast. They should be and are capable of being sufficiently robust as to express frank and honest views after taking reasonable care both as to the factual content and as to the opinion expressed. They will not shrink from the duty of taking reasonable care when they realize the importance of the reference both to the recipient (to whom it is assumed that a duty of care exists) and to the employee (to whom it is contended on existing authority that no such duty exists).[50]

This however is merely to assert rather than to prove.

In the absence of empirical evidence as to the behaviour of employers under a legal regime imposing liability for negligent references, the defendants' arguments could only be met by a priori reasoning based on clear and explicit assumptions about how those involved might rationally react to the imposition of a duty.

---

[49] Cf Diplock LJ in *Letang* v *Cooper* [1962] 1 QB 237, 242G–243C.
[50] [1994] 3 WLR 385F–H. Cf 375A–B Lord Goff and 376D–F Lord Lowry.

Adopting such an approach, it seems plausible to argue that though the giving of a careful reference might be costly for employers, it is a practice from which they themselves benefit in so much as it makes them attractive as employers. Subject to one caveat, the imposition of a duty of care is therefore unlikely to lead to employers as a class refusing to give references. The caveat is that whilst employers as a class might be unwilling to insert terms into their contract of employment that no references would be given, it seems naive to ignore the possibility that following an acrimonious end to an employment relationship a particular employer might refuse to give a reference in order to avoid further argument with a truculent employee over the terms of the reference. Unless the dispute is widely reported in the press, the consequential risk of damage to his reputation as an employer is likely to be fairly small and thus an acceptable price to pay. Consequently the risk of injustice to particular employees could only be avoided if their Lordships were prepared not only to impose a tortious duty to give references with reasonable care but also to imply into contracts of employment a term requiring employers to give references, at least in occupations where references are important. This was something to which only Lord Woolf was prepared to commit himself.[51] Thus their Lordships' consideration of the possibility of harmful consequences to employees was incomplete.

Turning to the argument that the prospect of liability to the subject will lead to prospective employers being harmed by excessively laudatory references, this seems unlikely. The crucial point is that it has always been assumed that the author of a negligent reference is liable to the recipient under the principle in *Hedley Byrne* for any consequential loss.[52] If referees are sufficiently responsive to the threat of litigation from the subject of the reference to avoid excessive criticism, they are likely to be equally sufficiently responsive to the threat of being sued by the recipient if they are too fulsome in their praise. This point is nowhere made explicit in their Lordships judgment but since the argument supports the result in fact reached this is perhaps not as serious as the possibility of negligently favourable references causing loss to the public.

---

[51] Ibid 402A–C. Cf 370F–G Lord Goff and contrast *Gallear* v *JF Watson & Son Ltd* [1979] IRLR 306. Lord Lowery declined to comment on the contractual position.   [52] Ibid 385 A–B Lord Slynn.

It is disturbing to note that no answer was given to Lord Keith's point that the public's need for protection from untrustworthy sellers of financial products is such that their former employers must be encouraged to convey the merest suspicion of dishonesty. For clearly the possibility of liability to the recipient will not be sufficient disincentive to excessive praise if the subject may in his new employment cause loss to the public without thereby causing actionable damage to the recipient. This does not seem to be a problem in the case of insurance salesmen who will normally cause damage by giving negligent professional advice to customers and for such advice the recipient employer will be vicariously liable. Consider, however the case of an employer wishing to give a reference with respect to a teacher about whom there are rumours of child abuse. Fear of being sued by the teacher may lead the author of the reference to consider not mentioning these rumours. Indeed that might pragmatically be a sensible course for if abuse is committed whilst the subject is in the employment of the recipient, the latter may not be vicariously liable and thus will have no cause of action against the author.[53] Thus whilst their Lordships' conclusion that harm to the public is unlikely to follow on the facts before them seems sound the decision fails to provide a touchstone for distinguishing those cases where the argument might have more substance.

III Negligent Misrepresentation:
Liability of Professional Agents

We have seen the House of Lords affirm within the period of this review that where a defendant commits a tort in the course of performing his own contract with the plaintiff, the plaintiff's right to sue in tort is unaffected by the mere existence of an action for breach of contract. This is because the duty in tort is part of the general law and is not effected by the mere presence of the contract. An analogous problem arises where the defendant commits the alleged tort in the course of performing a contract on behalf of his employer or negotiating a contract on behalf of his principal. It

---

[53] The extent of an employer's liability for deliberate and criminal wrongdoing by an employee is a difficult one: see generally B. S. Markesinis and S. E. Deakin, *Tort Law*[3] (Oxford, 1993), 508–517.

would seem to follow from their Lordships reasoning on concurrent liability that the plaintiff's contractual relationship with the employer/principal is in itself irrelevant to the defendant's liability in tort.

This point arose in *McCullagh* v *Lane Fox*.[54] The plaintiffs had taken the unusual step of exchanging contracts on a property for which they agreed to pay £875,000 a mere two days after their first viewing and without a survey. This they did in reliance on the defendant estate agents' oral representation that the house stood in 0.91 acres. This led the plaintiffs to believe that after demolishing the existing house they would be able to build the house of their dreams.

Unfortunately, the plot was only 0.48 acres and the plaintiffs' dreams were shattered. This being so their only recourse was against the estate agent because the contract of sale had effectively excluded any liability on the part of the vendors for the misrepresentations of their agent. Assuming that the statement was in fact careless one of the issues before Coleman J was whether the estate agent owed a duty of care. In particular, the defendant argued that even if the making of the same statement in the same circumstances by the vendor would have been subject to a duty of care, nevertheless no duty was owed by the defendants precisely because they had acted as agents for the vendors. In this they relied heavily on the earlier decision of Sir Donald Nicholls VC in *Gran Gelato* v *Richliff Ltd*.[55] There the solicitors to a sublessor had caused loss to the plaintiff sublessee by their negligent misrepresentations in response to inquiries before lease. The plaintiff pursued the solicitors because the solvency of the sublessor was in doubt. Nicholls VC held that there was no duty of care principally because the misrepresentation occurred in response to enquiries addressed to the sublessor. The sublessor was liable for any misrepresentations made by the solicitor on his behalf and it was not necessary to duplicate this remedy by giving a further remedy against the agent. That the principal might, as here, be insolvent was beside the point, this being one of the ordinary risks of every day life.[56]

The two cases were clearly indistinguishable in principle. If the

[54] [1994] 08 EG 118; (1994) 1 EGLR 48.   [55] [1992] Ch 560.
[56] Ibid 571F–G.

plaintiff in *Gran Gelato* was not permitted to escape the consequences of the insolvency of its chosen contracting partner, then a fortiori, in *McCullagh* the plaintiff could not be permitted to escape the consequences of having agreed that the vendor should not be liable for any misrepresentation by the estate agent. Accordingly Coleman J was required to decide whether or not to follow *Gran Gelato* and this his Lordship refused to do. The earlier decision depended upon the assumption that the plaintiff would (in the absence of a contractual exclusion clause) be able to sue the principal. However unless the agent were himself liable it would be difficult to see how this assumption could be justified. A defendant who is not personally at fault cannot be held liable in negligence unless he can be shown to be vicariously liable for the tort of his servant or, in certain limited circumstances, his agent acting within the scope of the employment or agency. This however presupposes the personal liability of the servant or agent. Eschewing the temptation to be an incrementalist, Coleman J rightly took the view that there was no reason for distinguishing the general principle either on the grounds that the case before him involved liability for an agent rather than an employee or that it involved liability for negligent misrepresentation rather than for personal injury or damage to property. His Lordship might indeed have added that since the rejection by the House of Lords in *Scruttons v Midland Silicones Ltd.*[57] of the doctrine of vicarious immunity and consistently with the logic of concurrent liability the presence of a contract between the defendant's employer/principal and the plaintiff is not regarded as sufficient per se to effect the duty of care of the servant/agent in tort. At the very least, the defendant has been required to show that the contract contained terms designed to exclude or restrict his liability. In some contexts, the law has been even stricter so that in the shipping context for example a stevedore employed by a shipowner who wishes to take advantage of exemptions in the contract of carriage must show that he is in fact a party to that contract.[58]

McCullagh is clearly correct as regards the existing law. It is worth asking however whether there might not be something to be said for the radical departure represented by *Gran Gelato*. The arguments were extensively reviewed in the minority judgment of

[57] [1962] AC 466.   [58] *The Eurymedon* [1975] AC 154 PC.

La Forest J in *London Drugs* v *Kuehne and Nagel*[59] in the Supreme Court of Canada. There the plaintiff entered into a contract for the storage of its goods on terms which limited the liability of the warehouseman. When the goods were damaged by the carelessness of an employee of the warehouseman the plaintiff sued the employee directly. La Forest J pointed out that in this situation the employee would traditionally be liable in tort unless he could somehow overcome the doctrine of privity of contract so as to be able to take the benefit of any exclusions of liability contained in the contract between the owner and the employer. The employer would be then be vicariously liable for the employee's tort. However where the employee's carelessness occurred whilst he was carrying out his employer's contract with the plaintiff, none of the traditional justifications for vicarious liability required both employer and employee to be liable. The need to ensure the distribution of loss via a deep-pocket could be met by confining liability to the employer: if the plaintiff had agreed to limit the liability of the employer that could only be because the parties had viewed the plaintiff as a superior channel for the distribution of losses. If the employer were insolvent that could be regarded as one of the risks of commercial contracting. Any perception that liability was needed to deter careless conduct could be met by the observation that placing liability on the employer would give him an incentive to monitor the conduct of his employees. Thus stated the argument is that (i) the purposes of vicarious liability can be fulfilled without making the employee personally liable and (ii) if they cannot, then if the plaintiff is in a contractual relationship with the defendant then he should be regarded as having contracted to bear the risk of the employer's insolvency and should not be permitted to evade this distribution of risk by suing the employee.

Contrary to the current position in English and indeed Canadian law, there may therefore be something to be said for employers being held liable for damage caused by the carelessness of employees in the course of their performance of the employer's contract without holding the employee personally liable. Be that as it may, the case of professional agents is clearly distinguishable. As regards loss distribution they are just as likely as their principals to be solvent. As regards deterrence, even if employee carelessness can

---

[59] (1992) 97 DLR (4d) 461.

be the deterred by imposing liability on employers, the position of professional agents seems altogether different. Given their professional expertise, the argument that imposing liability on the principal will lead the principal to monitor the work of the agent seems implausible. Moreover, where as in *McCullagh* the plaintiff is a private individual purchasing domestic property it seems wrong to remove the possibility of an action against the agent in the event of the insolvency of the principal.

IV Liability of Marine Surveyors

In *Marc Rich & Co. A.G.* v *Bishop Rock Marine Co. Ltd.*[60], the relevance to the defendant's liability in tort of the plaintiff's contract with a third party was again an important issue. The plaintiffs were the owners of cargo being carried on board the Nicholas H when it developed a crack in its hull. The shipowner called for a report on the damage from a surveyor employed by the defendant Classification Society. After temporary repairs had been carried out, the surveyor recommended that the vessel continue on its voyage. However the repairs proved inadequate and both the ship and the cargo were ultimately lost. Having recovered part of their loss from the shipowner, the plaintiffs claimed their remaining losses from the defendant alleging that the surveyor, having initially recommended permanent repairs (which would have required dry-docking and abandonment of the voyage) negligently allowed himself to be persuaded by the shipowner that temporary repairs would suffice[61] and that this carelessness had amounted to a breach of duty of care.

The question before the Court of Appeal was whether the Classification Society owed the plaintiffs a duty of care. The Court first held that even in a case involving physical damage rather than economic loss, foreseeability of harm was not per se sufficient to demonstrate the existence of a duty of care. It must be shown in addition that there existed a close relationship of proximity and that it is just and reasonable that a duty be owed,[62] although this would present little difficulty in cases where the defendant has

[60] [1994] 1 WLR 1071.
[61] Alternatively failed to check whether the temporary repairs were sufficient or properly done: ibid 1079F–G.
[62] Ibid 1077C–G Saville LJ; 1085F–H Mann LJ and 1087F Balcombe LJ.

directly inflicted physical harm.[63] On this point the Court's reasoning is impeccable and finds strong support in the law's reluctance to impose liability for failure to prevent third parties causing the plaintiff physical damage.[64] Much more questionable was the application of these criteria to the facts, for it was held that it was not just and reasonable for a duty to be owed principally because the plaintiffs had a contractual claim against the shipowner. This claim was subject to the Hague Rules which imposed certain limits on the shipowner's liability and it would, said the Court, be wrong to impose an unlimited liability on the Classification Society.[65]

The Court's focus upon the existence of a limited contractual claim against the shipowner is misconceived and approaches the problem from the wrong end. As *Henderson* suggests, the first question in this case should have been whether, disregarding the contract between plaintiffs and shipowner, the facts were such as to establish a duty of care. Then and only then was it appropriate to ask whether the terms of the Bill of Lading represented a reason why a duty should not be owed.

As it was, this first issue occupies only a quarter of one of the fourteen pages taken up by the judgments of the Court and is considered by only Saville LJ. He considered that no relationship existed between plaintiffs and defendant because there was no direct dealing between the two and because the plaintiffs did not rely upon the survey or even know that it had taken place. This seems to assume that the only relevant ground of liability on which the plaintiffs' case could succeed was liability for negligent misstatement or, more broadly, liability for the negligent breach of an undertaking to perform services given directly to and relied on by the plaintiff.[66] However even before the House of Lords decision in *Spring*, we already knew that in certain limited circumstances A might owe a duty of care to B in making a statement to C if the circumstances were such that reliance on A's misstatement by C might cause loss to B: *Ministry of Housing and Local Government* v *Sharpe*.[67] Saville LJ notes that insurers require that ships be

---

[63] Ibid 1077E–F Saville LJ; 1085G Mann LJ and 1088A–D Balcombe LJ.

[64] See for example *Hill* v *Chief Constable of South Yorks* [1989] AC 53 HL.

[65] [1994] 1 WLR 1080D–G Saville LJ; 1087D Mann LJ and 1089A–B Balcombe LJ.   [66] Cf *Hedley Bryne* v *Heller* supra note 12.

[67] [1970] 2 QB 223 CA.

maintained within class as a condition of cover. It seems plausible to infer therefore that the reason why the surveyor was instructed in this case was the owners desire to satisfy the insurers. If so, then it was at least arguable that the insurers' reliance on the defendant caused loss to the plaintiffs.

More damning still is the fact that the Court notes that Survey Societies are in effect the regulators of the shipping industry.[68] Governments regularly devolve to Survey Societies the enforcement of international conventions on maritime safety. Moreover, cargo owners *do* rely on Survey Societies for the due performance of their functions in the sense that no cargo would ever be placed on a ship which was not fully classed.[69] The Court should surely have considered the liability of the survey society as a quasi-public regulatory body. Not that this would necessarily have led to the conclusion that the defendant did owe a duty of care. Recent case law reveals a consistent refusal by the Courts to impose a duty of care on public regulatory bodies.[70] However, this refusal is based in part at least on a reluctance to see the deep-pocket of the public authority used as a source of compensation for wrongs for which others are primarily responsible. Survey Societies are in a different position being private bodies who accept large fees from ship-owners for the carrying out of their regulatory functions. Survey Societies compete amongst themselves for business. There is therefore an obvious temptation for Survey Societies to attract and retain the business of shipowners by charging low fees and making generous assessments of the condition of the relevant vessels. In such a situation, liability for negligence seems a wholly appropriate contrary incentive.[71] Be that as it may, it is clear that the question of the liability of the defendant Survey Society was not considered in its appropriate context.

Whether or not the facts were sufficient to justify the imposition of a duty of care on the Survey Society, the second issue, that of the impact of the limits on the shipowner's liability under the Hague Rules was quite straightforward. As stated in the previous section, English Law has imposed quite stringent conditions on the capacity of a defendant to avoid liability in tort on the basis of the provisions

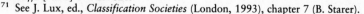

---

[68] [1994] 3 WLR 1078C–E.   [69] Ibid 1078H.
[70] Eg *Yuen Kun Yeu* v *Attorney-General for Hong-Kong* [1990] 2 AC 605; *Davis* v *Radcliffe* [1990] 1 WLR 821.
[71] See J. Lux, ed., *Classification Societies* (London, 1993), chapter 7 (B. Starer).

of a contract to which he is not a party. As a minimum, it must be shown that those provisions were intended to protect the defendant. The limits imposed by the Hague Rules by contrast are limits on the liability of the shipowner not that of Survey Societies. They could thus have been discounted without any consideration of the other problems arising from privity of contract and third party reliance on exemption clauses.

V Privity of Contract and Exclusion Clauses

If A voluntarily takes into his possession goods which he knows to belong to B, there will arise between A and B the relationship of bailor and bailee,[72] a simple example being the gratuitous loan of goods. The law of bailment has a number of characteristics peculiar to itself[73] and the issues which arose in the *Pioneer Container*[74] were seen as depending on the special features of the law of bailment. As we shall see, this is a pity, since the facts raised issues of general importance concerning the impact of privity of contract upon the availability of exclusion clauses as defences to actions in tort. Had the issues been discussed in more general terms this would have been of benefit to the future development of the law and led perhaps to a simpler resolution of the immediate dispute.

The plaintiffs were the various owners of goods lost at sea when the defendant's ship sank off Taiwan. In every case, the defendant shipowners had agreed to carry the goods pursuant to a contract which provided (cl.126) that any disputes were to be determined in Taiwan and the question before the Privy Council was whether the plaintiffs were bound by this clause. Some of the plaintiffs had contracted directly with the defendants and these plaintiffs clearly were bound. Others however had contracted with freight carriers who had then subcontracted the actual carriage to the defendants. As against these plaintiffs, the problem was therefore whether the plaintiffs were bound in the absence of privity of contract between themselves and the defendants. The facts thus raised a variant of the following common problem: A contracts with B for contractual performance which is in fact provided by C, a servant or independent contractor employed by B. The A-B and B-C contracts

[72] N. E. Palmer, *Bailment*[2] (London, 1991), 32–37.   [73] Palmer, ch 1.
[74] *BKH Enterprise (Cargo owners)* v *Pioneer Container (Owners)* [1994] 2 All ER 250 PC.

contain identical clauses designed to regulate the economic enterprise to be effected via this series of contracts. These clauses may for example exempt both B and C for damage to A's property, the idea being that A is to take out first party insurance. In the *Pioneer Container*, the relevant clauses where designed to insure that all disputes relating to the carriage of the goods be heard together in one jurisdiction, thereby saving considerable time and expense.[75] If A sues C in tort, C may attempt to rely upon an exclusion clause in the A-B contract and the legal difficulties created by the doctrine of privity of contract have already been discussed. Alternatively, the question may arise as to whether privity of contract equally prevents C (here the shipowner) relying on the clause in his own contract with B (the freight carrier) on the grounds that A cannot be bound by a contract to which he is not a party.

In the *Pioneer Container*, the defendants boldly argued that the plaintiffs were inevitably bound relying in this on the judgment of Donaldson J. in *Johnson Matthey & Co. Ltd v Constantine Terminals Ltd*.[76] Their argument was based on the view that the only relevant basis of liability was a breach of a bailee's duty to take reasonable care of the goods in his possession; and that the bailor-bailee relationship could only arise by consent. If so, the plaintiffs were on the horns of a dilemma: either they had consented to the terms of the subcontract, in which case they were bound by its terms or they did not consent, in which case no duty would be owed. Lord Goff giving the judgment of the Privy Council, rejected the consensual view of bailment,[77] preferring instead the view of Professor Palmer[78] that duties of a bailee are owed by any person who voluntarily takes into his possession goods which he knows to belong to another regardless of that other's consent. This seems correct: the alternative view makes it difficult to explain why a finder of goods becomes a bailee.[79] A bailee's duty being one which arises by operation of law. it followed that any attempt to qualify or limit the duty would be effective only if the owner consented.

[75] Ibid 255F–H.   [76] [1976] 2 Lloyd's Rep 215 QBD.
[77] Ibid 262D–E; though with the puzzling and irreconcilable caveat that where a bailee enters into a sub-bailment without the owner's consent it may be that no bailor-bailee relation arises between the owner and the sub-bailee (ibid 258E–F).
[78] Supra note 70.
[79] *Gilchrist Watt & Sanderson Pty Ltd v York Products Pty Ltd* [1970] 3 All ER 825, 831 Lord Pearson.

This too seems correct. What is disappointing, however, is his Lordship's failure to recognize that the issues were both simpler and of more general importance than at first appears. The defendants' argument amounted to an assertion that the plaintiffs were seeking to take advantage of their contract with the main contractor but circumventing the doctrine of privity by characterizing their claim as one based on bailment. If so, they clearly should have been bound by clause 126. In the same way, Steyn LJ was firmly of the view in *White* v *Jones*[80] that the liability of a solicitor to a disappointed beneficiary is regarded as tortious only because of the rigidity of the doctrine of privity of contract. It therefore followed in his Lordship's view that the beneficiary would be bound by any exclusory clauses in the solicitor-client contract.[81] However the duties owed by the sub-bailee to the owner cannot be characterized as covert exceptions to privity of contract: the duty arises as a matter of law upon the defendant's voluntarily taking possession of the plaintiff's goods. If so, then clearly that duty cannot be excluded by the terms of an agreement with the freight carriers to which the plaintiffs were not a party and did not consent; otherwise the manufacturer of a bottle of ginger beer would be able to rely upon exclusory clauses in his contract with the retailer as a defence to an action by an ultimate consumer injured by its contents.

On the facts however, the plaintiffs had consented to the terms of the subcontract. The defendants therefore argued that the plaintiffs were bound on the basis that a bailor is bound by the terms of a sub-bailment to which he expressly or impliedly consents. This argument was accepted by the Privy Council, thus affirming a doctrine first propounded obiter by Lord Denning in *Scruttons* v *Midland Silicones*[82] but never previously affirmed and applied other than at first instance.[83] There is obvious good sense in this both from a commercial and a doctrinal point of view. As to the former, the facts of the *Pioneer Container* show that where a single economic activity is effected by a network of contracts but is intended to be subject to standard terms, privity of contract can

[80] [1993] 3 WLR 730, 752D–G.   [81] Ibid 755 B–C.
[82] [1962] AC 466. The doctrine was approved, though again obiter, by the Court of Appeal in *Morris* v *C.W. Martin & Sons Ltd* [1966] 1 QB 716.
[83] By Steyn J in *Singer Co (UK) Ltd* v *Tees and Hartlepool Port Authority* [1988] 2 Lloyd's Rep 164.

have unacceptable consequences. As to the latter, full free and informed consent by a plaintiff that conduct by a defendant shall not be actionable, or not actionable otherwise than in a particular jurisdiction, should obviously be respected, at least in a commercial context.

Nevertheless, it is doubtful whether legal doctrine yet adequately reflects this good sense. Lord Goff's judgment seems to suggest that the doctrine represents a doctrine special to the law of bailment rather than an application of the doctrine of *volenti non fit injuria* as Lord Denning thought in *Scruttons*.[84] In principle, Lord Denning's view which attempts to state the doctrine in terms of a rational, generalizable principle seems preferable for two reasons. Firstly, the narrow view leads to some intolerable distinctions. If a defendant subcontractor provides services on terms which, with the consent of the main employer, limit its liability for negligence, then that limit will only avail against the plaintiff if the defendant comes into possession of the plaintiff's goods hence constituting the relationship of bailor and bailee. Those such as stevedores who do not obtain possession of the plaintiff's goods will have no defence unless they are protected by some clause in the main contract and can circumvent the difficulties of the *Eurymedon*.

Secondly, the narrow view will defeat the commercial purpose it is designed to fulfil when as often the law of bailment and the tort of negligence impose overlapping duties. Suppose that the owner of a car hires it out for reward on terms that the hirer is not to be liable for negligent damage to the car and that the hirer may subhire the car on the same terms. If the subhirer carelessly damages the car, he will have a defence if the owner alleges a breach of a bailees duty to take care of the goods. However, the facts are also sufficient to establish a breach of duty of care in the ordinary tort of negligence since in the case of direct damage to property such a duty almost invariably arises once the damage is shown to be foreseeable.[85] Therefore it is difficult to see why the subhirer does not owe the

---

[84] [1962] AC 446, 488–489. But see the rejection of this view (or at least a similar one based on non-contractual notices excluding liability) by Lord Simon of Glaisdale in *The Eurymedon* [1975] AC 154, 182B–H.

[85] Supra note 62 and following text. Contrast *Norwich City Council v Harvey* [1989] 1 WLR 828 CA, which ignores this point and is convincingly criticized by Palmer, 1651–1653.

same duty of care with respect to the car as any other road user[86] and on the narrow view the doctrine affirmed in the *Pioneer Container* does not apply. If there are sound reasons for giving legal effect to the plaintiff's consent to the terms of the subcontract, then this effect must encapsulated with the general law of tort rather than being viewed as some peculiarity of the law of bailment.

VI Strict Liability for Environmental Damage

In the case of *Cambridge Water Co Ltd v Eastern Counties Leather Plc*[87] the House of Lords was given the opportunity to consider the fundamentals of liability in nuisance. The case is important for the changes made to (or clarification of) the doctrine of private nuisance and other associated principles. However perhaps even more interesting is the general approach to the question of liability which was taken by Lord Goff who delivered the judgment of the House.

The defendant was a manufacturer of leather which used solvents in the tanning process. Over a period of years there were small but regular spillages when barrels of solvent were poured into the reservoirs of the degreasing machines. These spillages ended when a new system was installed whereby the solvent was delivered in bulk and stored in a tank from where it was piped to the degreasing machines. The Judge found that these spillages were the major cause of the pollution of the plaintiff's borehole. This borehole was located about 1.3 miles away from the defendant's factory and was used for the extraction of water. Before the plaintiff purchased the borehole it satisfied itself as to the quality of the water. However subsequent to the purchase there was a general increase in concern about the chemical pollution of drinking water. This was reflected in more stringent standards as to the permissible concentrations of certain substances in water intended for human consumption. An EC directive of 1980 (80/778/EEC) resulted in amendments to domestic legislation which reduced the previously permitted levels of certain pollutants. When tests were conducted by the plaintiff it was found that there were excessive quantities of solvent in their water and so the borehole was closed down. A major geological

---

[86] Cf *Awad v Pillai* [1982] RTR 266 CA criticized by N. E. Palmer and J. R. Murdoch [1983] 46 *MLR* 73.   [87] [1994] 2 WLR 53.

investigation followed which revealed that the defendant's factory was the source of the contamination and that due to the slow movement of the contamination and the possible 'pools' of solvent in the strata the period of pollution was indefinite; this despite the fact that the source of contamination had ended.

The plaintiffs sued the defendant in negligence, nuisance and under the rule in *Rylands v Fletcher*.[88] The actions in negligence and nuisance failed because the judge found that the defendant's employees could not have reasonably foreseen that the spillages would have resulted in detectable quantities of solvent being found in the aquifer let alone that those quantities would have a sensible effect upon the quality of water extracted from the borehole. This finding was not contested in the Court of Appeal and serves to emphasise the point that courts must resist the tendency to use the benefit of hindsight when considering a claim. Advances in knowledge which occur after the alleged tort was committed are not relevant to the proof of liability; a defendant's foresight must be related to the foresight of a reasonable person at the time of commission of the tort.[89]

In the Court of Appeal the finding that the defendants could not have reasonably foreseen the pollution which in fact ensued was not itself in question, but whether that finding was fatal to a claim in nuisance and under the rule in *Rylands v Fletcher* was very much in issue. The plaintiffs appealed on the ground that the defendants were strictly liable under the rule in *Rylands v Fletcher*. However the conclusion the Court of Appeal reached on the claim in nuisance made it unnecessary for them to consider the general scope of *Rylands v Fletcher* liability and, in particular, the necessity for and the meaning of, the frequently articulated requirement of a 'non-natural' use of land.[90] The conclusion which rendered otiose a consideration of *Rylands v Fletcher* was that there existed liability in nuisance based upon a proper consideration of the Court of Appeal's decision in *Ballard v Tomlinson*.[91] The Court of Appeal in the present case treated this earlier decision as authority for the proposition that 'where the nuisance is an interference with a natural right incident to ownership then the liability is a strict

---

[88] (1868) LR 3 HL 330, affg *Fletcher v Rylands* (1866) LR 1 Ex 265.
[89] *Roe v Minister of Health* [1954] 2 QB 66.
[90] See for example *Rickards v Lothian* [1913] AC 263, 279–280 Lord Moulton.
[91] (1885) 29 Ch D 115.

one'.[92] As this case was regarded as indistinguishable from the present case liability in nuisance was proven.

This conclusion is difficult to support. In *Ballard* v *Tomlinson* the plaintiff sought, inter alia, an injunction to restrain the defendant from pouring sewage and waste down a well on the defendant's land and thereby polluting a common source of percolating water which was drawn by the plaintiff in a well on his land and used to brew beer. Only one of the judgments in the Court of Appeal, that of Lindley LJ, appeared to proceed on the basis of nuisance; both Cotton LJ and Brett MR seemed to treat the case as falling under the rule in *Rylands* v *Fletcher*. Moreover the Court of Appeal in the present case did not seem to be sufficiently sensitive to the distinction between cases where an injunction is sought to stop a nuisance and one where damages were the only remedy sought. Statements in cases where an injunction was sought should not be treated as authority to support the proposition that liability in nuisance can exist in the absence of foreseeability because the foreseeability of risk is simply not in issue when that remedy is sought. This point has frequently been made by commentators[93] and is neatly summarised by Lord Goff in the House of Lords in this case when he says that

. . . where an injunction is claimed, its purpose is to restrain further action by the defendant which may interfere with the plaintiff's enjoyment of his land, and ex hypothesi the defendant must be aware, if and when an injunction is granted, that such interference may be caused by the act which he is restrained from committing.[94]

The defendants then appealed to the House of Lords against an award of damages amounting to over £1 million. In delivering the judgment of the House Lord Goff disposed quickly of the authority relied on in the Court of Appeal. He thought that the unreserved judgments in *Ballard* v *Tomlinson* simply did not develop the law of private nuisance in the way in which the Court of Appeal asserted. Rather he stated that there was nothing in that case which expanded the substantive heads of civil liability which are respectively known as the tort of private nuisance and the rule in *Rylands* v *Fletcher*.

---

[92]   Mann LJ delivering the judgment of the Court [1994] 2 WLR 64D.
[93]   See for example *Law Commission Report No 32* 'Civil Liability for Dangerous Things and Activities' at 25.   [94]   [1994] 2 WLR 75B–C.

The starting point of Lord Goff's analysis is interesting. Rather than seek a narrow authority which was dispositive of the case before him he preferred to commence his analysis with a broad historical survey of the development of nuisance and the rule in *Rylands* v *Fletcher*. For this historical account he drew upon an article written by Professor Newark in 1949[95] which sought to demonstrate that there had been a considerable, and in Professor Newark's view, unfortunate, cross-infection between the tort of nuisance and the emerging principles of negligence. Rather the article stressed the common origin of the modern tort of nuisance and the principle associated with the case of *Rylands* v *Fletcher* in actions on the case based upon strict liability. Lord Goff accepted that the modern tort of private nuisance was one of strict liability in the sense that a defendant may be liable notwithstanding that he has exercised all due care to avoid the interference. However he stressed that foreseeability of risk is a pre-requisite of liability. Thus a concept which was previously thought to be relevant only to the secondary issue of remoteness of damage[96] has been 'promoted' to the position of being determinative of primary liability. Lord Goff then turned his attention to the rule in *Rylands* v *Fletcher* and concluded that a similar requirement of foreseeability operated as a pre-condition of liability.

At a general level the approach of Lord Goff is as unusual as it is refreshing. Two things in particular are worthy of note. First is the influence of academic writing. For although the article by Professor Newark to which Lord Goff made extensive reference was primarily a historical analysis it obviously influenced considerably the way in which his Lordship conceived the various strands of civil liability which collectively comprise part of the protection accorded by the law of tort to interests in real property. Perhaps this should occasion no surprise when one remembers that Lord Goff was once himself a law tutor. Indeed it might be true to say that Lord Goff's influence upon the form and substance of the civil law of England might be attributable in greater measure to his own academic writing, particularly his co-authorship of Goff and Jones[97] than to his judicial role.

Second and undoubtedly related to the foregoing is the way in

---

[95] F. Newark, 'The Boundaries of Nuisance' (1949) 65 *LQR* 480.
[96] *The Wagon Mound (No 2)* [1967] 1 AC 388.
[97] R. Goff and G. Jones, *The Law of Restitution*[4] (London, 1993).

which Lord Goff analysed the law. He perceived the need for the protection accorded to a particular interest by the law of tort to function as a harmonious whole. It has been a frequent criticism of recent developments of the law of tort that they are unsynchronised and as a result are poorly integrated and sometimes pursue competing policy objectives. In a recent edition of a long established textbook the editor laments:[98]

I hope I am not alone in thinking that we seem to have made the law of negligence inordinately doctrinally complex in the last decade: the issues with which the court has to grapple in making the pragmatic decision whether or not a duty of care is owed are sometimes intensely difficult ones, but it is not clear that their resolution is aided by having three or four overlapping legal concepts.

A particular matter of complaint has often been the poorly orchestrated efforts at law reform by the agencies of the courts and the legislature. This has produced multiple avenues of redress for a single problem with many subtle, obscure and inexplicable differences between them. Consider for example the interaction of the liability introduced in *Dutton* v *Bognor Regis U.D.C.*[99] and the provisions of the Defective Premises Act 1972. No less unfortunate is the overlap between the liability for negligent misstatement established by *Hedley Byrne* v *Heller*[100] and section 2(1) of the Misrepresentation Act 1967. Lord Goff's answer in the sphere of environmental protection is to avoid such conflict between law making agencies by emphasising the greater skills and resources at the disposal of the legislature when considering such matters. It is hoped that if the general approach of Lord Goff finds favour in our appellate courts overlapping spheres of responsibility will be avoided and the common law will in a sense become more common and, thereby, avoid the same fate as that suffered by the tort of negligence.

VII Remedies For Misrepresentation

It is often said that damages in tort for misrepresentation, whether fraudulent, negligent, or pursuant to section 2(1) of the Misrepresentation Act 1967 have the advantage for plaintiffs that they

[98] *Winfield and Jolowicz on Tort*, 14th ed by W. V. H. Rogers, (Cambridge, 1994) at p v.
[99] [1972] 1 QB 373 overruled in *Murphy* v *Brentwood District Council* [1991] 1 AC 398.   [100] [1964] AC 465.

undo the consequences of a bad bargain.[101] This is said to follow from the fundamental principle governing damages in tort, namely that the Court should award

> that sum of money which will put the party who has been injured in the same position as he would have been in if he had not sustained the wrong . . .[102]

In recent years asset values in the United Kingdom have fluctuated widely in value. The expectation of price inflation has led to speculative purchases financed by equally speculative loans; the disappointment of those expectations has led the losers, both purchasers and borrowers to test the true limits of the principles governing damages in tort for misrepresentation.

In the typical case, the purchaser buys property in reliance on a misrepresentation by a surveyor employed by the lender financing the transaction as to its condition or value. When it subsequently transpires that the surveyor has been negligent, the purchaser claims damages from the surveyor. If the purchaser defaults on the mortgage the lender may find the security insufficient and bring its own action for misrepresentation against the surveyor. If the property market has fallen since completion, the question is whether damages will be assessed so as to permit the plaintiff to transfer to the misrepresentor the effects of the fall in the market.

William Sindall Plc v *Cambridgeshire County Council*[103] was different in that the action was brought against the vendor but raised the same issue. In the late 1980s Sindall joined the long list of developers seeking to profit from the efforts of public bodies to raise money by selling real property assets. In March 1989 they bought a school playing field for £5 million. This was at the height of the property boom. By October 1990 however, the market had collapsed so that the site was worth only £2 million and interest on the loan used to finance the purchase was accruing at a rate of £2,000 per day.

At that point, Sindall sought salvation in a sewer. The sewer in question was discovered running across the site in October 1990 and neither vendor nor purchaser had been aware of its existence at completion. The sewer was not a serious problem but the

---

[101] H. McGregor *McGregor on Damages* 15th ed., 1992, para 1721.
[102] *Livingstone* v *Rawyards Coal Co* (1880) 5 App Cas 25, 39 Lord Blackburn.
[103] [1994] 1 WLR 1016 CA.

purchasers sought to allege that they had brought the property in reliance on a misrepresentation by the vendor that there were as far as it could reasonably be ascertained no such easements effecting the property.

The Court ultimately held that there was no actionable misrepresentation but nevertheless expressed a view as to the principles governing a claim for damages under section 2(1) of the Misrepresentation Act 1967. Even assuming in the plaintiffs' favour that they would not have purchased the property had they known the truth, Evans LJ thought that damages would not include the subsequent drop in the market.[104] Hoffman LJ, albeit with some hesitation, took the opposite view.[105]

Their Lordships' uncertainty is no doubt due to the state of the authorities. The leading cases on the point are *Waddell* v *Blockey*[106] (fraud) and *Perry* v *Sidney Phillips*[107] (negligence). These decisions are often said to stand for the proposition that where the plaintiff purchases property in reliance on a negligent misrepresentation, damages are to be assessed as the difference between the price paid for the property and its actual value at the date of acquisition.[108] However the decisions are much narrower in their effect. Thus in *Perry* the plaintiff discovered the truth soon after the property was acquired. Clearly, any further loss was due to the plaintiff's decision not to resell and was thus a failure to mitigate the loss.[109] *Waddell* is narrower still: the defendant fraudulently represented that certain investments which he had purchased on the plaintiff's behalf had been purchased on the open market. In fact he had simply transferred identical instruments then standing in his own name, but there was no evidence that the plaintiff thereby paid too high a price. Prior to the discovery of the fraud the investments fell in value and were resold at a loss. The Court of Appeal held that damages should be assessed as the difference between the price paid and their value on acquisition, thereby denying the plaintiff the right to shift to the defendant the subsequent drop in the market. The reason why the date of

[104] [1994] 1 WLR 1046C–F.
[105] Ibid 1037F, 1036F–G. Russell LJ agreed with both judgments.
[106] (1879) 4 QBD 676 CA.   [107] [1982] 3 All ER 705 CA.
[108] Jackson, R., & Powell, J., edd., *Professional Negligence* 3rd ed, London, 1992, 270 par 3–120 (Iain Hughes).
[109] [1982] 3 All ER 710G Megaw LJ. Cf the facts of *Ward* v *Phillips* [1956] 1 WLR 471 and see McGregor, para 1215.

acquisition was chosen as the date for the assessment of damages emerges clearly from the judgment of Bramwell LJ:[110] the plaintiff was a perfectly willing buyer who would have purchased the investments and suffered the decline in the market even if the misrepresentation had not been made. In a case where the plaintiff would have completed the purchase (albeit at a lower price) had the misrepresentation not been made, it is clearly correct to confine damages to the difference in value. In such a case the plaintiff would have suffered the decline in the market even if the tort had not been committed. Thus the leading cases do not address the situation where the plaintiff purchaser would not have bought the property at all had the truth been known and where ignorance of the true position prevented him mitigating the loss through re-sale.

Two more recent decisions have served only to confuse the picture. In *Watts* v *Morrow*,[111] the plaintiffs purchased a house for £170,000 in reliance on the defendant surveyor's negligent mis-representation that it needed no substantial repairs. The very significant repairs in fact required meant its market value on acquisition was £15,000 less than the purchase price but the plaintiffs quite reasonably remained in occupation and spent £33,000 on repairs. The Court of Appeal confined damages to the difference between price paid and actual value at the date of acquisition despite the plaintiffs' argument that this was inappro-priate since had the truth been known they would not have negotiated a reduction in the price but rather purchased similar alternative accommodation in a better state of repair. On this basis, the plaintiffs argued that the costs of repairs were recoverable since they were considerably less than the costs involved in sale followed by equivalent repurchase of alternative accommodation.[112] The plaintiffs' argument in *Watts* v *Morrow* seems compelling and the decision unjust. Nevertheless the significance of the Court of Appeal's refusal to distinguish *Perry* v *Sidney Phillips* in a case where there would have been no purchase if the truth had been known should not be overstated. It was recognized that damages were not invariably confined to the difference between price paid

---

[110] (1879) 4 QBD 676, 681. [111] [1991] 1 WLR 1421.
[112] Ibid 1434A–D.

and actual value.[113] Hence *Watts* v *Morrow* probably does no more than rule out claims for the cost of repairs. It confuses but does not answer the question of whether damages for negligent misrepresentation can include any loss caused to the plaintiff by a decline in the value of the property after the date of acquisition where the property would not have been purchased if the truth had been known.

Equally confusing is the decision of the House of Lords in *Swingcastle* v *Gibson*.[114] Property had been purchased on the basis of a negligent valuation by the defendant valuers. The plaintiffs however were the lenders, the purchasers having defaulted. The Court of Appeal reluctantly held itself bound by the authority of *Baxter* v *F. W. Gapp & Co Ltd*[115] to award as damages all sums left unpaid by the defaulting borrowers, including contractual interest. Lord Lowry giving the judgment of the House of Lords decided that it was wrong in principle to make the valuers liable for contractual interest since this would in effect make them guarantors of the loan. *Baxter* v *Gapp* was therefore overruled. What is material for our purposes however is that Lord Lowry approved[116] as correct the alternative approach set out by Neill LJ in the Court of Appeal. The starting point was to ask what the plaintiff would have done had the defendant supplied an accurate valuation. In a case like *Swingcastle*, where no money whatsoever would have been lent, the plaintiff should then be awarded the capital sum (together with interest), less any sums received from the borrower and the sale of the security. The crucial point is that according to Lord Lowry credit is only to be given for the value of the security at the time of sale, thus transferring to the valuer any loss caused by a fall in its value subsequent to the making of the loan.[117] If this is so however, a similar allocation of loss ought also to occur where the plaintiff is the purchaser. However, in the recent case of *Smith New Court* v *Scrimgeour Vickers (Asset Management) Ltd*,[118] the Court of Appeal relying on *Waddell* v *Blockey* accepted without question that in such a case damages should normally be assessed when the

---

[113] Ibid 1435E–F Ralph Gibson LJ and cf the decision in *County Personnel (Employment Agency) Ltd* v *Alan R. Pulver & Co* [1987] 1 WLR 916 which was approved in *Watts*.   [114] [1991] 2 AC 223.
[115] [1938] 4 All ER 457 CA.   [116] [1991] 2 AC 237A–B.
[117] Cf Jackson and Powell, *Professional Negligence*, 261 para 3–137 where *Swingcastle* is cited for the proposition that valuers bear the risk of a fall in the market.   [118] [1994] 1 WLR 1271 CA.

property was acquired.[119] The conventional understanding of the authorities would lead to an indefensible difference in result depending on whether the plaintiff is the purchaser or the lender. Within the review period the issue has however been thoroughly considered by Phillips J. in *Banque Bruxelles Lambert S.A. v John D. Wood and Others.*[120] This case arose from a series of property transactions organized by one Markovits. The basic pattern was for Markovits to introduce the plaintiff bank to purchasers of commercial property. The plaintiff was induced to lend to the purchaser more than the purchase price in the belief that the properties were worth significantly more. The plaintiff was willing to make the advance only on the basis of satisfactory valuations. These were provided by a valuer chosen by Markovits, who awarded the contract to whichever firm of valuers gave the highest preliminary valuation. When the borrower defaulted, the plaintiff lost considerable sums of money and sued inter alia the defendant valuers. Phillips J held that the defendant's valuation of the properties was in excess of their actual value at the time of the loan and that this overvaluation was a breach of a duty of care owed to the plaintiff. However, the plaintiff's losses had been aggravated by the collapse in the property market which had caused a sharp fall in the value of the securities. Phillips J therefore had to decide whether this further loss was recoverable. The plaintiff's case was a simple one. If the properties had been valued at or near their actual value, the plaintiff's would still have been willing to advance a smaller sum. However, Markovits and the purchasers would not have been willing to proceed. Therefore it could be said that 'but for' the defendant's misrepresentation the transactions would not have occurred at all and the plaintiff would not have been exposed to the ensuing fall in the market.

Phillips J rejected this argument and confined recoverable losses to the difference between the sum lent and actual value of the security at the time of the loan. The reasoning was that the plaintiff was relying on the valuations only in order to verify the current value of the securities. The risk of subsequent fluctuations was one

---

[119] On the facts *Smith New Court* was correctly decided since, had the truth been known, the plaintiff would have continued with the transaction though at a lower price; but the case was not decided on this basis.

[120] *The Times*, 7 March 1994: hereafter references are to the transcript. The decision was followed on indistinguishable facts by Arden J in *Mortgage Express Ltd v Bowerman & Partners, The Times*, 19 May 1994.

which the plaintiff would bear with the help of credit risk insurance.[121] On these facts, his Lordship's conclusion was that regardless of the foreseeability of the fall in the market,

I do not see how the negligent adviser can fairly be said to have caused that loss unless his advice has been relied upon as providing protection against the risk of that loss.[122]

Such a conclusion was open to Phillips J only because he was prepared to regard *Swingcastle* v *Gibson* as deciding only that a plaintiff who lends on the faith of a negligent valuation cannot recover contractual interest left unpaid by the borrower. This seems a very narrow view of the ratio decidendi of the earlier decision and it remains to be seen whether the Court of Appeal will take a similar view. Nevertheless Phillips J's decision seems correct on principle. The defendant's representation was only as to the current value of the property. The plaintiff was prepared to risk future falls in the value of the property because, on the basis of information for which the defendant was not responsible, it believed that the market would continue to rise and because it had credit risk insurance. Losses caused by the fall in the market can thus be said to have been caused not by the negligent survey but by a *novus actus interveniens*, namely the plaintiff's voluntary and informed decision to run what it perceived as a very small risk of market collapse. The reasoning would seem to apply in any case where the plaintiff whether purchaser or lender has taken an interest in property in reliance on a misrepresentation by the defendant valuer or vendor as to its current condition. In such a case damages cannot include any additional loss caused by a decline in the market subsequent to its acquisition: further loss is caused not by the defendant's negligence but by the plaintiff's decision to run the risk of a fall in the market.

It is significant that the decision turns on causation rather than on the question of duty or of foreseeability. The emphasis on causation will ensure that where property is purchased or security taken in reliance on a misrepresentation as to its current value, then the allocation of losses arising from a subsequent fall in the market will remain the same whether the plaintiff's cause of action is under *Hedley Byrne* v *Heller* (as in *Banque Bruxelles*), section 2(1) of the Misrepresentation Act 1967 or the tort of deceit. Had the emphasis

---

[121] Supreme Court Transcript p. 120.   [122] Ibid 127.

been on duty or foreseeability, then a different result would have followed in the latter two cases. In neither case does liability depend on the concept of duty and in neither case is it limited by a principle of remoteness dependent on foreseeability.[123] This seems wholly appropriate. More generally, the case is an illustration of the fact that while satisfaction of the 'but for' test may be a necessary condition of liability in the tort of negligence it is not sufficient. The requirement that the defendant's conduct be a cause of the plaintiff's damage is more stringent and sophisticated.

If the decision in *Banque Bruxelles* is correct then it helps to clarify another point which troubled the Court in *Sindall*. Assuming the contract to have been induced by a misrepresentation, the plaintiff had purported to rescind: the return of the land in exchange for the purchase price would clearly have reversed the result of the bargain. The defendants accordingly invoked section 2(2) of the Misrepresentation Act 1967 and asked the Court to award damages in lieu of rescission. The Court was therefore required to ascertain how those damages should be assessed. The plaintiffs argued that the tortious measure applied and that, assuming they would not otherwise have purchased the property, they should therefore recover the fall in value of the land after acquisition. The Court's response was that this would subvert the purpose of section 2(2) which was to protect misrepresentors against the harsh consequences of rescission. On the plaintiff's view damages in lieu of rescission would always have the same effect as rescission. Accordingly, both judges thought that the contractual measure namely the difference between the value of the property as it was represented to be and its actual value was appropriate.[124] The astonishing conclusion that an unincorporated pre-contractual misrepresentation can attract contractual damages seems misconceived. The preference for the contractual measure seems to be based on an acceptance of the plaintiff's premise that the tortious measure would invariably result in their recovering any decline in the value of the property subsequent to acquisition. However if *Banque Bruxelles* is correct, the premise is false. In cases like *William Sindall*, the tortious measure of damages will not, unlike

---

[123] See *Doyle v Olby (Ironmongers) Ltd* [1969] 2 QB 158 (fraud) and *Royscott Trust Ltd v Rogerson* [1991] 2 QB 297 (s. 2(1)).

[124] Or in an appropriate case the cost of repair: ibid 1038A–C Hoffman LJ; 1045H Evans LJ.

rescission, allow the plaintiff to escape the consequences of a bad bargain because unlike rescission damages are limited by the concept of causation. Accordingly the right to rescind will be curbed in just those cases where its operation would be harshest on the misrepresentor, namely where the plaintiff is seeking to escape the consequence of a risk he freely undertook but which materialized in a manner adverse to his interests.

IX Personal Injuries: Damages for the Cost of Care

Hunt v *Severs*[125] involved the interaction not of tort and contract but rather tort and restitution. The case involved a variant on a common and, in human terms, tragic problem. Typically, the defendant (D) negligently causes severe personal injury to a plaintiff (P) whose disability is such as to require long term care. If the care were provided on a commercial basis, for example by a private nurse, then its cost would undoubtedly be an item of recoverable damage. In fact however, the care is provided at no cost to P by a third party, often a relative (C). What then is the legal significance of C's generosity?

Since 1974, the orthodox analysis has been that supplied by Megaw LJ in *Donnelly* v *Joyce*.[126] According to his Lordship, the fact that P's need is met gratuitously by C rather than commercially does not extinguish the loss. The loss for which D must pay compensation is the existence of the need for care not the cost of providing it so that this loss remains undiminished by C's generosity. If P and C had entered into a contract to provide the services then P would undoubtedly be under an obligation to reimburse C and Megaw LJ suggested that such an obligation might be imposed as a matter of law. Similarly, Lord Denning had suggested in *Cunningham* v *Harrison*[127] that the P would hold the damages 'on trust' for C. Nevertheless Megaw LJ was at pains to emphasize that this was irrelevant to the ascertainment of what was quite genuinely a loss to P.

Hunt v *Severs* involved a factual variant which provoked a challenge to the orthodox analysis. P was a passenger on a motor

---

[125] [1993] 3 WLR 581 CA, [1994] 2 WLR 602 HL.
[126] [1974] QB 454 CA.
[127] [1973] QB 942. For a contrary view, see the judgment of the Court of Appeal (*per incuriam*) in *Housecroft* v *Burnett* [1986] 1 All ER 332, 343D.

bike driven by D which crashed owing to D's admitted negligence. P suffered crippling injuries. D cared for her devotedly over the ensuing years and indeed they had married by the time of the trial of her action for damages. P claimed damages inter alia for the costs of the care provided by D so that this case differed from the standard pattern in that P's need for care was met not by a third party but by D. Thus C in this case is more properly designated C/D.

The Court of Appeal held that this made no difference and consequently that P was entitled to claim cost of care damages from C/D qua tortfeasor even though the care had in fact been provided by C/D himself. This followed logically from Megaw LJ's analysis in *Donelly* v *Joyce*: if P's loss was the need for care regardless of the source from which it was met then this loss remained even if the carer were the defendant.[128] In addition, the Court noted that this would not in reality involve the defendant's meeting the need twice over, since the damages would be paid by C/D's liability insurers and that C/D would most probably benefit from the sums so paid.[129] In addition, the Court noted that any other result would be contrary to public policy since it would encourage P and C/D in a case like this to enter into a contract for the provision of care.[130]

The House of Lords allowed D's appeal. Lord Bridge with whom all the other judges concurred was disposed to doubt Megaw LJ's analysis which if correct would allow plaintiffs to recover medical costs even when they had been treated by the NHS.[131] More important however than a nice conceptual analysis was the need

to recognize that the underlying rationale of the English Law ... is to enable the carer to receive proper recompense for his or her services. . . .[132]

Consequently, any damages recovered under this head were held by P 'on trust' for C. It was therefore evident that there could be no ground for requiring C/D qua tortfeasor to pay P a sum of money which P would immediately be liable to repay to C/D qua carer.

Lord Bridge's willingness to have regard to the underlying purpose of the applicable law is to be welcomed. Nevertheless, the decision is ultimately wrong for reasons which illustrate the importance of combining an awareness of the purposes of the law with a precise analysis of the concepts through which these

---

[128] [1974] QB 569F–G. [129] Ibid 570B–C. [130] Ibid 570D–E.
[131] [1994] 2 WLR 609H. [132] Ibid 611E–F.

purposes are effected. The unexplored conceptual ambiguities are concealed in the phrases 'proper recompense' and 'on trust'.

The starting point should clearly have been a rigorous analysis of the effect of C's generosity on P's claim for the cost of care in the ordinary case where C is not also the tort-feasor. This however is difficult since the law has been conspicuous in its failure to develop consistent principles to deal with the effect on the assessment of damages of benefits accruing to the victim following the commission of the tort.[133] Nevertheless, one principle which the law might appropriately adopt would be that gratuitous benefits should not affect the assessment of damages unless they were both offered and received with the intention of diminishing the defendant's liability.[134] Payment by a third party will not extinguish a debt unless at the very least it is both offered and received with the intention of reducing liability[135] and it is difficult to see why the same should not apply to the obligation to pay damages in respect of personal injuries. It is easy to assume that applying this principle to a case where C is also the tortfeasor leads to a diminution of damages but this would follow only if C/D's offer of assistance were made with the intention of mitigating C/D's liability and accepted as such. However, C/D may have very good reason for not offering assistance on this basis, most obviously because C may be insured and wish P to benefit from monies paid out by the liability insurers. Moreover, P may not wish to accept assistance in lieu of damages, particularly with respect to future care. This is because a general damages payment which is reduced or extinguished because of C/D's generosity leaves P very vulnerable should C/D die or the relationship deteriorate. For the same reason the Court of Appeal in *Housecroft* v *Burnett* were surely wrong to assess damages at less than the commercial cost of care in a case where C had not given up full time employment.[136]

If this is correct it follows that, despite Lord Bridges doubts, C's generosity does not prejudice P's claim for damages against D. It is

---

[133] See generally, A. S. Burrows *Remedies for Tort and Breach of Contract*[2] (London, 1994) 124–127.

[134] For recognition of the importance of the intention with which the benefit is provided see the judgment of Lord Reid in *Parry* v *Cleaver* [1970] AC 1, 14A–B. For doubts as to its juristic relevance see Burrows, 125–126.

[135] See generally, J. Beatson and P. B. H. Birks 'Unrequested Payment of Another's Debt' (1976) 92 *LQR* 188.   [136] [1986] 1 All ER 343.

P who has a claim in tort in respect of the cost of care against D. C's claim, if any, must be against P and have a quite different basis. It is this point which is obscured by Lord Bridge's suggestion that the rationale of this area of English Law is the 'recompense' of C. This suggests, contrary to the above analysis, that C's claim is in some sense a claim in tort against D.[137] The point is important because a claim by C in tort would clearly be impossible where C was also the tortfeasor.

The next question is the nature of C's claim against P. Their Lordships describe the damages received by P as being held 'on trust', but it is difficult to justify the evocation of the trust concept in this context. In so far as it suggests a proprietary claim, this is problematic since the money is neither paid by D on trust for C nor is there in most cases any evidential basis for a declaration of trust by P. It would also give C a priority on insolvency not accorded to commercial carers, which seems difficult to justify. Moreover the characterization of the claim as a trust claim is enormously significant where as in *Hunt* v *Severs*, C is also the tortfeasor, for in that case P would be seeking an award of damages which would immediately be held on trust for the defendant— clearly an absurdity.

It is suggested however that a more secure basis for C's claim can be found in the law of restitution. Such a claim requires that P be enriched at C's expense in circumstances such that the law regards it as unjust that the enrichment be retained.[138] On our typical fact pattern, C clearly enriches P through the provision of services which P either requests or, in the case of severe disability can be regarded as factually necessary.[139] As to why retention of this enrichment is unjust, it is fanciful to regard most carers as having an intention to charge P for those services. More plausible however, is to regard the services as being provided on the basis that they are

---

[137] Cf *The Esso Bernicia, Esso Petroleum Ltd* v *Hall Russell & Co Ltd and Shetland Islands Council* [1989] AC 643 HL, where the defendants' negligence had caused oil to spill from a ship owned by the plaintiffs on to property owned by local crofters. The plaintiffs who had paid to rectify the damage as they were bound to do under an industry agreement, sought to recoup these sums from the defendants relying inter alia on the tort of negligence. The claim failed because loss suffered by a plaintiff who has paid out money for the benefit of the victim of a tort is not a form of economic loss protected by the tort of negligence.

[138] See generally Birks, *Restitution* (supra note 5) 9–16.

[139] Cf *Re Rhodes* (1890) 44 Ch D 94.

to remain gratuitous only so long as P's loss remains un-compensated. Once however compensation for the cost of care is awarded, the basis or consideration[140] on which the services were to remain gratis fails and P accordingly comes under an obligation to make restitution.[141] An analogous claim though it is rarely pursued seems to be available to an indemnity insurer against the insured when the insurer has paid an insured loss only for the insured to recover in respect of the same loss against a tort-feasor. In *Darrell* v *Tibbitts*[142], Thesiger LJ said that

> It appears to me that this suit may be supported . . . as an action for money had and received to recover the sum upon which they paid upon the ground that money was paid upon the conditions, that the person to whom it was paid had sustained a loss, that in point of fact no loss has been sustained, and therefore that the money paid by the company ought in justice to be returned to them.[143]

Once it is recognized that C's claim is a personal restitutionary claim rather than a trust claim then the result reached in *Hunt* v *Severs* becomes highly questionable. The analysis then is that the services were offered by C/D and accepted by P on the basis that they should not diminish C/D's liability in tort but that P should be liable to make restitution of the value of the services on receipt of the damages payment. Thus P's claim will be or could be met by a restitutionary counterclaim. However, this is crucially different from saying that the claim and counterclaim cancel each other out because in the presence of liability insurance the claim provides a fund from which the counterclaim is met. Claims and counter-claims for equivalent sums where both causes of action are in tort are well known: see *Smith* v *W.H. Smith & Son Ltd.*[144] It should make little difference that the counterclaim is restitutionary.

---

[140] There is a lively debate about whether the factor making the enrichment unjust in a case such as this should be seen as failure of consideration, as argued here, or as free acceptance. See generally A. S. Burrows 'Free Acceptance and the Law of Restitution' (1988) 104 *LQR* 576 and contrast Goff and Jones, *Restitution*[4] 18–19 and 413–414. This is not a case however where the result of the debate is likely to lead to a different result.

[141] Though if the parties remain on friendly terms this obligation is unlikely to be enforced.   [142] (1880) 5 QBD 560.

[143] Ibid 588. See also 562–3 Brett LJ. In fact, insurers normally rely on their subrogation rights: see generally *Lord Napier & Etrick* v *Hunter* [1993] AC 713.

[144] [1952] 1 All ER 528 discussed in *Atiyah's Accidents, Compensation and the Law* 5th ed. by Peter Cane (London, 1993) 208–209.

CRIMINAL LAW

Jim Stephens

I. Introduction

As usual, in the field of criminal law there have been a number of incremental developments since the publication of last year's *Annual Review*, but the review period has been characterised by a number of substantial developments which have resulted from the decisions of the courts. The time of the legislature has, of course, during the period in question, been taken up with the Criminal Justice and Public Order Bill which at the time of writing still has not received royal assent. It has been subject to substantial change and amendment—some at the last minute—giving the impression of afterthought. However, it seems that the criminal law and the legal system continue to reflect a number of underlying uncertainties which permeate other aspects of our social life. For example, is conduct to be categorised as criminal merely because of what is done or based on the state of mind of the offender? A weakening in the sense of shared values may, in part, be the cause of a weakening in an agreed prospective and coherent analysis of our social problems. The major changes, economic and social, which have occurred in recent times must eventually reflect and be reflected in our perceptions of crime, criminals and the criminal justice system. These perceptions, in turn, are reflected in the suggestions for change to cope with the perceived increase in criminal activity. The changes introduced by the Criminal Justice and Public Order legislation have been the subject of considerable modification and debate. However, even with this major piece of legislation an impression of vacillation has arisen—an impression of making policy on the hoof—without proper reflection and careful consideration. Also, the failure to implement some proposals and the unfortunate disregarding of some of the recommendations of the Royal Commission on Criminal Justice has not helped. For example, the proposed modifying of the so-called right of silence has produced much disagreement reflecting considerable differences of opinion. The proposal that the defendant's failure to respond to questioning and accusation can be the subject of a judge's comment to the trial jury flies directly in the face of the conclusion arrived at by the Royal Commission.

The underlying social and moral consensus has become increasingly weakened as diversity and individualism are increasingly acceptable. This is true not only of the politician, the man in the street but also of the lawyer. There is no agreement on the causes of our problems or, for that matter the solutions to them. Nature and nurture debates raise fundamental issues of legal responsibility as well as of ethics. Modifying behaviour by controlled and stimulating regimes have been seen by some as rewarding criminals by giving them opportunities which non-offenders from the same background would not have. For example, challenging character-building holidays are justified as likely to modify unacceptable behaviour but criticised, by some, as over generous. Others consider that containment in the form of custodial sentences work to the extent at least of protecting society while such persons are incarcerated. Interesting and stimulating as such arguments and debates are, the criminal law cannot await an authoritative outcome. It does not have the luxury of existing in a vacuum. Decisions and policies have to be given effect in legislation and in the day to day operation of the criminal justice system but the system has to continue about its task irrespective of any furore raging around it.

Yet protection of the 'innocent' from defined harm would seem, if anything, to be as pressing a matter as ever—whether that individual is someone terrorised in a ghetto estate or a person 'mugged' in a middle class district. However, even this observation begs an important question on which there is no agreement. The cry of 'something should be done' is a frustrated response reflecting the apparent impotence of people to live without fear of crime. However, although such a cry is common it begs two questions. The first is the debate about what can be done? The second concerns the issue whether criminal law should be based on the harm suffered by the victim (and society) or should it primarily be concerned with the defendant's conduct and his precise state of mind? Traditionally, guilt was associated not only with carrying out the prohibited conduct but also with the defendant's mental state when he did it. Even this traditional approach is currently under question—if not attack. We are told we should be concentrating more on the victim not the accused. However, we should be careful, when considering whether the balance between the two interests is correct, to ensure that any proposed changes do not themselves turn the accused into yet another victim—a victim of the criminal justice system! If the problems which led to the setting up of the Royal Commission are called to mind, the danger would seem to be that there are too many cases coming to light where the criminal justice system itself has failed and created victims. It is hoped that more such victims will not result from an overzealous response to the cry 'something must be done.' Some of the matters discussed below represent an overt resort to principle rather than precedent and in their own way represent substantial change. Perhaps the judges too are trying to respond to modern times. They are growing in increasing confidence, and in some cases moving away from precedent and appealing directly to principle, as a means of responding to the desire for something to be done. Such developments, for example, in the contexts of reckless manslaughter, involuntary intoxication (in the Court of Appeal) and mischievous propensity were all approached from that point of view.

II Actual Bodily Harm

The Court of Appeal has had to consider actual bodily harm in the context of mental anxiety and took advantage of the opportunity to bring the criminal law into line with the concepts currently employed by the civil courts. The question which had to be decided was, is mental anxiety or severe distress actual bodily harm? In *Chan-Fook*[1] the defendant's fiancée told the defendant that she believed the victim, M (a foreign student living with the family), had stolen her engagement ring. The defendant searched M's room. Then after close questioning (M being unable to explain the absence of the ring) the defendant dragged M upstairs and locked him in a second floor room. M alleged that he had been struck about the head, kneed and at one point his head had hit a wall. M alleged that the defendant had threatened him with further violence. M's account was he was frightened that the defendant

[1] [1994] 2 All ER 552.

would return and assault him further. This fear caused M to tie his sheets into a rope which he connected to the curtain rail. He climbed through the window intending·to escape to the ground below. However, he fell and sustained a fractured right wrist, a dislocated pelvis, tenderness to the groin and bruising on his face. Although the defendant admitted dragging M upstairs by the collar of his jacket and locking M in his room he denied that he had struck M or caused any injury. The defendant was charged with occasioning actual bodily harm contrary to section 47 of the Offences Against the Person act 1861. The defendant's case was that the physical 'harm' which M had sustained was the result of the fall and not attributable to his conduct. At trial the prosecution argued that even if the physical harm was not attributable to the defendant's violent conduct he had nevertheless put M into a nervous state which itself constituted actual bodily harm. The only evidence in support of this proposition was M's testimony that he felt abused, humiliated and frightened of further violence from the defendant. No medical or psychiatric evidence was introduced in support of this contention. Was this nervous state sufficient to constitute actual bodily harm? Judge Bernard Charles QC at trial adopted the traditional definition found in *Archbold*[2] and directed the jury in the following terms:

What is meant by 'actual bodily harm?' It does not have to be permanent. It does not have to be serious. It is some actual harm which interferes with the comfort of the individual, for the time being, described as any hurt or injury calculated to interfere with the health or comfort of Mr. Martins, in this case.[3]

He directed the jury on the alleged physical harm and then went on

Equally the Crown says that his mental state, which caused him to lock the door and take the extreme action of climbing out of a window, tying sheets together, indicates that he was in a nervous, maybe hysterical condition. It is a matter for you to judge what his condition was. That in itself is capable of amounting to actual bodily harm.[4]

The defendant appealed on the basis that there was no psychological evidence capable of supporting the allegation of

---

[2] *Archbold's Pleading, Evidence and Practice in Criminal Cases*, 44th ed., 1992, Vol 2, para 19–197: 'an assault which causes an hysterical and nervous condition is an assault occasioning actual bodily harm. . . .'

[3] Ibid 556.

[4] Ibid 556.

mental actual bodily harm. On appeal, Hobhouse LJ adopted the approach approved of by the House of Lords,[5]—giving words their ordinary and natural meaning. He said that the danger of elaboration is that it may distract the jury from the ordinary meaning or cause elision of ideas. He said of actual bodily harm,

These are three words of the English language which require no elaboration and in the ordinary course should not receive any. The word 'harm' is a synonym for injury. The word 'actual' indicates that the injury (although there is no need for it to be permanent) should not be so trivial as to be wholly insignificant. The purpose of the definition of s.47 is to define an element of aggravation in the assault. It must be an assault which besides being an assault (or assault and battery) causes to the victim some injury.[6]

He turned to the matter of what was meant by the word 'bodily.' He referred to *Miller*[7] where a wife who was separated from her husband was forced to undergo intercourse without consent. There was evidence of acute mental and emotional distress as a result. Lynskey J said,

There was a time when shock was not regarded as bodily hurt, but the day has gone by when that could be said. It seems to me now that if a person is caused hurt or injury resulting, not in any physical injury, but in an injury to the state of his mind for the time being that is within the definition of 'actual bodily harm.'[8]

Hobhouse LJ was critical of that dictum and of its being treated subsequently as an accurate definition of the offence. He criticised the direction on three bases. The first was that Lynskey J was concerned with the issue whether the indictment should be quashed. Secondly, the concept of state of mind was capable of engendering confusion and thirdly the paraphrase in *Archbold* was inaccurate. However, he went on to say that Lynskey J was correct in holding that bodily harm was not confined to skin, flesh and bones. He accepted that the use of the phrase nervous shock was no longer appropriate and stated that the body of the victim could

[5] *Smith* [1961] AC 290, 334 Viscount Kilmuir quoting Martin J in *Miller* [1951] VLR 346, 357, ' "there does not appear to be any justification for treating the expression 'grievous bodily harm' or other similar expressions used in the authorities upon this common law question which are cited as bearing any other than their ordinary and natural meaning. . . ." In my opinion, the view of the law thus expressed by Martin J is correct.'   [6] Ibid 557.
[7] [1954] 2 QB 282; 2 All ER 529.   [8] Ibid 292.

include all parts of his body, including organs, nervous system and brain. He added, that bodily injury could include injury to any of those parts of the body responsible for mental and other faculties. He said,

the phrase 'actual bodily harm' is capable of including psychiatric injury. But it does not include mere emotions such as fear or distress or panic nor does it include, as such, states of mind that are not themselves evidence of some identifiable clinical condition. The phrase 'state of mind' is not a scientific one and should be avoided in considering whether or not a psychiatric injury has been caused; its use is likely to create in the mind of the jury the impression that something that is no more than a strong emotion such as extreme fear or panic, can amount to actual bodily harm. It cannot. . . . Where there is some evidence that the assault has caused some psychiatric injury, the jury should be directed that that injury is capable of amounting to actual bodily harm; otherwise there should be no reference to the mental state of the victim following the assault unless it is relevant to some other aspect of the case. . . .[9]

In adopting this approach he was following the distinction which had been developed by Lord Wilberforce[10] between actual psychiatric illness, on the one hand, e.g. anxiety, neurosis or reactive depression and 'strong emotion' on the other. He said that it was a matter for expert evidence and in the absence of substantive evidence the issue should not be left to the jury.

III Mistake and Reasonable Force

When a person claims to be using force in self defence or under the powers conferred by the Criminal Law Act 1967 section 3 when, in fact, the force is inappropriate, does the defendant have a defence? Does the defendant's mistake effect his legal liability? The cases where a defendant has used force when it is inappropriate, had been thought to have established two general propositions. The first proposition is that if the mistake is about whether the circumstances confer on the defendant the right to use force. The courts will take the circumstances as the defendant believes them to be and ask whether they provide a legal justification for the use of force. It is clear that the subjective mistaken belief of the defendant can

[9] [1954] 2 QB 282; 2 All ER 559.
[10] *McLoughlin v O'Brian* [1983] 1 AC 410, 418; *Attia v British Gas plc* [1988] QB 304; *Alcock v Chief Constable of the S. Yorkshire Police* [1992] 1 AC 310.

provide a justification for the use of force even where the facts do not. The court is engaged in a hypothetical analysis—considering the facts to be as the defendant believed them to be. Would such facts if they had existed entitle the defendant to use force? Secondly, given that the courts regard the use of some force as legitimate in the circumstances as the defendant believes them to be, the next question is was the force which was used reasonable? Traditionally, this has been considered as a purely objective question. It does not matter whether the defendant believes the force to be a reasonable response or the force used was reasonable. It is for the court to decide this issue using objective criteria.

The effect of such an objective approach is to prevent an enormously disproportionate force being used and justified merely because the defendant considers the amount of force to be reasonable. If the law were to reflect a subjective approach the use of a machine gun could be justified as a reasonable response when a person is being attacked by fists, provided the defendant honestly regarded the response as reasonable force in the circumstances. Traditionally, in policy terms, the courts set the limits of reasonableness—not the defendant. This traditional approach was recently considered in the case of *Scarlett*[11] where the defendant was a landlord of a public house who refused to serve a potential customer who came into the public house 'the worse for drink.' The customer refused to leave voluntarily and when the defendant tried to take hold of him he wheeled round. The defendant believing that he might be struck from these gyrations pinned the man's arms by his sides from behind, and bundled him to and through the door. He left the man with his back against the lobby of the public house from where the man fell backwards down a flight of five steps into the street. He struck his head sustaining an injury from which he died. At trial for manslaughter the prosecution alleged that the defendant had used more force than was necessary in the pub and thus his act became unlawful so that the defendant was guilty of constructive manslaughter. The defendant was convicted and sentenced to nine months imprisonment. There were two central issues. The first was whether there was an unlawful and dangerous act and the second was whether the conduct of the defendant was the cause of the victim's death.

[11] [1993] 4 All ER 627.

On appeal, Beldam LJ had to consider the direction of the trial
judge about the essential ingredients of the offence. In summary, he
concluded, that the tenor of the judge's direction was that if the jury
concluded that the appellant had used more force than was
necessary in the circumstances in the bar, and if they were satisfied
that that caused the deceased to fall and strike his head, he was
guilty of manslaughter. For there to be unlawful-and-dangerous-act
manslaughter three matters had to be proved. The first was that the
act was unlawful, the second was that the act was dangerous and
the third that the act caused the death of the victim. Beldam LJ
considered the issue of dangerousness quoting Lord Salmon in
Newbury and Jones[12] approving the judgment of Edmund Davies J
in *Church*[13] that,

The test is still the objective test. In judging whether the act was dangerous
the test is not did the accused recognise that it was dangerous but would all
sober and reasonable people recognise its danger.

Beldam LJ then turned to the issue of unlawfulness. He pointed out
that both in *Newbury and Jones* and *Church* the conduct was
clearly unlawful. He went on to point out that the legal principle
was more complicated when the issue was whether the act was
unlawful in the context of the use of reasonable force under section
3. He quoted from *Williams*[14] and, in particular, referred to the
observation of Lane CJ that, 'The mental element necessary to
constitute guilt is the intent to apply *unlawful* force to the victim.
We do not believe that the mental element can be substantiated by
simply showing an intent to apply force.' As Beldam LJ pointed out
in *Williams* the point in issue was whether there was a right to use
reasonable force in the circumstances as the defendant believed
them to be. There was no question of excessive force being used—
assuming that there was a right to use reasonable force. What
principle was to operate when the defendant's mistake related not
to whether reasonable force could be used but whether the force
used was believed by the defendant to be reasonable?

Beldam LJ gave two reasons why the conviction was not safe. He
said,

The principle we have quoted that the mental element necessary to
constitute guilt of an assault is the intent to apply *unlawful force*[15] to the

¹² [1977] AC 500, 507.   ¹³ [1966] 1 QB 59, 70.
¹⁴ [1987] 3 All ER 411, 413.   ¹⁵ My emphasis.

victim was approved by the Board of the Privy Council in *Beckford*.[16] . . .
If the mental element necessary to prove an assault is an intention to apply
unlawful force to the victim, and the accused is to be judged according to
his mistaken view of the facts whether that mistake was on an objective
view reasonable or not, we can see no logical basis for distinguishing
between a person who objectively is not justified in using force at all but
mistakenly believes he is and another who is in fact justified in using force
but mistakenly believes that the circumstances call for a degree of force
objectively regarded as unnecessary.[17]

This clear observation seems to suggest that a mistake about the
amount of force necessary must be considered subjectively—at least
where there is a legal right to use force. This observation would
seem to open up new possibilities. Provided the defendant believes
that the circumstances call for the degree of force that he uses, he is
not to be convicted even if his belief is unreasonable. This would
seem to suggest that if a person considers that he is entitled to use
an automatic pistol when he is being attacked—provided he can
convince the jury that such was his considered judgment—he
should be acquitted. This is certainly, as it stands, a novel
development. But will it be extended to circumstances where the
defendant also mistakenly believes that he is entitled to use force—
when, in fact, such is not the case? For example, if the defendant
mistakenly believes that he is being attacked (when he is not) and
uses excessive force believing that he is entitled to use such force in
the circumstances he should be acquitted on the 'new' test as laid
down. He continued,

Further they should be directed that the accused is not to be found guilty
merely because he intentionally or recklessly used force which they
consider to have been excessive. They ought not to convict him unless they
are satisfied that the degree of force used was plainly more than was called
for by the circumstances as he believed them to be and, provided he
believed the circumstances called for the degree of force used, he is not to
be convicted even if his belief was unreasonable.[18]

However, there is another possible reason for the decision of the
Court of Appeal. Beldam LJ went on to state,

Where as in the present case, an accused is justified in using some force and
can only be guilty of an assault if the force used is excessive, the jury ought
to be directed that he cannot be guilty of an assault unless the prosecution

---

[16] [1988] AC 130.   [17] [1993] 4 All ER 636.   [18] Ibid 636.

prove that he acted with the mental element necessary to constitute his
action an assault, that is, that the defendant intentionally or recklessly
applied force to the person of another. . . .[19]

On the basis of this direction he concluded that the direction to
the jury at trial was inadequate on the ingredients of the assault.
What subsequent cases will make of this judgment is difficult to
say. It may be followed on the wide principle or, alternatively,
confined to situations where there was a right to use reasonable
force and the defendant believed that that excessive force was
reasonable.

IV Involuntary Intoxication

For many years involuntary intoxication has been the subject of
much academic speculation. Recently, the courts have had to
consider the legal effect of involuntary intoxication and fit the
decision into the current analysis of mens rea, actus reus and
intoxication.

Although mens rea can exist without actus reus there can be no
crime unless also there is an actus reus. Unless the defendant did the
act he must be acquitted—whatever the state of mind when he did
not do it![20] Although the precise actus reus of each offence will
depend on the statutory or common law definition of the offence in
question,[21] the traditional method of analysing offences is, of
course, to divide the definition into conduct (act or omission),
consequences, surrounding circumstances and an absence of a
justification or excuse. An act is defined in terms of a 'willed'
muscular movement. There is no liability if the defendants conduct
was involuntary.[22] At one time, it was argued that the act of the
defendant was not voluntary and that he was an automaton when
the defendant moved his muscles in spasm, while hypnotised or
while asleep. The rationale was that there was no mental control of
the muscles so the defendant was not *'acting'*.[23]

What is missing . . . appears to most people as a vital link between mind
and body; and both the ordinary man and the lawyer might well insist on
this by saying that in these cases there is not 'really' a human action at all

[19] Ibid 636. Beldam LJ refers to R v *Venna* [1976] 1 QB 421, 429 James LJ.
[20] *Deller* (1952) 36 Cr App R 184.   [21] *Dadson* (1850) 2 Den 35.
[22] *Hill v Baxter* [1958] 1 QB 277.   [23] *Bratty* [1963] AC 386.

and certainly nothing from which anyone should be made criminally responsible however 'strict' legal responsibility may be.[24]

Of course, the concept of automatism is not a defence in the strict sense of a defence to a fully constituted crime. It is an imprecise and elliptical way of describing the situation where the prosecution cannot prove all the essential ingredients of actus reus of the offence in question beyond reasonable doubt. Automatism was confined to 'involuntary movement of the body or limbs of a person.' This means that even if the crime was one with an element of 'strict' liability the defendant could nevertheless argue that he had not committed the offence. The defence was still available because this mental element of control by the defendant was thought to be categorised as part of the actus reus and not mens rea. There was no actus reus and therefore the fact that no corresponding mens rea was required to a particular element of the actus reus was not relevant. The essential element was a total lack of muscular control. Partial lack of control was not suffice to give rise to automatism.[25]

A distinction was drawn between this lack of control which came from some internal factor[26] where the court treated the lack of control as insanity, and sane automatism which came from an external source. Sane automatism resulted in the defendant being acquitted,—the prosecution having failed *in limine*. Insanity resulted in the defendant being found not guilty by reason of insanity and disposed of under Criminal Procedure (Insanity and Unfitness to Plead) Act 1991. Two matters need further elaboration. The first concerns conduct during sleep. The second is conduct while involuntarily intoxicated. The tendency of the courts seems to be restrict the scope of the defence of automatism as it can lead to an acquittal especially if the uncontrolled conduct is likely to reoccur. At another level this restriction becomes understandable because a defendant can be treated today as insane and as a result the courts have a discretion, in appropriate circumstances, to use a number of non custodial resolutions.

---

[24] H. L. A. Hart, 'Acts of Will and Responsibility' first published in Marshall, O. R., ed., *The Jubilee Lectures of the Faculty of Law, University of Sheffield*, Sheffield, 1960, 137; reprinted as chap. IV of Hart, H. L. A., *Punishment and Responsibility*, Oxford, 1968, 90, 107.
[25] *Broome v Perkins* [1987] Crim LR 271; *Issit* [1987] Crim LR 159.
[26] *Sullivan* [1984] AC 156.

CONDUCT WHILE ASLEEP

External causal factors said to give rise to automatism were thought to included blows to the head (concussion), responding under authorised medication and hypnosis. Ordinary stress and disappointments of life are not sufficient to constitute an external factor.[27] Although sleep 'acting' has been considered in *Boshears*[28] as a defence, recently the courts have treated sleep killing as an example of insanity as it was said to arise from an internal factor[29] and presumably would be likely to reoccur. This was the result of the decision in *Burgess*.[30] Should conduct under hypnosis be treated differently from conduct which occurs when asleep? In principle, they both can constitute a threat—a recurrent threat to others. A contrary argument might be that it is the conduct of a third party which is responsible for the hypnotised defendant's conduct. This is assuming (by analogy to intoxication) that the defendant in agreeing to be hypnotised or succumbing to hypnosis is not himself guilty of reckless conduct. This approach would have much to commend it if the hypnotist 'puts an idea' for action in someone's mind but what if the effect of the hypnosis is merely to remove a control so that the subject does what he wants to do but would not otherwise do because of self control? Is this nevertheless to be treated as the subject's conduct even though he would not have 'acted' had he not been hypnotised? Does this distinction exist? If it does it will determine which conduct is criminal or not? This will be considered further below.

CONDUCT WHILE INTOXICATED

Voluntary intoxication (from drugs[31] or alcohol[32]) can be argued to be the one established exception to the rule that there can be no criminal liability for an involuntary act—even though it is described in the cases in terms of negativing intent. There is a crime even though—through drunkenness—the defendant is not fully aware of his actions (i.e. that he was moving muscles, bringing about consequences or aware of the surrounding circumstances). The

[27] *Rabey* (1977) 37 CCC (2nd) 461.   [28] [1961] *The Times*, 8 February.
[29] I. Dennis (1992) 45 *CLP Annual Review* 43–46.
[30] [1991] 2 QB 92.   [31] *Lipman* [1970] 1 QB 152.
[32] *Majewski* [1977] AC 443.

rationale put forward by the courts is that the defendant was 'reckless'[33] in taking alcohol or drugs. However, this established exception is qualified in two circumstances. The first circumstance is that, in crimes of 'specific intent', voluntary intoxication can be a defence.[34] It may negative mens rea depending on the view that jury takes of the evidence. To all basic intent crimes (i.e. non specific intent crimes) voluntary intoxication is no defence. The defendant is regarded as acting with mens rea even when intoxicated.[35] However, if the loss of control arises from taking sedative or soporific drugs, then provided the defendant was not reckless in taking the drug, the defendant can be regarded as not having the requisite state of mind and acquitted[36]—there being no mens rea.

It has been a matter of some academic debate whether involuntariness is to be regarded as relevant to mens rea or actus reus.[37] The view taken by *Smith and Hogan* was that the distinction between whether automatism was to be considered as negativing mens rea or actus reus is 'a matter of convenience only.'[38] This approach is based on the fact that even with crimes of strict liability there are some actus reus element which require mens rea. In dismissing the importance of the categorisation they write,

The fallacy in this argument lies in the proposition that offences of strict liability require 'no *mens rea*' and the assumption that this means that the whole of the mental element involved in *mens rea* may be lacking. This is not so. If the mental element is part of the *actus reus* there is certainly no

[33] *Bailey* [1983] 2 All ER 503, 507: 'The question in each case will be whether the prosecution has proved the necessary element of recklessness. In cases of assault, if the accused knows that his action or inaction are likely to make him aggressive, unpredictable or uncontrolled with the result that he may cause some injury to others and he persists in the action or takes no remedial action when he knows it is required, it will be open to the jury to find that he was reckless.'

[34] *Beard* [1920] AC 479; *Majewski* [1977] AC 443.

[35] *Majewski* [1977] AC 443.

[36] *Hardie* [1984] 3 All ER 848, 853 Parker LJ: 'if the effect of a drug is merely soporific or sedative the taking of it, even in some excessive quantity, cannot in the ordinary way raise a conclusive presumption against the admission of proof of intoxication for the purpose of disproving mens rea in ordinary crimes, such as would be the case with alcoholic intoxication or incapacity or automatism resulting from the self-administration of dangerous drugs.'

[37] Commentators considering it an element of mens rea include Radzinowicz, L., and Turner, J. W. C., *Modern Approach to Criminal Law*, 195; Turner in *Kenny's Outlines of Criminal Law*, Cambridge, 1966, 23; Hart in *Jubilee Lectures*, cit. n. 23. Commentators considering it an element of actus reus include Williams, G., *Criminal Law, The General Part*, London, 1961, s.8 and Ingrid Patient [1968] Crim LR 23.   [38] Smith, J., and Hogan, B., *Criminal Law*[7], 1992, 39.

way of dispensing with it; but it does not follow that it must be dispensed with where an offence is held to be one of strict liability.[39]

The courts had to consider the effect of involuntary intoxication in the recent decision in *Kingston*.[40] The defendant was a paedophile with homosexual tendencies. In collusion with the defendant's two business associates, P, lured a fifteen year old boy to his flat. P administered drugs to the boy who passed out. While the youth was drugged P invited the defendant to the flat and invited him to sexually abuse the boy. This the defendant did. The defendant was photographed and audio-taped indecently assaulting the boy. It was intended that these materials would subsequently be used for the purpose of blackmail. The flat contained three types of sedative drug. The defendant argued that, like the boy, he had been drugged and could remember nothing after seeing the boy lying on the bed. He believed that he had been given drugged coffee. Medical evidence was that the drugs would induce calm, drowsiness or sleep and could cause amnesia and impaired judgment. The verdict of the jury was that the assault and the circumstances of indecency were intended. Potts J directed the jury,

In deciding whether Kingston intended to commit this offence, you must take into account any findings that you may make that he was affected by drugs. If you think that because he was so affected by drugs that he did not intend or may not have intended to commit an indecent assault upon [the boy], then you must acquit him; . . .

Later he added,[41] 'a drugged intent is still an intent.' The jury convicted and the defendant was sentenced to five years imprisonment.

On appeal, the Court of Appeal, had to consider the legal effect of involuntary intoxication. Lord Taylor CJ examined observations in previous authorities,[42] the Law Commission[43] and textbooks[44]

---

[39]   Smith, J., and Hogan, B., *Criminal Law*[7], 1992, 38.

[40]   [1993] QB 81; [1993] 4 All ER 373 CA; [1994] 3 WLR 520; [1994] 3 All ER 353 HL.   [41] Quoting *Sheehan, Moore* [1975] 2 All ER 960, 964.

[42]   Hale, M., *History of the Pleas of the Crown*, London, 1736, Vol 1, 31: 'if a person . . . by the contrivance of his enemies, eat or drink such a thing as causeth such a temporary or permanent phrenzy . . . this . . . equally excuseth him'; *Pearson's Case* (1835) 2 Lew CC 144, 145; 168 ER 1108 Park J: 'If a party be made drunk by stratagem, of the fraud of another, he is not responsible.'

[43]   Law Commission Report No 127 *Intoxication and Criminal Liability* (1993) para 2.28: 'Involuntary intoxication is always taken into account in determining the existence of a subjective mens rea.'

which all suggested that involuntary intoxication negativing mens rea would be a defence. He concluded, however, that the question could be best answered by turning to first principles. He said,

the purpose of the criminal law is to inhibit, by proscription and penal sanction, antisocial acts which individuals may otherwise commit. Its unspoken premise is that people may have tendencies and impulses to do those things which are considered sufficiently objectionable to be forbidden. Having paedophiliac inclinations and desires is not proscribed; putting them into practice is. If the sole reason why the threshold between the two has been crossed is or may have been that the inhibition which the law requires has been removed by the clandestine act of a third party, the purposes of the criminal law are not served by nevertheless holding that the person performing the act is guilty of an offence.

. . .

If therefore drink or a drug, surreptitiously administered, causes a person to lose his self-control and for that reason to form an intent which he would not otherwise have formed, it is consistent with the principle that the law should exculpate him because the operative fault is not his. The law permits a finding that the intent formed was not a criminal intent or, in other words, that the involuntary intoxication negatives the mens rea.

On the ground that the direction by the trial judge may have prevented a sufficient ventilation of the issues the Court of Appeal quashed the conviction considering it a case when the use of the proviso would be inappropriate because the court could not be sure that, if the appropriate direction had been given to the jury, they would have convicted.

On appeal to the House of Lords the decision of the Court of Appeal was reversed. Lord Mustill categorised the case as one of 'disinhibition'. By this he meant that the defendant had the latent intention (inclination) to do the act but as a result of the involuntary administration of alcohol or drugs his inhibiting controls were overcome resulting in the defendant acting on his underlying intention.

Lord Mustill considered three possible arguments in favour of the decision of the Court of Appeal. These were that: (1) immunity

---

[44] *Smith and Hogan*, 220: 'Evidence of intoxication negativing mens rea is a defence . . . to all crimes where the drink or drug was taken involuntarily'; *Archbold*, vol 2, p 2004, para 17–138: 'In crimes of basic intent, the House of Lords recognised in *Majewski* that involuntary intoxication negativing mens rea would be a defence. . . .'

flows from general principles; (2) the immunity is established by authority; and (3) the justice of the case requires a new common law defence.

(1) General Principle

He said that the Court of Appeal had adopted this approach and had concluded that an accused person can be acquitted where, although his act was intentional, the intent arose out of circumstances for which the accused was not to blame. Lord Mustill stated,

My Lords, with every respect I must suggest that no such principle exists or, until the present case, had ever in modern times been thought to exist.[45]

In support of rejecting the suggested defence, as he saw it, based on a moral principle, Lord Mustill cited *Yip Chiu-cheung*[46] heard earlier in the year where the advice of the Privy Council was delivered by Lord Mustill. He said it stood for the opposite contention than that adopted by the Court of Appeal. In that case an undercover agent was charged with a conspiracy to traffic in dangerous drugs. He was trying to break a drug ring but the Privy Council advised that although no moral guilt attached to his acts nevertheless he must be taken to have had sufficient intention to commit the offence.[47] Lord Mustill said that, in general terms, mens rea did not refer to the moral condition of the defendant's conduct but the criminality of the act in terms of a proscribed state

---

[45] Smith and Hogan, 360.

[46] [1994] 2 All ER 924.

[47] Ibid 518 Lord Mustill: 'it was submitted that the trial judge and the Court of Appeal were wrong to hold that Needham, the undercover agent, could be a conspirator because he lacked the necessary mens rea or guilty mind required for the offence of conspiracy. It was urged upon their Lordships that no moral guilt attached to the undercover agent who was at all times acting courageously and with the best of motives in attempting to infiltrate and bring to justice a gang of criminal drug dealers. . . . The crime of conspiracy requires an agreement between two or more persons to commit an unlawful act with the intention of carrying it out. It is the intention to carry out the crime that constitutes the necessary mens rea for the offence.. . . there can be no doubt that the method he chose and in which the police in Hong Kong acquiesced involved the commission of the criminal offence of trafficking in drugs by exporting heroin from Hong Kong without a licence. Needham intended to commit that offence by carrying the heroin through the customs. . . .'

of mind.[48] In that he would have general support. He concluded on this argument,

I would therefore reject that part of the respondent's argument which treats the absence of moral fault on the part of the appellant as sufficient in itself to negative the necessary mental element of the offence.[49]

It would seem difficult to disagree with the wide proposition of Lord Mustill. The system of justice according to law could be undermined if the extent of the law was determined by justice which is a subjective and highly variable concept. However, it was not a general moral justification exculpating from criminal responsibility which was being advanced before the Court of Appeal, but the limited moral principle that, where drink or a drug, surreptitiously administered, causes a person to lose his self-control the operative 'fault' is the fault of the person administering the alcohol not the defendant whose conduct is called into question.

It was unfortunate, to say the least, that the Lord Chief Justice expressed himself in his judgment in two essentially different ways. The first was in terms of intent that did in fact exist but which the defendant would not otherwise have formed, 'the law permits a finding that the intent formed was not a criminal intent.' This suggests that involuntary intoxication is a defence to a fully constituted crime and left the judgment open to the criticism that there was the necessary intent despite the involuntary intoxication and that an intoxicated intent is nevertheless an intent which can support a conviction. The second formulation by Lord Taylor CJ was based on the principle that, 'the involuntary intoxication negatives the mens rea.' This means that, in principle, there being no mens rea there is, *ex hypothesi*, no offence. Criminal liability fails *in limine*. This distinction between a defence to a fully constituted crime and a set of circumstances which prevent an element of an offence being proved have caused problems elsewhere in the criminal law, for example in connection with the 'defence' of mistake.

Lord Mustill also wondered whether this approach—whereby involuntary intoxication negatived an ingredient of the crime—was the basis on which the Court of Appeal operated. He said,

[48] Ibid 360: 'Certainly the 'mens' of the defendant must usually be involved in the offence; but the epithet 'rea' refers to the criminality of the act in which the mind is engaged, not its moral character.' [49] Ibid 361.

I have however wondered whether the Court of Appeal meant something different and more narrow,[50] namely there is no mens rea if the intent is set in motion by a condition which the defendant did not bring about by his own deliberate act.[51]

It is submitted that is precisely what the Court of Appeal had in mind. However, dealing with his own speculation Lord Mustill stated,

This proposition was not separately argued and I hesitate to say anything about it, except that if it were right as a matter of general law an irresistible influence brought about by any inherent medical condition, would aside from all questions of insanity and diminished responsibility, be a defence at common law; which it is not.[52]

To say the least, the judgment of the Court of Appeal when subjected to detailed criticism[53] was unfavourably received, in part, because of Lord Taylor CJ's double formulation and has even been described as contrary to principle.[54] Professor Griew considered that the effect of the judgment of the Court of Appeal was to create a new defence.

Lord Mustill did not analyse further the possibility of involuntary intoxication operating so as to negative an ingredient of an offence. It might have been helpful if he had done so. Involuntary intoxication arising from the actions of third parties, could have been treated as negativing liability for any offence—provided the jury are content that the conduct would not have occurred but for that intoxication. How can there be an 'intention' if as a result of intoxication there is insufficient ratiocination to form judgment or to foresee accurately? How can there be recklessness (by analogy with voluntary intoxication) if the defendant is unaware that he is taking alcohol or drugs? Also, it might have been productive to have considered whether the involuntary imbibing by the defendant could possibly be considered to produce involuntary action. Although the courts have come over the years to narrow the defence of automatism, can there be said, in such circumstances, to be an act which is attributable to the defendant if the cause of the act was 'disinhibition' through involuntary intoxication?

---

[50] I.e., than good motive exculpating from what otherwise would be criminal intent.   [51] [1994] 3 WLR 519, 528.   [52] Ibid 528.
[53] G. Sullivan [1994] Crim LR 272.
[54] J. Smith [1993] Crim LR 784; J. R. Spencer [1994] *CLJ* 6; E. Griew, *Archbold News* 28 May 1993, 5.

By analogy, it has often been suggested that hypnosis would mean that the defendant's act could be regarded as automatic. Why? The reason seems to be that despite the controlled muscular action the defendant's muscular movement are not to be regarded as his voluntary acts. If the defendant in *Kingston* had been drugged to the extent that he was akin to someone hypnotised why should he not be entitled to the defence of automatism? What justifies different legal treatment? Of course, the answer to that question should not be limited by the repugnant facts of the case.

Even if Lord Mustill had considered involuntary intoxication as giving rise to a limited defence based on the conduct of another, (by analogy with duress), involuntary intoxication could have been seen not as negativing mens rea but as a defence to fully constituted crime. Such an approach would have allowed the courts to acknowledge the existence of the defence but on terms. For example, involuntary intoxication could have operated as a defence in certain sets of circumstances only or to certain offences only.

One central issue needs further consideration. Should it make any difference that the ability to control may be taken away rather than the suggestion to act be implanted? Lord Mustill considered that this was a crucial distinction. He said,

Thus we are concerned here with a case of disinhibition. The drug is not alleged to have created the desire to which the respondent gave way, but rather to have enabled it to be released.[55]

Also, there may be a distinction between irresistible impulse which comes from an internal desire to act and the releasing of a desire—otherwise controlled—by the secret conduct of a third party? One can understand the evidential problems of drawing a distinction between an impulse which the defendant could not resist and one which could have been resisted albeit with difficulty. However, whether the jury could have difficulty in determining whether because of the involuntary intoxication the essential elements of the offence were present, on the facts of *Kingston* is doubtful. The jury would have to be convinced that the defendant did the act and at the appropriate time had the mens rea. The lacing of drinks by a third party would only provide a defence if the jury believed that there was no mens rea/actus reus as a result of the lacing. Surely this would not impose too demanding a task—especially as medical

[55] [1994] 3 WLR 519, 525.

evidence could be adduced? It is true that it would be a difficult
hypothetical question but is that a sufficient justification for
refusing to allow the defence?

(2) Authority

Lord Mustill concluded after a consideration of the older cases[56]
that there was an absence of guidance from English authorities. He
also considered the case of *Majewski*[57] concluding that where
intent is proved the case does not add a further defence of
involuntary intoxication. He considered the Scottish authorities. In
Ross[58] the defendant was charged with attempted murder. The can
of lager beer which he had been drinking had been laced with
temazepam and LSD. Lord Weir[59] said,

> At the time in question the accused must have been suffering from a total
> alienation of reason rendering him incapable of controlling or appreciating
> what he was doing, that such alienation was caused by an external factor
> and that this factor was neither self induced nor one which he was bound
> to foresee. Anything short of this will not suffice.

This was followed in *Cardle* v *Mulrainey*[60] where Lord Hope,
remitting the case to the sheriff, said,

> The sheriff found ... that the respondent's ability to reason the
> consequences of his actions to himself was affected by his ingestion of the
> drug. The finding narrates that he was unable to take account in his actions
> of the fact that they were criminal in character and to refrain from them.
> But this inability to exert self control, which the sheriff has described as an
> inability to complete the reasoning process, must be distinguished from the
> essential requirement that there should be a total alienation of the
> accused's mental faculties of reasoning and of understanding what he is
> doing.

Lord Mustill concluded that the effect of the Scottish authorities
was that a mere disinhibition was insufficient to found a defence.
He went on to examine a Canadian case and the US Model Penal
Code,[61] and concluded,

---

[56] *Pearson's Case* (1835) 2 Lew CC 144; 168 ER 1108 and Hale, *Pleas of the Crown*, Vol 1, 32.   [57] [1977] AC 443.   [58] [1991] SLT 564.
[59] Ibid 532, 577.   [60] [1992] SLT 1152, 1160.
[61] American Law Institute, *Model Penal Code*, Part I, 363: 'Involuntary intoxication, however, excuses only if the resulting incapacitation is as extreme as that as would establish irresponsibility had it resulted from mental disease.'

I cannot find in this material any sufficient grounds for holding that the defence relied upon is already established by the common law, any more than it can be derived from general principles.[62]

(3) Creation of a New Defence

Given that the authorities did not establish the existence of the defence, should a new defence be created? It is to be noted that the House of Lords considered without legal argument that it had the right to create a new defence—presumably on the basis of a residual common law power. Historically, the judges created all the present general defences. However, on the reasoning that there is no residual jurisdiction to create new offences, it might be thought that, although the judges can extend and develop existing defences, they no longer have a residual jurisdiction to create new defences. The matter has been indirectly considered by the House of Lords in *Lynch*[63] where the defendant who was charged with aiding and abetting murder raised the defence of duress. He had been forced by terrorists to drive them to where they killed a policeman. Lord Kilbrandon said,

I remain convinced that the grounds on which the majority propose that the conviction of the appellant be set aside involve changes in the law which are outside the proper functions of your Lordships in your judicial capacity. If duress per minas has never been admitted as a defence to a charge of murder, and if the proposal that it should now be so admitted be approved, it seems to me that your Lordships, in countenancing a defence for many years authoritatively (though not in your Lordship's House) denied would be doing what, in the converse, was firmly and properly disapproved in *R v Knuller*. . . .

The argument which he advanced against the residual power to create new defences was that

An alteration of a fundamental doctrine of law, such as this appeal proposes, could not properly be given effect to save after the widest reference to interests, both social and intellectual, far transcending those available in the judicial committee of your Lordship's House. Indeed general public opinion is deeply and properly concerned. It will not do to claim that judges have the duty—call it the privilege—of seeing to it that the common law expands and contracts to meet what the judges conceive to be the requirement of modern society. Modern society rightly prefers to

---

[62] [1994] 3 WLR 535.   [63] [1975] AC 653.

exercise that function for itself, and this it conveniently does through those who represent it through Parliament.

However, Lord Mustill seems to have assumed that there was a residual jurisdiction to create new defences. He considered that any new defence such as that argued for, would imply five character-istics. First it would apply to all mens rea offences. Secondly, the defence would give rise to an acquittal. Thirdly, the intoxication must be the result of the conduct of a third party. Fourthly, the onus of disproving the defence is on the prosecution. Fifthly, the defence is subjective—were the defendant's inhibitions overcome by the effects of the drug? He considered that the creation of such a defence would be a bold step fraught with theoretical and practical implications.

(i) Theoretical Implications
These Lord Mustill listed as:–

(a) It would be necessary to reconcile the new defence with the law concerning irresistible impulse where the defendant contends that he acted under the 'direction' of his subconscious mind. This is no defence if solely of an internal origin[64] and cannot even be the foundation of the defence of insanity.[65] The defence contended for would have to be reconciled with the circumstances where conduct resulted from a combination of innate drives and disinhibition.

(b) It would be necessary in the context of murder to determine how the defence would work in the context of diminished responsibility[66] (involving abnormality of mind and substantial impairment of mental responsibility) which the new defence would resemble.

(ii) Practical Implications
These he listed as:–

(a) The jury would be faced with difficult speculative psycho-logical evidence about the defendant's personality in order to

---

[64] *Kopsch* (1925) 19 Cr App R 50.
[65] *Att-Gen for South Australia v Brown* [1960] AC 432.
[66] Homicide Act 1957 s 2.

assess the likely disinhibiting effect of any involuntary intoxication. He described the matters involved as 'elusive concepts'.[67]

(b) The defence could open the door to spurious claims.

(c) If the form of the defence was that the defendant would not have done such things but for the disinhibiting effect of the involuntary intoxication and evidence from well wishers was in support of that proposition it would be difficult, in practice, for the prosecution to introduce evidence to rebut such evidence and to counter such a proposition.

Lord Mustill went on to conclude that the new defence would require an adjustment of existing principles and the adoption of new trial techniques, and that these, though not themselves an irrefragable argument against acceptance of new rules of law, constituted an argument against accepting the proposed defence. However, he asserted, it would only be necessary to undertake such a disturbance to principle and practice if the interests of justice required the undertaking of such a course. He concluded that the ability to adjust the sentence by the judge was a more just way of taking involuntary intoxication into account rather than a straight acquittal or conviction by the jury. He felt that the existence of the mandatory life sentence for murder (which he described as 'an anomalous relic of the history of the criminal law') was not a sufficient argument to 'force on the theory and practice of the criminal law an exception which would otherwise be unjustified.'[68]

Although he allowed the appeal, Lord Mustill suggested that the work of the Law Commission should be expanded to consider whether 'a merciful, realistic and intellectually sustainable statutory solution could be newly created. For the present, however, I consider that no such regime now exists, and that the common law is not a suitable vehicle for creating one.'[69]

This case creates a number of interesting issues but perhaps the central one is whether there is something different between disinhibition and other cases of suggestion. If a hypnotist convinces a subject that all women are available for sexual purposes (whether or not they have consented) and when freed from the hypnotic state the defendant has non-consensual intercourse with a woman, will he be guilty of rape? Would it be different if the hypnotist had directed the defendant to rape the woman? In the first case it would

---

[67] [1994] 3 All ER 353, 371.　　　[68] Ibid 371.　　　[69] Ibid 372.

be argued that the defendant had the innate desire/intention to have sex with women (with or without their consent) and, therefore, he was guilty of rape even if the only reason why he committed the act of penetration was hypnotic disinhibition. The Freudian assumption that all men want to sleep with as many partners as possible (with or without consent?) is open to question. But what would be the legal position if it proved to be judicially accepted? Would a basic 'drive' over which all any person has is 'self-control' be regarded as sufficient evidence of an intention in respect of which the disinhibition is irrelevant—except, that is, as a factor to mitigate sentence?

Although the evidential issues are very difficult, in principle, if a person is disinhibited because of hypnosis or involuntary intoxication should this be considered irrelevant when guilt is in question? Also, the whole issue of the basis of criminal liability should be kept in mind in considering this question. At common law criminal liability is based not only on conduct but also on the state of mind of the defendant when he does the act. If he has no control (because an outside agency has removed his normal disinhibiting processes without the defendant's consent) how can it be his actus reus or mens rea? Perhaps this is where the matter should be considered. Although it might be argued that there is an underlying mens rea which comes to light because of disinhibition if the matter had been considered as a matter of actus reus it could be argued that there was no effective control of the act. If a person is involuntarily injected with a drug which removes control is any spasmodic movement of the defendant the defendant's act? This is the question which remains to be considered. Even if there is the mens rea because there is an underlying intention to do the act it does not mean that what occurs is an 'act of the defendant.' It may well be that if this line of analysis had been adopted the problems with the underlying existence of a desire/intention to carry out the conduct could have been avoided.

V Reckless and Grossly Negligent Manslaughter

Historically, manslaughter was a crime which could be committed by gross negligence. After *Caldwell*[70] and *Lawrence*[71] the courts

[70] [1982] AC 341.   [71] [1982] AC 510.

had to consider the question what was the precise relationship between gross negligence and the new concept of 'objective recklessness' which the House of Lords had introduced. It was thought that after the decisions in *Seymour*[72] and *Kong Cheuk Kwan*[73] which had addressed this issue the test of gross negligence had been supplanted by the new test of reckless manslaughter to such an extent that the old test no longer operated. The *Caldwell* loophole (which was considered in last year's *Review*[74]) was thought to apply equally to cases of reckless manslaughter which previously had been considered cases of gross negligence. In theory, this meant that where a defendant had caused the death of another after (1) giving thought to the possibility of causing harm to another and (2) erroneously concluding that there was no risk of such harm, he would be acquitted of the offence of manslaughter. Under the old test of gross negligence the defendant's consideration of the risk was not relevant. If the defendant considered that there was no risk of harm to another (where there was such risk of harm obvious to the reasonable man) the defendant's erroneous foresight was not relevant to the issue of liability. It was purely an objective matter and provided the defendant's failure was considered by the jury to be gross he would be found guilty.

Recently, the issue of reckless and gross negligence manslaughter fell to be considered and, in particular, the courts had to decide what is left of the old gross negligence test? In the compound report of three appeals the Court of Appeal had to consider this issue. In *Prentice, Adomako and Holloway*[75] the court had to consider three directions given on this issue at three separate trials. In *Prentice* a young doctor gave a wrong drug in the process of administering a lumbar puncture and the patient died. In *Adomako* an anaesthetist failed to notice that the patient's breathing tube had become disconnected during an eye operation. The patient died. In *Holloway* the defendant electrician had been responsible for wiring a central heating system and a person was electrocuted because a circuit breaker had been left inoperative because of inappropriate wiring. In *Prentice* the direction of the trial judge was in terms of

[72] [1983] 2 AC 493. [73] (1985) 82 Cr App R 18.
[74] (1994) 47 *CLP Annual Review*, 64–68. [75] [1993] 4 All ER 935.

the *Lawrence/Caldwell* test.[76] Counsel complained that this test
prevented the jury from taking into account the mitigating
circumstances in determining whether the high degree of gross
negligence had been established for manslaughter. In *Adomako* the
trial judge gave a gross negligence direction quoting from a number
of conflicting authorities about what was meant by 'gross.' Counsel
objected saying that the appropriate direction should have been
that of objective recklessness. In *Holloway* the trial judge directed
on the *Lawrence/Caldwell* test. Counsel argued that this test
prevented the jury from considering whether the failure was gross.

Lord Taylor CJ considering the legal authorities referred to
Bateman[77] and *Andrews*[78] and concluded, 'But negligent inattention characterised as "mere inattention" does not create criminal
liability. To do so, the inattention or inadvertence must be, in the
jury's view, grossly negligent.'[79] In support of this view he quoted
Geoffery Lane LJ in *Stone and Dobinson*[80] where a high degree of
negligence was held to be required. Lord Taylor CJ went on to
consider and trace the history of the Diplock test in *Caldwell*[81] and
Lawrence[82] as confirmed in *Reid*.[83] In *Seymour*[84] the House of
Lords decided that causing death by dangerous driving and motor
manslaughter were to be tried using the objective recklessness test.

The Court of Appeal were faced with the question whether the
judgment in *Andrews* had survived the *Reid* approach? Lord Taylor

[76] 'What do the prosecution have to prove for recklessness? You must be satisfied
of three factors: (1) that the defendant whose case you are considering created a
serious risk of causing serious harm to Malcolm Savage ... Next, you have to be
satisfied that that risk would have been obvious to any ordinary prudent doctor of
the experience, of the knowledge and of the status of the defendant being considered
when performing the task which the defendant was performing. Thirdly, you have to
be satisfied that the defendant gave no thought to the possibility of there being any
such risk.'   [77] (1925) 19 Cr App R 8.
[78] [1937] AC 576, 583 Lord Atkin: 'Simple lack of care such as will constitute
civil liability is not enough. For purposes of the criminal law there are degrees of
negligence, and a high degree of negligence is required to be proved before a felony is
established. Probably of all the epithets that can be applied 'reckless' most nearly
covers the case.'   [79] Ibid 940.   [80] [1977] QB 354.
[81] Recklessness occurs '. . . if (1) he does an act which in fact creates an obvious
risk that property would be destroyed or damaged and (2) when he does the act he
either has not given any thought to the possibility of there being any such risk or has
recognised that there was some risk involved and has nonetheless gone on to do it.'
[82] 'without having given any thought to the possibility of there being any such
risk or, having recognised that there was some risk involved, had none the less gone
on to take it.' [1982] AC 510, 527.   [83] [1992] 3 All ER 673.
[84] [1983] 2 AC 493.

CJ considered that both *Andrews* and *Stone and Dobinson* had not been disapproved of in the subsequent cases. Secondly, he concluded that *Reid* had qualified the *Caldwell/Lawrence* test by emphasising the need to take into account excuses and explanations put forward by the defendant. Such an approach, he contended, would be inappropriate if a strict application of the Diplock test were employed. Against this background Lord Taylor CJ drew a distinction between the three cases before the Court of Appeal and another category of cases. He said that the serious and obvious risk test, although appropriate to everyday circumstances where any reasonable person would be aware of the risk, was not appropriate where there were duties of a different character. He said,

> However, it is a basic premise of Lord Diplock's formulation that the defendant himself created the obvious and serious risk. This is entirely appropriate in a case of driving, or setting fire to a hotel. Unless and until the defendant drives, or strikes a match, there is no risk. But breach of duty cases such as those involving doctors are different in character. Often there is a high risk of danger to the deceased's health, not created by the defendant, and pre-existing risk to the deceased's health is what causes the defendant to assume the duty of care with consent. His intervention will often be in situations of emergency. Further, the 'obvious risk' of Lord Diplock's formulation in *R. v. Caldwell* meant obvious to the 'ordinary prudent individual'. Everyone knows what can happen when you strike a match, and practically everyone, whether as driver or passenger, knows the risk of the road. But in expert fields where duty is undertaken, be it by a doctor or electrician, the criteria of what the ordinary prudent individual would appreciate can hardly be applied in the same way.'[85]

Lord Taylor CJ said that except in cases of motor manslaughter (where the Court of Appeal regarded itself as bound by *Seymour*) 'the proper test in manslaughter cases based on breach of duty is the gross negligence test established in *Andrews* . . .' The result was that the appeals of *Prentice* and *Holloway* were allowed. That of *Adomako* was dismissed. The decision has been criticised.[86] Although the Court of Appeal refused Adomako leave to appeal to the House of Lords the appeal committee gave leave, though in the event *Adomako's*[87] appeal was dismissed and the decision of the Court of Appeal confirmed. After a review of the authorities Lord Mackay LC confirmed that the decision in *Andrews* 'remains the

---

[85] Ibid 943.   [86] S. Lai (1994) 58 Jo Cr L 303–9.
[87] [1994] 2 All ER 79.

most authoritative statement of the present law . . .'[88] He said that, having considered whether there was a breach of duty the jury would have to consider

whether that breach of duty should be characterised as gross negligence and therefore as a crime. This will depend on the seriousness of the breach of duty committed by the defendant in all the circumstances in which the defendant was placed when it occurred. The jury will have to consider whether the extent to which the defendant's conduct departed from the proper standard of care incumbent upon him, involving as it must have done a risk of death to the patient, was such that it should be judged criminal.

He went on to state that the decision in *Seymour* concerning motor manslaughter should no longer apply. He considered it an unnecessary exception introducing undesirable complexity into the law. Similarly, he confirmed that although the word 'reckless' could be used in its ordinary sense it was not necessary to refer to the formulations in *Lawrence*.[89]

This case represents two important developments. It confirms that, at least in duty situations, there has to be a gross failure of duty. The second is a retreat by the House of Lords from the doctrine of objective recklessness at least in the case of motor manslaughter. The doctrine of objective recklessness, although strictly a matter of statutory interpretation, was based on the fact that the House of Lords lacked confidence in the subjective recklessness test. It is true that only the thick and uncaring are likely to convince a jury that they did not foresee the possibility of bringing about a prohibited consequence obvious to anyone with common sense. The effect of objective recklessness is that such unthinking persons will be guilty and not acquitted because of their lack of foresight. The possible acquittal of such undeserving defendants was the reason why the judges had a theoretical objection to the use of subjective recklessness.

However, the use of the objective recklessness test seems to place little confidence in the jury. Surely, human nature being what it is,

---

[88] [1994] 2 All ER 86.

[89] '. . . it is perfectly open to a trial judge to use the word "reckless" if it appears appropriate in the circumstances of a particular case as indicating the extent to which the defendant's conduct must deviate from that of a proper standard of care. I do not think it right to require that this should be done and certainly not right that it should incorporate the full detail required in *R v Lawrence*': ibid 89.

the more obvious the risk the more unlikely the jury would be to believe a plea by the defendant that he did not foresee the possibility. It is hoped that the traditional confidence in the jury system will continue to be reaffirmed and the House of Lords will resile increasingly from the objective test—imposing liability as it does where there is no 'active' thought process in the defendant's mind which could be considered as at 'fault'. Many have considerable confidence in the jury system and welcome the House of Lords step back at least to the point where *Caldwell/Lawrence* can be confined to statutory offences using the word 'recklessness' or one of is derivatives. Such a position is consonant with the rationale of Lord Diplock himself in *Caldwell*. In principle, criminal liability should be based on the active content of the defendant's mind. In this light the judgment of the House of Lords is to be welcomed even if it does leave the difficult question about what is sufficient to constitute gross as opposed to ordinary negligence.

VI Attempt and Recklessness

It is axiomatic when considering the crime of attempt to assert that the prosecution has to prove not only an act that is more than preparatory but also that the defendant has the necessary mens rea—which, in general, at common law is the mens rea of the substantive offence.[90] At common law the mens rea for an attempt is intent.[91] This was given statutory effect in the Criminal Attempts Act 1981 section 1(1).[92] Intent under the statute means the same as it did at common law.[93] Where it is alleged that an offence has been attempted the jury has to consider whether the defendant intended to bring about the consequence in the sense of he had it as his purpose to bring about the consequence or foresaw the consequence—as defined in the substantive offence—as virtually certain to occur.[94] If the substantive offence can be committed recklessly—in the subjective sense—as laid down in *Cunningham*[95] recklessness

---

[90] Murder can be committed only with an intention to kill. An intention to cause grievous harm is insufficient. [91] *Mohan* [1976] QB 1.

[92] 'If with intent to commit an offence . . . a person does an act which is more than merely preparatory to the commission of the offence, he is guilty of attempting to commit the offence.' [93] *Pearman* (1984) 80 Cr App R 259.

[94] *Walker* (1989) 90 Cr App R 226. [95] [1957] 2 QB 396.

in the sense of foresight of the possibility of bringing about the prohibited consequence is not sufficient to support a charge of attempt.[96]

Conceivably, the position could be different if the crime attempted relates to a consequence crime which can be committed objectively recklessly. It can be argued that provided the reasonable man will foresee the consequence as likely to come about if the defendant does the act deliberately that is sufficient mens rea— following the *Caldwell/Lawrence*[97] test. Such an interpretation would, of course, fly in the face of the statute which requires an intent to commit an offence. It would be a strange consequence of the dual definition of recklessness if the result of the categorisation would be that one group of offences (objective recklessness offences) could be attempted and the other (subjective recklessness cases) could not. However, the same argument would not pertain if the crime is an 'act crime.' By definition, all that has to be proved to give rise to an attempted act crime is an intent to do the act. There is a sustainable distinction between act and consequence crimes provided there is a scientific discrimination in categorising offences into the appropriate category. The question arose in *Att-Gen's Ref (No 3 of 1992)*[98] which concerned the offence of attempted aggravated arson contrary to subsections 1(2) and (3) of the Criminal Damage Act 1971.[99] There had been a number of attacks on property owned by the complainants and so they sat and kept watch over their premises from their car. In the early hours the defendants drove to the scene with a milk crate containing petrol bombs, matches, a petrol can and some rags. The defendants threw a petrol bomb towards the complainants and two men to whom they were talking, standing on the pavement. The petrol bomb passed over the complainants' car and smashed against an adjacent garden wall. On the count with which we are concerned, namely, being reckless as to whether life would be endangered, the learned

---

[96] *Millard and Vernon* [1987] Crim LR 393.
[97] [1982] AC 341 and 510.   [98] [1994] 2 All ER 121.
[99] 'A person who without lawful excuse destroys or damages any property, whether belonging to himself or another—(a) intending to destroy or damage any property or being reckless as to whether any property would be destroyed or damaged; and (b) intending by the destruction or damage to endanger the life of another or being reckless as to whether the life of another would be thereby endangered; shall be guilty of an offence. (3) An offence committed under this section by destroying or damaging property by fire shall be charged as arson.'

judge directed in terms of the general observations referred to above. She reasoned (1) that there can be no attempt unless the defendant intends to commit the substantive offence; (2) the evidence could not support an allegation that the defendants intended by the destruction of the car to endanger the life of its occupants; (3) *it is impossible to intend to be reckless* as to whether the life of an other would be endangered by damage to property; and (4) it is, therefore, impossible in law to convict of an attempt to commit aggravated arson if all that can be proved is recklessness as to whether life would be endangered by the damage.

The point of law was referred by the Attorney-General.[100] Of course, the recklessness relevant to the offence is not subjective recklessness but objective recklessness as defined by *Caldwell*.[101] It is established that the threat to life must result from the destruction or damage to the property.[102] It would make no difference to the issue referred whether the damage resulted from fire or some other cause. Shiemann J, giving the judgment of the Court of Appeal, began by stating what needs to be established to prove a subsection 1(2) offence. He said,

In the case of the completed aggravated offence the prosecution needs to prove (1) the defendant in fact damaged property, whether belonging to himself or another; and (2) that the state of mind of the defendant was one of the following, (a) he intended to damage property, and intended by the damage to endanger life of another or (b) he intended to damage property and was reckless as to whether life of another would be thereby endangered or (c) he was reckless as to whether any property would be damaged and was reckless as to whether life of another would be thereby endangered.[103]

He stated that the central issue was whether the offence with the postulated mens rea in 2(b) above could be attempted—when the defendant did an act that was more than preparatory? The Criminal Attempts Act 1981 section 1 lays down that an attempt occurs where the defendant does an act which is more than preparatory 'with an intent to commit an offence.'

First, he considered the simple offence under subsection 1(1) and said that attempted intentional criminal damage required intention

---

[100] The reference was, 'Whether on a charge of attempted arson in the aggravated form, . . . , in addition to establishing a specific intent to cause damage by fire, it is sufficient to prove that the defendant was reckless as to whether life would thereby be endangered?'   [101] [1982] AC 341.   [102] *Steer* [1988] AC 111.
[103] [1992] 2 All ER 125.

to do the act and an intention to damage property. Recklessness about the possibility of causing criminal damage, in the objective sense, was considered insufficient to sustain a conviction for an attempt by the Court of Appeal in *Millard*.[104]

Would the same principle operate in respect of the aggravated offence? Assuming that the act or omission bringing about the criminal damage was intended and there was an intention thereby to endanger life clearly the mens rea is sufficient to support a charge of attempt provided the defendant's act is more than preparatory. Of course, that was not the point at issue. What is the position if the defendant does an act not intending thereby to endanger life but the circumstances suggest to the reasonable man that there would be a risk of such an endangerment? Can there be an attempt in such circumstances? Is objective recklessness as to this possibility sufficient to enable an attempt to be established. In other words, would an intention to cause criminal damage by itself be sufficient to support the charge of an attempted aggravated offence? In principle, it might be argued it should not. Above all attempt is a crime based on the defendant's mental state—the proscribed thought processes in the defendant's mind. If, in fact, there is nothing actually in the defendant's mind either (a) by way of forethought of possible consequences, or, (b) knowledge of surrounding circumstances which would alert him to the possibility, he does not, as a fact, have a mind which subjectively contains these ingredients referring to the possible consequences. If the defendant did not intend the prohibited consequence he could not have in his brain the thoughts—the mens rea—for the offence when he did the act. In principle, a principle which commended itself to the learned judge, intention is required. Objective recklessness would not do. However, the subsection 1(2) offence can be committed where there is only objective recklessness. This means (omitting consideration of the loophole) that the courts do not have to consider what the defendant has in his mind but what the reasonable man in the defendant's position would have foreseen as a possibility. If the possibility of causing criminal damage (section 1 offence) or causing, thereby endangerment of life (subsection 1(2) offence) is obvious to the reasonable man, the substantive offence can be

[104] 1987] Crim LR 393 where Mustill LJ stated that mere recklessness was insufficient, 'the prosecution had to show .. it was [damage to the stand] which each appellant had decided, so far as in him lay, to bring about'

committed. What are the 'knock on' effects when an attempted subsection 1(2) offence is charged—bearing in mind that the 1981 Act speaks of an intent to commit an offence?

The conclusion of the Court of Appeal, disagreeing with the trial judge, (that recklessness as to the consequences of such damage for the lives of others was not enough for an attempt though it was sufficient for the completed offence) advised that, 'The defendant must intend to damage property, but there is no need for a graver mental state than is required for the full offence.'[105]

The rationale for this was that for an attempt to be established all that had to be proved was the state of mind required for the completed offence and that the defendant intended to supply the missing physical element of the completed offence. Of course, in the instant case that could be established by proof of an objectively reckless endangerment.

This raises a number of interesting questions. In the simple subsection 1(1) offence objective recklessness could not support a charge of attempted criminal damage, but in relation to the aggravated offence contrary to subsection 1(2) the other component—recklessness as to whether the life of another would be endangered—is sufficient to support an attempt. Why? One answer is that the criminal damage is analysed as a consequence of the defendant's conduct, whereas the recklessness as to the endangerment is not a consequence which has to be proved but only a surrounding circumstance. The difference between recklessness as to consequences and surrounding circumstances may be a key analytical distinction. *Caldwell* clearly establishes that objective recklessness would be sufficient to establish liability. In relation to surrounding circumstances usually the prosecution has to prove knowledge of the surrounding circumstances. If it fails to do so the prosecution fails *in limine*. There is no offence.[106] This common law position has been the subject of statutory modification in the case of some offences e.g. rape.[107] It is interesting that it was the offence of rape which the court employed by way of analogous reasoning in *Att-Gen's Ref (No 3 of 1992)*. They referred to *Khan*[108] where attempted rape was charged. The defendant argued that he could not be convicted of a attempted reckless rape but this

---

[105] [1994] 2 All ER 127.   [106] *Morgan* [1976] AC 182.
[107] Sexual Offences (Amendment) Act 1976, s 1.
[108] [1990] 1 WLR 813; 2 All ER 783.

argument was not accepted by the Court of Appeal, where Russell LJ stated,[109]

> The only difference between the two offences [rape and attempted rape][110] is that in rape sexual intercourse takes place whereas in attempted rape it does not, although there has to be some act which is more than preparatory to sexual intercourse. Considered in that way, the intent of the defendant is precisely the same in rape and attempted rape and the mens rea is identical, namely an intention to have intercourse plus a knowledge of or reckless as to the woman's absence of consent. ... No question of attempting to achieve a reckless state of mind arises; the attempt relates to the physical activity; the mental state of the defendant is the same. ... Recklessness in rape and attempted rape arises not in relation to the physical act of the accused but only in his state of mind when engaged in the activity of having or attempting to have sexual intercourse ... the attempt does not require any different intention on the part of the accused from that of the full offence of rape.

The Court of Appeal followed this approach on the basis that there was no argument of policy or principle why *Khan* was not correctly decided. It is submitted that this decision needs to be thought about carefully especially as there may now be a distinction between consequences and surrounding circumstances. This distinction has been seen as unworkable, for example, by the Law Commission in its first version of the draft criminal code.[111] However, in relation to consequence crimes the consequence has to be desired—recklessness is not enough for an attempt, not even subjective foresight.[112] In relation to surrounding circumstances, the general rule is that to commit the offence or to attempt it the prosecution have to prove knowledge of the surrounding circumstances.[113] Either there is knowledge or there is not. Recklessness in the sense of foresight seems inappropriate in the context of a surrounding circumstances. It can be argued that it is only in connection with objective recklessness that ignorance of the existence of these surrounding circumstances may support a conviction for an attempt. This seems to be one of the possible consequences of the use of the concept of objective recklessness in the criminal law. It is the hypothetical state of mind of the

---

[109] [1990] 1 WLR 813, 818-195   [110] My supplement.
[111] Law Commission Paper No 143, *Codification of the Criminal Law*, HMSO, 1985.   [112] *Mohan* [1976] QB 1.
[113] *Morgan* [1976] AC 182; *Gardiner* [1994] Crim LR 455.

reasonable man which is called into question not the defendant's. Perhaps, an example would help. If X throws a petrol bomb trying to damage a statue of a famous politician but he misses he can be found guilty of attempted criminal damage. If there is a courting couple sitting behind the statute can he be guilty of an attempted subsection 1(2) offence? Clearly, if he intends by the damage, to injure the couple there can be no doubt. If he does not know that there is anyone sitting there can he be found guilty of an attempt? Knowledge of surrounding circumstances is usually required at common law for a common law offence unless there is some reason of principle[114] or statutory provision which requires less than this. In the case of rape the statute makes it clear that recklessness about whether the victim was consenting (a surrounding circumstance) is sufficient for the substantive offence although the courts have had some difficulty assigning a precise meaning to the concept in relation to surrounding circumstances. In the case of offences contrary to subsection 1(2) the courts have interpreted the offence similarly. *Smith and Hogan* have suggested that,

The decision [in *Khan*] is limited to attempted rape but consistency will surely requires the application of the same principle . . . to other offences where recklessness as to circumstances suffices, conspicuously offences of obtaining by deception.[115]

It is to be noted that the authors are not considering objective recklessness as to consequences. They add,

The recklessness required in rape and obtaining offences is, it is submitted, *Cunningham* recklessness, i.e. advertent, subjective recklessness, and the law should draw the line at this. *Caldwell/Lawrence* recklessness should have no place. It would be wrong to hold that a person intended and attempted to commit a crime when he had not even adverted to an element of it. Still less should strict liability have any place on a charge of attempt.[116]

Even in the case of rape—objective recklessness does not suffice (there must be at least indifference to a foreseen possibility[117]).

In criminal damage non-advertence to the possibility of damage or destruction endangering life suffices. The test is whether the reasonable man would have foreseen the possibility of the endangerment of life:

---

[114] *Sweet* v *Parsley* [1970] AC 132.   [115] Ibid 306.
[116] Ibid 306.   [117] *Pigg* [1982] 2 All ER 591.

The substantive crime is committed if the defendant damaged property in the state of mind where he was reckless as to whether the life of another would thereby be endangered. We see no reason why there should not be a conviction for attempt if the prosecution can show that he, in that state of mind, intended to damage property by throwing a bomb at it.[118]

The definition of the aggravated offence reads as far as relevant, 'being reckless as to whether the life of another would be thereby endangered.' Seemingly, objective recklessness suffices for this element. However, the endangerment of another could be regarded as a consequence in which case a reckless attempt would not constitute an offence. By using the analogy of the principle in *Khan* (which was based on statutory recklessness about a surrounding circumstance) the courts have drawn a principle concerning surrounding circumstances and applied it to recklessness as to a hypothetical possibility or consequences. However, Shiemann J decided,

What was missing in the present case was damage to the first named property, without which the offence was not complete. The mental state of the defendant in each case contained everything which was required to render him guilty of the full offence. In order to succeed in a prosecution for attempt, it must be shown that the defendant intended to achieve that which was missing from the full offence.[119]

He was critical of the trial judge's distinguishing of *Khan* and said he could see no reason of principle for distinguishing the two cases.

It is submitted that if the Court of Appeal had regarded the reckless endangerment of life on general principle as a surrounding circumstance it would have asked if it were appropriate to extend the principle of recklessness to a surrounding circumstance. Analogous reasoning from a statutory offence which was the subject of a subjective approach might not be thought appropriate for an objective recklessness offence not specifically defined in such terms. If objective recklessness as to the endangerment is treated as a state of mind of the reasonable man by definition this does not refer to the defendant's actual knowledge. This raises an issue of principle which could be best dealt with by rejecting the concept of objective recklessness. However, for the present, the court has, therefore, taken a step further in the direction of objectivity in the

[118] *Att-Gen's Reference (No 3 of 1992)* [1994] 2 All ER 121, 126.
[119] Ibid 128.

context of attempts. Each extension must be looked at carefully because attempt as suggested above is essentially an offence which is in the defendant's mind and decidedly not in the mind of the reasonable man.

VII Mischievous Propensity

It has long been understood that children are to some extent exempt from criminal liability. This is based on the doubtful assumption that some children cannot discern 'good from evil.'[120] The modern rule concerning children between 10 and 14 years is that they are exempt from criminal liability unless a mischievous discretion can be proved by the prosecution. This is an understanding which is additional to all the usual ingredients of the offence charged. The modern law was thought to have been stated in *Gorrie*[121] where Slater J defined mischievous propensity in terms of the defendant knew that he was doing was gravely wrong, seriously wrong. This was qualified in *JM (a minor)* v *Runeckles*[122] from a knowledge of the moral wrongfulness to an awareness that it was more than naughty or mischievous. The child's conduct before[123] during and after the offence can provide evidence which can prove this additional element. The younger the child the more 'evidence' is required to prove the mischievous propensity. The usual way of describing this process was in terms of a presumption[124] that children of that age are *doli incapax*. This presumption could be rebutted by evidence of the mischievous propensity. The nature of that presumption came before the courts in *C*[125] where a twelve year old boy and friend were found tampering with a chained and locked motor cycle in a private driveway. When two police officers approached they ran away leaving a crowbar in the cycle chain. The defendant climbed a wall trying to escape and was arrested on the other side by another constable. They were charged with interfering with a motor cycle with the intention of committing theft.[126] The magistrates were of opinion that the substantial

---

[120] Hale, *Pleas of the Crown*, Vol 1, 630.   [121] (1919) 83 JP 136.
[122] (1984) 79 Cr App R 255.   [123] *R v B, B v A* [1979] 3 All ER 460.
[124] *A* [1992] Crim LR 34 where Bingham LJ said, 'children have the benefit of the presumption which in this case and some others seems to me to lead to results inconsistent with common sense.'   [125] [1994] 3 All ER 190.
[126] Criminal Attempts Act 1981, s.9(1).

damage to the cycle and the running from the police indicated that the defendant knew that he had done something seriously wrong. It was argued for the defendant that the prosecution had adduced no evidence and that the magistrates were not entitled to draw such an inference. It was further argued that running away and damage to the cycle could take the matter no further. After a thorough examination of the cases, Laws J concluded that they demonstrated that for the presumption to be rebutted, there must be clear evidence that the defendant knew that the act was seriously wrong and that the evidence of the acts themselves was insufficient evidence of this knowledge. He said that there was no such evidence in the case and the defendant ought to be acquitted. However, he did not leave the matter there but went on to consider the nature and utility of the presumption. He said,

Whatever may have been the position in an earlier age, when there was no system of compulsory education and when, perhaps, children did not grow up as quickly as they do nowadays, this presumption at the present time is a serious disservice to our law. It means that a child over ten who commits an act of obvious dishonesty, or even grave violence, is to be acquitted unless the prosecution specifically prove by discrete evidence that he understands the obliquity of what he is doing. It is unreal and contrary to common sense; . . .[127]

He went on to say that this additional requirement of mischievous propensity was out of step with the general law of mens rea. His third objection was that the doctrine of knowledge of what was 'seriously wrong' was 'conceptually obscure'. It cannot, in principle, mean knowing that it is against the law (everyone is presumed to know the law) and the authorities suggest that it was not necessary to prove that he knew it was morally wrong. He concluded, 'But if "seriously wrong" means neither "legally wrong" nor "morally wrong" what other yardstick remains?'[128]
He went on to add,

The rule is divisive and perverse: divisive, because it tends to attach criminal consequences to the acts of children coming from what used to be called good homes more readily that to the acts of others; perverse, because it tends to absolve from criminal responsibility the very children most likely to commit criminal acts. It must surely nowadays be regarded as obvious that where a morally impoverished upbringing may have led a teenager

[127] 1994] 3 All ER 196.   [128] Ibid 197.

into crime, the fact of his background should go not to his guilt, but to his mitigation; . . .'[129]

He said that if the law were otherwise immunity would be conferred on the very children who should be managed on a remedial basis within the criminal justice system and not left unchecked outside the system.

It is precisely the younger whose understanding of the difference between right and wrong is fragile or non-existent who is more likely to get involved in criminal activity. Yet this outdated and unprincipled presumption is, no less precisely tailored to secure his acquittal if he is brought before the court. The prosecution are in effect required to prove, as a condition of his guilt, that he is morally responsible: but it is because he is morally *irresponsible* that he has committed the crime in the first place.[130]

He said that the rule was the product of its time when the harsh criminal laws were often regarded as ferocious in the case of young children. His final resume was that, 'This presumption has no utility whatever in the present era. It ought to go.'

He rejected the three arguments advanced for retaining the presumption, (1) that its rejection would have a retroactive effect on criminal liability, (2) that it is long established and should be abolished only by parliament or the House of Lords, (3) precedent. The latter point was rejected on the basis that the presumption that there had never been a decision of the Court of Appeal where the existence of the presumption was a distinct issue. It had been assumed to be operative. He concluded,

I would hold that the presumption relied on by the appellant is no longer part of the law of England. The appeal should therefore be dismissed.[131]

This provides an interesting example, of the courts adapting what was thought to be a long established rule by taking into account the realities of modern life. This process, which the courts employed in relation to marital rape, has not been without criticism as being unsystematic, incomplete and, possibly, unconstitutional.[132]

---

[129] Ibid 198.   [130] Ibid 198.   [131] Ibid 200.
[132] I. Dennis (1993) 46 *CLP Annual Volume*, 41–42.

PROPERTY LAW

Alison Clarke

In a year of significant but quite disparate developments in property law, attention will be focussed here on three main areas. The first is a group of cases on identifiability of the subject matter of property interests, which raise questions about the fundamental nature of property interests in general. The second involves a consideration of formalities rules governing the creation and disposition of property interests, where changes in the law have led to a reappraisal of the nature of equitable interests. The third, much narrower in scope, covers the most recent developments in the continuing saga of the continuing liability of tenants under leases after assignment.

I Property, certainty and identifiability

As a general principle, the subject matter of property must be certain. If property can be defined as an interest in relation to a thing, it is axiomatic that the thing must exist. It might be intangible rather than tangible, but nevertheless if the thing does not exist at all no-one can have a proprietary interest in it. Thus, you cannot have a proprietary interest in a thing not yet in existence, even if it will necessarily come into your hands if it ever does come into existence—you have no copyright in a song you have not yet written.[1]

The same applies if the thing exists, but is not yet in the right hands: if you have no interest in a thing, you cannot vest an interest in that thing in anyone else.[2] So, if A, who owns no caravans, promises you that she will transfer or charge to you all caravans she acquires this may give you all sorts of rights against A, but it gives you no interest in any caravan.[3]

---

[1] *Performing Right Society* v *London Theatre of Varieties* [1924] AC 1.
[2] Although your interest need be no more extensive than a power of disposition (for example, a power of appointment over someone else's property), you must have some interest.   [3] Unless and until A acquires one.

The position is precisely the same, only slightly more difficult to see, if the thing is a chose in action. A present right of action exists as a thing in its own right, even if it relates to another thing which is not yet in existence or not yet in the right hands. There is a complicating factor in that, in our jurisdiction at least, not all rights of action are capable of forming the subject matter of property.[4] Nevertheless, assuming that a right of action is of a type that is recognised as proprietary, if it exists it can be the subject matter of property, but if it does not yet exist, or is not yet in the right hands, it can not. Thus, if A promises B for consideration to transfer future property to C, B holds an existing thing—the promise, which is a chose in action—and can dispose of it now by transfer or declaration of trust, either to C or to someone else.[5] This distinction between future things and present rights to future things is best exemplified by *Williams* v *CIR*[6]—a beneficiary entitled to the net income from a trust fund can assign his interest in the income, or half or any other share of his interest in the income, but what he cannot do is make a valid assignment of the £500 he expects to receive next year as the first instalment of next year's net income, even if there is no doubt whatsoever that next year's income will total several thousand pounds. The New Zealand Court of Appeal rejected an argument to the effect that this amounted to the same thing as assigning part of his right to the income: 'He did not assign part of his right to income; he assigned a right to a part of the income, a different thing.'[7]

So, certainty of subject matter is essential in the sense that you cannot have a property interest in a thing that does not exist, nor can you acquire from A a proprietary interest in a thing which is not, or not yet, in A's hands. However, does it necessarily follow that the thing must also be *identifiable*? If the thing in

---

[4] F. Lawson and B. Rudden *The Law of Property*[2] (Oxford, 1982), 22–28. This is of course not unique to rights of action—we might also as a matter of policy decide not to recognise property rights in other sorts of things, such as air or human bodies.

[5] *Fletcher* v *Fletcher* (1844) 4 Hare 67 and see further G. Moffat *Trusts Law: Text and Materials*[2] (London, 1994), 133–141 and also Hanbury and Martin, *Modern Equity*[14] Martin, J. E., ed., (London, 1993), 130 for convincing criticism of dicta to the contrary in *Re Cook's Settlement Trusts* [1965] Ch 902 by Buckley J. For policy reasons (circumvention of the privity rule) the courts may be reluctant to find that B has in fact transferred or declared a trust of the promise: *Beswick* v *Beswick* [1968] AC 58.

[6] [1965] NZLR 395, a decision of the New Zealand Court of Appeal.

[7] Ibid 399 Turner J.

question is in existence, and is in the hands of A, is it possible for B to claim a proprietary interest in the thing if it is impossible to distinguish it from other like things also in existence and also in the hands of A?

This question lies at the heart of three otherwise apparently diverse cases decided by the courts this year: *Hunter* v *Moss*,[8] where an employee claimed that 50 of the 950 shares in his company employer which were held by the defendant were held on trust for him, *In re Stapylton Fletcher Ltd*,[9] where pre-paying customers claimed an interest in wine ordered and stored for them by a now insolvent wine merchant, and *Re Goldcorp Exchange Ltd*,[10] where pre-paying customers who had contracted with a company to order and store bullion for them claimed an interest in the bullion held by the company when it went into receivership.

These cases raised a number of very different issues, but in each case each plaintiff faced essentially the same problem: he claimed that he owned x out of the x+y items held by the defendant, but could not say of any one item in the hands of the defendant that it was or was not his. Does this difficulty—essentially one of identification—rule out a proprietary claim?

Before looking at each case in detail, there are two preliminary points to be made. First, it is worth looking more closely at the difficulty here. If B holds x+y like items, and A claims x of them but cannot tell us which x, why should we perceive that as a difficulty? There are several possible reasons. The first is conceptual: if a thing must exist before a person can be said to have a proprietary interest in it, does it make any sense to say that someone has a property interest in a thing when we cannot say what that thing is? More compellingly, there are practical reasons why we need to be able to say with certainty (ignoring evidential difficulties) whether or not a proprietary interest exists in relation to any given thing. First, there is the possibility that the total stock (x + y) might be increased by reproduction or depleted by loss or damage to some of the items. Deliberate or blameworthy depletion of the stock by B is not a problem: any item which he disposes of, or destroys, or diminishes in value by creating a charge over it, we can

---

[8] [1994] 1 WLR 452 CA.
[9] [1994] 1 WLR 1181 Ch D, also reported at [1994] BCC 532 *sub nom Re Ellis, Son & Vidler Ltd.*   [10] [1994] 2 All ER 806 PC.

deem to be his own rather than A's.[11] However, this is not appropriate for other reproductions/depletions. If even one of the items has offspring, or attracts a bonus (one of a holding of 400 premium bonds or lottery tickets wins a prize), or is damaged in transit, or broken, we need to know whether it was one of A's or one of B's. Secondly, third parties proposing to take an interest in a thing need to know what other property interests are subsisting in relation to that thing. For example, a creditor can take a charging order over, or levy distress on, property beneficially owned by the debtor but not property held by the debtor on trust for someone else, or property in the possession of the debtor but owned by someone else. In the case of each item in B's stock, the creditor therefore needs to know which is B's and which is A's. Thirdly, ownership of things can attract personal liability: if one sheep in a flock contracts a notifiable disease, we need to know whether it is A's sheep or B's sheep.

Nevertheless, pressing as these practical reasons are, they do not necessarily apply with equal force, or indeed at all, to all types of thing in all circumstances. This becomes apparent as one examines the practical problems in the context of each specific case.

Before doing so, however, there is the second preliminary point to be made. We need to distinguish this situation—where A claims a specific number of unidentified items from the total stock held by B—from the situation where A claims a *proportion* of the stock, in the sense of an undivided share in it. If B holds 500 items, to say that A is entitled to 25% of the total rather than to 125 items may seem like a distinction without a difference, but it is not. If A has a proportion of the stock, in the sense of an undivided share, it means that A has a 25% share in each of the 500 items, rather than a 100% share in each of 125 items. Reproductions and depletions are thus shared proportionately. There is therefore a real difference here, although not always reflected in the terminology used, and not always intended by those electing for one formula rather than the other.

---

[11] Cf the tracing rule in *Re Hallett's Estate* (1880) 13 Ch D 696: a fiduciary paying out money from an account in which trust money is mixed with his own money is deemed to exhaust his own money first.

IDENTIFIABILITY AND CHOSES IN ACTION: *HUNTER* v *MOSS*[12]

This is the most straightforward of the three cases. Robert Moss held 950 of the 1000 issued shares in Moss Electrical Company Ltd. The judge at first instance found as a fact[13] that in 1986 Robert Moss orally declared that he held 50 of his shares on trust for the finance director, Mr Hunter.[14] Subsequently the company was taken over by another company, Bennett & Fountain, which took a transfer of the entire share capital in Moss Electrical Company Ltd and in exchange gave Mr Moss 13,500,000 shares in Bennett & Fountain and £150,000 in cash. Mr Hunter claimed he was entitled to a sum equivalent to 5% of the value of those shares and cash paid to Mr Moss.

It was argued on behalf of Mr Moss that no valid trust was created by the oral declaration since the subject matter of the trust was uncertain—the 50 shares to be held on trust for Mr Hunter were not identified. Therefore, counsel for Mr Moss argued, Mr Hunter had no interest in the Moss Electrical Company Ltd shares, and consequently no interest in the Bennett & Fountain shares and cash exchanged for them.

The Court of Appeal rejected this argument and found for Mr Hunter. Dillon LJ, giving the only reasoned judgment,[15] said that a specified number of shares of a certain class in a certain company was sufficiently certain to form the subject matter of a trust, even if there is no indication of which of the identical shares held by the trustee are to be held subject to the trust and which are to be held by the trustee beneficially. He gave two reasons. First, he pointed out that a bequest by Mr Moss of 50 of his shares to Mr Hunter would have been a valid bequest which his executors would have been bound to have carried into effect.[16] This, although disputed by counsel for Mr Moss, is surely correct (and, as Dillon LJ pointed

---

[12] [1994] 1 WLR 452 CA.
[13] On somewhat equivocal evidence: the finding was challenged on appeal but the Court of Appeal declined to disturb the judge's conclusion: ibid 457 Dillon LJ.
[14] Throughout the decision, the alternative formulae of 50 shares and 5% of the shares are used interchangeably, but it is apparent that they are both being used to describe a specified number of shares, rather than an undivided share in Mr Moss's total shareholding.
[15] Mann and Hirst LJJ agreed without adding anything further.
[16] Ibid 457–8.

out, supported by authority[17]) but hardly conclusive. A bequest does not of itself vest property in the beneficiary, it merely operates as a direction to the executor to transfer an asset to the beneficiary.[18] The degree of certainty of subject matter required is therefore no more than is necessary to enable the executor to carry out the instructions, which may involve leaving it up to the executor or even the beneficiary to select the precise item to be transferred.[19]

Dillon LJ's second reason is more compelling. He points out that if someone wishes to transfer, say, 50 out of her 500 ordinary shares in ICI she does not have to specify which ones. She merely hands over to the transferee or a broker a share transfer form specifying the number of shares to be transferred, together with her own certificate for her 500 shares. These are then transmitted to the company, which alters the register and issues a certificate for 50 share to the transferee and a new certificate to the transferor in respect of the retained 450 shares. If you can transfer 50 unidentified shares, why should you not be able to declare a trust of them? Were it not for authority, this could be met by the same argument as that just put in relation to a bequest of shares: the share transfer form is merely a direction to the company to transfer the shares, and so the level of certainty required is only that necessary to enable them to do so—precise allocation of property occurring only when the name of the transferee is entered in the company's books. However, as Dillon LJ said, it was held in *Re Rose*[20] that on a transfer of shares, property passes in equity as soon as the share transfer form and share certificate are handed over by the transferor. The facts of that case were that Mr Rose

---

[17] *In re Clifford* [1912] 1 Ch 29 and *In Re Cheadle* [1900] 2 Ch 620.

[18] *Commissioner of Stamp Duties* v *Livingston* [1965] AC 694.

[19] See for example *Re Barlow's Will Trusts* [1979] 1 ALL ER 296, a decision on certainty of conditions precedent, where a provision in the testator's will that any of her family and friends should be allowed to purchase 'any of' the pictures in her valuable collection at below market value was held *not* void for uncertainty. *Re Golay's Will Trusts* [1965] 1 WLR 969 is also interesting in this connection. The testator directed his executors to 'let Tossy . . . enjoy *one of my flats* during my lifetime and . . . receive a reasonable income from my other properties [and] if she so wish, to wear any of my jewellery, car etc until her death'. The decision is reported only in relation to whether 'a reasonable income' was sufficiently certain to form the subject matter of a trust (it was held that it was and that in context 'reasonable' was an objective yardstick) but presumably 'one of my flats' was judged sufficiently certain by either the Court (Ungoed-Thomas J) or the parties.

[20] [1952] Ch 499.

executed two transfers of his shares in a private company, one in favour of his wife and another in favour of trustees. It was held that in respect of the shares transferred to his wife, he held them on trust for her from the moment when the share transfer form and share certificate were handed over to her until the moment when the company registered her as the shareholder (whereupon she acquired legal title). This decision causes all sorts of theoretical and practical problems and has been much criticised,[21] but no-one has suggested that it is challengeable on the grounds that during this period we cannot say in respect of any one share whether it was held by Mr Rose on trust for Mrs Rose or on trust for the trustees.

It would seem, therefore, that there is no objection in principle to allowing A to claim 50 unearmarked shares out of a larger holding of identical shares in the same company. Nor is it easy to see any objection in practice. None of the three practical reasons given above for disallowing a proprietary claim to a specified number of unidentified items in a bulk applies here. Shares in a company cannot be lost or destroyed. Whilst they can attract bonuses, in the shape of dividends or rights issues, these accrue uniformly to shares of the same class.[22] They can be damaged, in the sense of suffering a diminution in value through being charged, but third parties do not take security (or seek to acquire any other property interest) in specific shares, but in shareholdings or numbers of shares. Thus, someone seeking to take a charge over or purchase 450 shares out of 500 of the same class held by B will be unperturbed to hear that 50 of B's shares (but we do not know *which* 50) are claimed by A. And finally as to liability attaching to shareholdings, whilst it is just conceivable that liability could rationally be made to attach to ownership of some but not other shares within the same class, depending on whether or not the share had a specified individualising characteristic,[23] the likelihood is so remote as to be hardly worth considering.

---

[21] Moffat, *Trusts Law*, 103–107.

[22] Even a rights issue of, say, one Class B share for each holding of Class A share would define the holding of Class A shares by reference to a specified *number* of shares held, not by reference to a feature identifying specific shares (such as one Class B share for every two Class A shares with a reference number which includes a 7). If it did the latter, it would not be treating the Class A shares as all of one class

[23] Perhaps a double or half rate of capital tax leviable on transfer of shares which had been transferred more than five times in the previous ten years—although it is difficult to see what the point of such a distinction might be.

The reality of the situation is that shares of the same class in the same company are for all practical purposes identical and indestructible. In respect of things which are identical and indestructible, there seems no reason at all why we should not allow someone to claim a proprietary interest in a specified number of unidentified objects.

IDENTIFIABILITY OF GOODS: *IN RE STAPYLTON FLETCHER*[24] AND *RE GOLDCORP EXCHANGE*[25]

The problem with goods is more complex. They might well be identical for all relevant purposes, in the sense of being fungible, or, to adopt Professor Rudden's classification, for so long as they are fulfilling the role of things as 'wealth' rather than things as 'thing'[26] Professor Rudden's distinction is useful here since it depends on function, that is on whether a thing is valued for itself or for the wealth it represents. He distinguishes this from fungibility:

> The distinction between the uniqueness of things considered for themselves and their total convertibility when treated as wealth does not follow the classic lines of fungibility: a pound of flour is unique if its owner wants to make bread with it; a Vermeer in the hands of a pension fund is just another investment. Nor is the distinction necessarily tied to the nature of the subject in question: most things can be either possessed for their own sake or held as investments for their income stream or in the hope of capital appreciation.[27]

Adopting this classification, it can be said that any goods in a bulk are identical when they are fulfilling the function of 'wealth' rather than 'thing'.

However, whilst goods can easily be identical in this sense, they can never be indestructible in any relevant sense—even a cargo of diamonds can be depleted by losing one overboard.

Moreover, in the case of goods there is the additional complicating factor of section 16 of the Sale of Goods Act 1979. This provides that:

> Where there is a contract for the sale of unascertained goods no property in the goods is transferred to the buyer unless and until the goods are ascertained.

[24] [1994] 1 WLR 1181.   [25] [1994] 2 All ER 806 PC.
[26] B. Rudden, 'Things as Thing and Things as Wealth' (1994) 14 *OJLS* 81.
[27] Ibid 83.

This applies not only to goods that are unascertained in the sense of not yet being in existence. It also applies to what have been described as 'generic goods' and 'goods sold ex-bulk'. The latter are the ones relevant here. The distinction between the two was explained by Lord Mustill in *Re Goldcorp Exchange Ltd*:[28]

'generic goods' . . . are [goods] sold on terms which preserve the seller's freedom to decide for himself how and from what source he will obtain goods answering the contractual description . . . 'goods sold ex-bulk' [are] goods which are by express stipulation to be supplied from a fixed and a pre-determined source, from which the seller may make his own choice (unless the contract requires it to be made in some other way) but outside which he may not go. For example, 'I sell you 60 of the 100 sheep now on my farm'.[29]

The parties cannot contract out of section 16. Sections 17 and 18 set out the rules for identifying the point at which property passes once the goods have become ascertained. This will be the point at which the parties intend property to pass,[30] and section 18 sets out rules (applicable unless a different intention appears) for ascertaining this intention. Rules 5(1) and 5(2) are relevant to goods sold ex-bulk:

Rule 5(1) Where . . . goods of that description and in a deliverable state are unconditionally appropriated to the contract, either by the seller with the assent of the buyer or by the buyer with the assent of the seller, the property in the goods then passes to the buyer; and the assent may be express or implied, and may be given either before or after the appropriation is made.

(2) Where, in pursuance of the contract, the seller delivers the goods to the buyer or to a carrier or other bailee or custodier (whether named by the buyer or not) for the purpose of transmission to the buyer, and does not reserve the right of disposal, he is to be taken to have unconditionally appropriated the goods to the contract.[31]

At first sight, therefore, the Sale of Goods Act 1979 is a significant bar to a proprietary claim to a specified number of unidentified goods in a bulk or stock. However, it is important to note its limitations. First, it deals only with legal title, not with the

---

[28] [1994] 2 All ER 806. [29] Ibid 814.
[30] s 17(1). S 17(2) provides that for the purpose of ascertaining the intention of the parties 'regard shall be had to the terms of the contract, the conduct of the parties and the circumstances of the case.' [31] S 18 Sale of Goods Act 1979.

creation of equitable interests. Therefore, for example, it would have had no application to a case such as *Hunter* v *Moss*[32] even if the things in question there had been goods rather than shares, since the legal title in the total shareholding remained throughout in Mr Moss.

Secondly, it deals only with cases where a pre-existing bulk is sub-divided by sale. It has no application where goods (or any other things) in which A has an interest are mixed with goods of a like nature in which B has an interest, to form an inseparable bulk or mixture. The problem in these mixing cases, whether the mixture is what Professor Birks calls fluid or granular,[33] is whether the mixture belongs to A and B in common in undivided shares, or belongs wholly to one or another or neither of them, or whether they each continue to have a separate interest in their own (still existing but now evidentially non-identifiable) goods. Although, as is apparent from the *Stapylton Fletcher* case, these mixing problems tend to be closely allied in practice with separation from bulk problems, it is important to bear in mind that section 16 of the Sale of Goods Act 1979 applies to the latter but not to the former.

Despite these limitations, it is generally recognised that section 16 causes significant problems in practice, and in 1993 the Law Commission in its Report on Sale of Goods Forming Part of a Bulk[34] recommended that it should be modified. Broadly, the modification recommended is that on a sale of a specified quantity of unascertained goods ex bulk, the buyer should (subject to agreement to the contrary) acquire a proportionate undivided share in the bulk as soon as the *bulk* is identified and at least part of the

---

[32] See above note 8.
[33] See P. B. H. Birks, 'Mixing and Tracing: Property and Restitution' (1992) 2 *CLP* 69. Fluid mixtures correspond to the Roman law *confusio*, a mixture of inseparable objects such as wine from two different owners poured into the same vessel, whereas granular mixtures are separable in the sense that each particle retains its own identity (as in the Roman law *commixtio* where separable objects belonging to different owners are mixed, like two flocks of sheep put together in a single field) although inseparable in practice 'for want of marks of identification' (ibid 72). As Professor Birks points out, although modern science demonstrates that the apparent difference between the two is illusory (at the atomic level the particles retain their integrity in every case) 'yet we can still sympathise with the Roman view and acknowledge its reality as a matter of day to day perception.'
[34] Law Commission Report No 215.

price is paid by the buyer, or at such later stage as the parties may agree.[35]

Meanwhile, pending implementation of these recommendations, the courts are having to find their own way round these problems. The rather different outcomes in *Stapylton Fletcher* and *Goldcorp* are indicative of the difficulties involved.

IN RE STAPYLTON FLETCHER LTD[36]

In 1992 Nigel Baring[37] bought up all the shares in two independent wine merchants, Ellis, Son & Vidler Ltd and Stapylton Fletcher Ltd. Within a matter of weeks joint administrative receivers were appointed of the two companies by their debenture holder, National Westminster Bank Plc. The administrative receivers sought directions under s 35 of the Insolvency Act 1986 to determine the ownership of the stocks of wine held by the companies.

It became clear that the two companies had rather different ways of running their businesses. Ellis, Son & Vidler Ltd ('ESV') had been in business for nearly 200 years, and latterly at least its attention to stock management and control had been punctilious, largely thanks to the efforts of one of its employees, a Mr Steedman. It kept its own trading stock of wine in one warehouse unit, and maintained a separate warehouse unit as a Customers' Reserve. When a customer ordered a specified quantity of a specified wine which was kept in the trading stock, the appropriate quantity was physically removed from the trading stock unit to the Customers' Reserve. Customers were charged a rental for storage of these wines in the Customers' Reserve, and they could also store wine bought elsewhere there, at a slightly higher rental. The company was responsible for insurance in respect of major risks but invited customers to take out additional cover if required. All wine in the Customers' Reserve was fully paid for by customers. It was stored there in stacks by type and vintage. Although individual bottles and cases were not usually marked as belonging to specific customers, attached to each stack was a card showing the names of

---

[35] See Part IV, and Part VI Summary of Recommendations. See in particular para 4.9 for the somewhat over-complicated rules proposed for the severance of the undivided share.   [36] [1994] 1 WLR 1181.

[37] and/or his company Nigel Baring & Co Ltd.

customers and the numbers of cases allocated to each of them. When a customer directed that its wine should be delivered to it or sold, the appropriate quantity was taken off the top of the stack and the card was marked accordingly. On the very rare occasions when a bottle or case was lost or damaged it was either replaced from the trading stock or assigned to a customer with a large holding who was given a credit for it. Mr Steedman could not recall an occasion when a customer had refused to accept this and insisted on replacement in specie, but he said that if this had happened he would have tried to buy a replacement in the market (presumably at the company's cost).

ESV also held wine in a bonded warehouse. Some of this had been bought en primeur by customers direct from wine producers through ESV, the rest had been bought by ESV for customers from other sources and imported by ESV into bond and retained there for the customers until required. All customers' wine in the bonded warehouse had been fully paid for, and customers could get their wine out of bond at any time on 14 days notice by paying ESV the duty and VAT and any other outstanding charges. Wine in bond was identified by rotation numbers used as a check by the customs. If one customer ordered a large quantity of a particular wine, the consignment was given its own unique customer rotation number. If several customers had each ordered a smaller quantity of a particular wine, the total consignment was given a group customer rotation number. Rotation numbers given to ESV's trading stock held in bond were quite different from customer rotation numbers.

In all the company's paper work, including its annual accounts, its insurance policies, and the debentures under which the administrative receivers were appointed, customers' stocks, whether held in the Customers' Reserve or in bond, were clearly treated as belonging to customers and not to the company.

However, just before the administrative receivers were appointed, Mr Steedman's meticulous stock systems were disrupted by Mr Baring ordering all the Customers' Reserve to be removed to his private house. Although a semblance of order was later restored by Mr Steedman (retained for this purpose by the administrative receivers) some of the stacks were broken up, some of the cards were lost, and some wine disappeared.

At Stapylton Fletcher, matters were conducted differently. As at ESV, the company maintained a duty paid warehouse and stock at a bonded warehouse. At the duty paid warehouse each item of customers' stock was clearly labelled as belonging to a specific customer. At the bonded warehouse, on the other hand, no system was used to differentiate trading stock from customers' stock, nor to label any stock as belonging to any particular customer. As at ESV, all customers' wine was fully paid for.

As the judge Paul Baker QC remarked,[38] the customers of both companies could have been forgiven for assuming that they would have no difficulty in recovering their wine from the wine merchants, despite the insolvency of the businesses. From the customers' perspective, they had bought and paid for wine some time ago and had since paid for its storage. Moreover, the company had indeed acquired and stored the wine as directed, and had always treated it as belonging to the customers rather than to themselves, and there the wine still was. Who could possibly have a stronger claim to it than the customers?

In fact the receivers admitted claims in respect of wine labelled as belonging to a specific customer, or in a stack whose card showed that all the wine in that stack belonged to one customer,[39] or in bond under a single customer rotation number. They denied all other claims. In the case of ESV customers, these contested claims fell into the following categories:

1 Customers claiming wine held in bond under a group customer rotation number.
2 Customers claiming wine held in composite stacks in the Customers' Reserve, where the stacks were still intact.
3 The same as Category 2, except that the stacks were now dispersed and the contents not distinguishable from like wine of other customers.
4 Customers whose wine had been bought elsewhere but stored at the Customers' Reserve and could not now be distinguished from like wine of other customers.
5 Customers who had paid for wine en primeur, where the wine

---

[38] [1991] 1 WLR 1181, 1191–1192.

[39] Including those where the card showed that the stack had originally contained wine for several different customers, but amounts tallying with the orders of all but one of the customers had been removed, leaving an amount that tallied exactly with the order of the one remaining customer: this is appropriation by exhaustion, held to be sufficient by Roche J in *Wait & James* v *Midland Bank Ltd* (1926) 24 Ll L Rep 313.

had not yet been dispatched from the vineyards, and in some cases had not yet been bottled.

In addition, the receivers contested all claims of Stapylton Fletcher customers claiming wine in bond ("the SFL claims").

All these customers faced two immediate problems. The first was section 16 of the Sale of Goods Act 1979. In order to circumvent the section they had to show either that their wine had been sufficiently ascertained to allow property to pass under the section, or that the company was holding the wine for them in some sort of fiduciary capacity and that they consequently had an equitable proprietary interest or claim to the wine to which section 16 did not apply.

Their second problem was the decision of Oliver J in *In re London Wine Co (Shippers) Ltd*, decided in 1975 but not fully reported until 1986.[40] The *London Wine* case concerned the ownership of wine in bond, none of which had been specifically allocated to any particular customer. The company solicited orders for wine for investment purposes, the contract providing that the company would store the wine in bonded warehouses for a rental fee plus a charge to cover insurance. The company issued customers with a certificate of title which stated that the customer was 'sole and beneficial owner' of a specified amount of wine of a specified description, but there was no means of marrying the certificates of title to any particular bottle or case or consignment held by the company at any warehouse. Although full records of customers' holdings were kept and these allocated wine at specified warehouses to each order, there was no system at the warehouses for allocating any specific wine to any specific customer, nor indeed for distinguishing it from the company's own trading stock. The warehouses only became involved with the movement of customers' wine if it was either withdrawn to be delivered to the customer (in which case an appropriate amount was simply withdrawn from the company's general stock) or pledged by the customer. In the latter event, the warehouse issued the pledgee with a document stating that it held specified wine of the customer to the pledgee's order, but this document too contained no means of identifying any particular bottle or case. When the company's debenture holder

---

[40] [1986] PCC 121. A full transcript of the judgment was however published as an appendix to R. M. Goode, *Proprietary Rights and Insolvency in Sales Transactions* (London, 1985): see now the 2nd edition (1989), 111.

appointed a receiver, there was ample stock in the company's bond to satisfy all the customers' claims. However, Oliver J held that none of the claims were made out,[41] and therefore all the wine went to the debenture holder.

The claims in the *London Wine* case fell into three categories. The first category was of customers who had each purchased what amounted to the company's total stock of that particular wine at the time of purchase. The second category was of customers whose aggregate purchases exhausted the whole of the company's stock of that particular wine at that time, although the stock was held in several different warehouses. The third category was similar to the second except that (a) the aggregate purchases did not exhaust the company's stock but (b) each customer's mortgagee had received an acknowledgement by a warehouseman that an appropriate quantity of wine was held to its order.

The *London Wine* customers in categories 1 and 2 argued that legal title to the wine had passed to them, and that even if it had not, either the wine was held on trust for them, or that they had a specifically enforceable contractual right to it, and hence a pre-existing equitable interest in it which took priority over the debenture holder's equitable charge over it. Customers in category 3 did not attempt to argue that legal title had passed, but adopted the same arguments on interests under a trust and equitable interests by virtue of a specifically enforceable contract right. All of these arguments were rejected.

In *London Wine*, the arguments that legal title had passed, and that a trust had been declared in favour of the customers, all ultimately failed on essentially the same point: on the facts, Oliver J was unable to find a sufficient link between the stocks held by the company and the wine contracted to be sold to the customers. Stock was not allocated to orders, nor was there sufficient evidence of intention that orders should be fulfilled from stock rather than from another source. There was therefore no appropriation for the purposes of sections 17 and 18 of the Sale of Goods Act 1979, and insufficient certainty of subject matter to create a trust. As Oliver J put it in relation to the trust argument:

[41] Except those of a small category of customers whose wine had been segregated and appropriated, although later mixed in with other batches to form a now inseparable granular mixture (as to which see n 33 above). These claims the receivers admitted: p 134 of the report.)

. . . to create a trust it must be possible to ascertain with certainty not only what the interest of the beneficiary is to be but to what property it is to attach.

I cannot see how, for instance, a farmer who declares himself to be a trustee of two sheep (without identifying them) can be said to have created a perfect and complete trust whatever rights he may confer by such declaration as a matter of contract. And it would seem to me immaterial that at the time he has a flock of sheep out of which he could satisfy the interest . . .[42]

In *Stapylton Fletcher* the same clearly applied to the SFL claims— no sufficient connection could be made between the wine ordered and paid for and the undifferentiated stock at the bonded warehouse. These claim was therefore rejected. In respect of the ESV claims, however, the judge declined to follow the *London Wine* decision:

I do not regard that decision as inevitably governing the case before me. One obvious difference in the present case is the segregation of the wine purchased by the customers in a separate part of the warehouse and the careful maintenance of records within the company. Further as the London Wine Co was free to sell its stock and satisfy the customers from any other available source, there was no ascertainable bulk in that case.[43]

The correct legal analysis of what happened at ESV, he said, was that customers did not, as they did at London Wine, enter into a single contract for the sale of goods. Instead they entered into two separate if related contracts—the first to buy the goods, and the second to store them. Property in the wine passed to the customers when the wine was segregated from the company's stock. The wine was then notionally passed back to the company for storage. What then happened was a mixing of wine belonging to different customers. Since the customers must have been aware that thereafter their wine would be mixed with like wine and that they would not necessarily get back the very bottles or cases stored for them (because good stock management dictated that the wine should be disturbed as little as possible) this was mixing by consent, and the proper inference to draw was that each customer intended to become a tenant in common of the mixture (ie of all the wine in a stack at the Customers' Reserve, or under a group rotation number at bond).

---

[42] Ibid 137.
[43] [1994] 1 WLR 1181, 1194.

The judge held that this analysis applied to all but category 5 of the ESV claims, and consequently all these claims succeeded. It clearly had no application to category 5, where the wine was still part of the vineyards' generic stock and could not by any stretch of the imagination be said to be ascertained for the purposes of the sale contract between ESV and the customer.[44]

In relation to the other categories, there are several points to be made about the judge's analysis.

First, it relation to the wine in Customers' Reserve stacks, it is relatively easy to see how each customer's wine was ascertained for the purposes of section 16 of the Sale of Goods Act 1979—specific bottles and cases were physically moved there to match each order, either from trading stock or from outside sources. As Judge Paul Baker said, the result was the same as if the company had called the customer in to take delivery of the wine and then hand it over again for storage.[45] It is however less easy to see how ascertainment occurred in relation to the wine in bond, and this is really the nub of the matter. Judge Paul Baker said that where, as here, goods are to be kept by the seller for storage, ascertainment for the purpose of section 16 must take place on 'segregation of the stock from the company's trading assets, whether done physically or by giving instructions to a bonded warehouse keeper'.[46] The difficulty with this in relation to the wine in bond was that even in the case of ESV the company did not appear to have given *separate* instructions to the warehouse keeper in relation to each customer: in most cases it appears that a single consignment was bought for several customers, in which case there was presumably a single instruction to the warehouse keeper in relation to the group of customers. There was never any actual or notional dealing with individual customers' orders, equivalent to the physical transfer that took place in the Customers Reserve. Judge Paul Baker dealt with this point as follows:

It could not be doubted that if, by agreement with a number of customers, the aggregate number of cases of a specific vintage bought by them were handed over en bloc to another company to hold on their behalf, the cases

---

[44] The judge also rejected a claim that ESV held the purchase money on trust for these customers, as in *Re Kayford Ltd* [1975] 1 WLR 279: as he pointed out, the wine was used, and intended to be used, to purchase wine from France, there was no intention of holding it on trust pending import of the wine into this country ([1994] 1 WLR 1201). [45] Ibid 1199. [46] Ibid 1199.

would be ascertained. The selling company would not be seeking any interest in them. . . . Where goods were to go to another company for storage there would be an actual delivery. Where the selling company was going to store them and *segregated them for that purposes*, there will be a constructive delivery . . .[47]

Logically this cannot be faulted—if the seller has no interest against the customers as a group, how can it maintain an interest against them individually? Whether it is wholly reconcilable with previous authorities, and with dicta of Lord Mustill in *Re Goldcorp* (as to which see below) is more difficult.[48] The judge concluded:

. . . if a number of cases or bottles of identical wine are held, not mingled with the trading stock, in store for a group of customers, those cases or bottles will be ascertained for the purposes of section 16 of the Sale of Goods Act 1979 even though they are not immediately appropriated to each individual customer. Property will pass by common intention and not pursuant to section 18 rule (5). They will take as tenants in common.

This is a welcome conclusion, in line with the Law Commission's recommendations,[49] although it has to be said that it makes those recommendations largely redundant.

The second point to make about the judge's analysis is this. Whilst it may be doubted whether customers did indeed intend to hold an undivided share in the company's stock of the wine they had ordered, rather than to acquire absolute ownership of specific bottles and cases, this is not crucial to the analysis. The fact of the matter is that wine intended for different customers *was* mixed. Provided it is accepted that *before* the mixing the wine was the separate property of individual customers, it does not matter whether the mixing was done with the consent of customers, or wrongfully by the companies, or (most likely) without the knowledge of customers who would however probably not have objected if they had known. In any of these cases the mixing could only have resulted, as between the customers, either in co-ownership of the mass or in continued separate ownership.[50] Either of these would have been sufficient to establish the customers'

---

[47] [1994] 1 WLR 1199–1200.
[48] See in particular the authorities cited in note 24 to para 2.7 of the Law Commission *Report on Sale of Goods Forming Part of a Bulk* (Law Com. No 215).
[49] Law Com No 215, as to which see text to n 35 above.
[50] See Birks, (1992) 2 *CLP* 69, 74–75 and text to n 33 above.

claims as against the debenture holder. Continued separate ownership would have caused evidential difficulties as between customers, but since there was enough stock to cover all customers' claims, the difficulties would have been theoretical only.[51]

Finally, the judge's analysis has the considerable merit of yielding an eminently sensible and fair result. In this particular case customers' stocks were always regarded by the company as belonging to their customers, and were represented as such to the debenture holder. It would therefore represent a windfall for the debenture holder if it was allowed to have recourse to these stocks. And in more general terms, the businesses of procuring and storing goods for customers carried on by these companies were perfectly legitimate commercial enterprises, and as far as one can gather they were being carried on honestly and competently. In such circumstances, the law ought not to be allowed to defeat the legitimate expectations of the customers. It would be a pity if dicta in *Re Goldcorp* should be taken as casting doubt on the decision.

RE GOLDCORP EXCHANGE LTD[52]

This third case of the trio can be dealt with more briefly, although a wide range of points of current importance in property law were canvassed in the Privy Council. Unfortunately, although the Privy Council judgment was delivered more than a month after the reserved judgment of Judge Paul Baker in *Stapylton Fletcher*,[53] it contains no reference to that case, nor to the Court of Appeal decision in *Hunter v Moss*. This is unfortunate since several general remarks made obiter in the Privy Council are not easily reconcilable with these decisions.

This was an appeal to the Privy Council from a decision of the New Zealand Court of Appeal. The judgment of the Privy Council

---

[51] In fact, even if there had been de facto mixing without the customers' consent, there is authority to the effect that the result would have been co-ownership rather than continued separate ownership: *Spence* v *Union Marine Insurance Co Ltd* (1868) LR 3 CP 427 (mixing of cotton bales). However, as Birks points out, this case. although one of granular mixture, was based on fluid mixture cases, and if the co-ownership rule is established to also apply to granular mixtures (such as bottles and cases of wine) 'it will be almost impossible to defend the then anomalous rule for money [where mixing results in continued separate ownership] to change which will, however, have serious implications for tracing': (1992) *CLP* 83.

[52] [1994] 2 All ER 806 PC.   [53] [1994] 1 WLR 1181.

was given by Lord Mustill. The facts of the case are superficially similar to those of the wine cases in that Goldcorp Exchange Ltd, a dealer in New Zealand in gold and other precious metals (and in particular in gold coins and ingots as consumer products) entered into contracts with customers whereby it agreed to buy and store bullion for customers, providing customers with a certificate of title whilst the bullion was in store. When its debenture holder appointed a receiver the customers claimed to be entitled to the bullion stocks held by the company. There however the resemblance with the wine cases ends. In this case the stocks held by the company, although no doubt valuable, were nowhere near sufficient to meet the customers' claims. Whilst the documentation led customers to believe that there would be physical bullion kept in store for them, in fact the company had neither bought bullion in response to each customer's order, nor had it made any attempt to ensure that it held enough trading stock to satisfy all orders. Instead it aimed (not, as it transpired, with any great accuracy) to merely hold enough stock to meet likely demands for delivery.

This shortfall in the stock dramatically broadened the scope of the customers' claims, to include not only claims to the bullion stock but also to all other assets of the company. The customer claimants fell into three categories, only two of which are relevant here.[54] The first of these consisted of the 'non-allocated claimants', comprising the vast majority of customers, who had ordered bullion to be purchased and stored where no appropriation of bullion had been made towards their contracts. The second category were referred to as the 'Walker & Hall claimants'. These were customers of Walker & Hall, a company taken over by Goldcorp in 1986. Until then it ran the same sort of business as Goldcorp, but in a rather more orthodox (or honest) way. Until about 1983 at Walker & Hall specific bullion was bought for each customer to match each order and was stored and recorded separately. Thereafter all the customers' stock was pooled, but it was kept separate from the company's stock and the quantity

---

[54] The third category consisted solely of a Mr Liggett, who had the misfortune of being noteworthy mainly because his claim was very large (which, as Lord Mustill said, entirely explained his special indignation, without however going any way towards his claim to be treated as a special case) and because he had originally ordered 52 gold maple coins for immediate delivery, but when he went to collect them, after he was shown them he was persuaded to change his order to one for 1,000 coins to be kept in store. His proprietary claims failed in total.

precisely matched customers' orders. When Goldcorp took over the company it absorbed this customers' stock into its own trading stock.

These claims raised a number of important issues, which cannot be done full justice here. Consideration here will be confined to those dealing with the identifiability problem. Lord Mustill himself saw this as central to the whole case. The principal claim of the non-allocated claimants (although the one clearly least likely to succeed) was that they had acquired title to bullion by virtue of their sale contracts. Lord Mustill unequivocally rejected this, on the basis that this was a purchase of unascertained goods and there had been no ascertainment of the bullion which was the subject matter of the contract to satisfy s 18 of the Sale of Goods Act 1908 (New Zealand), which corresponds to s 16 of the UK Act. On the facts, this is hardly surprising, but Lord Mustill proceeded to enlarge on the point because, as he said 'the reasons for this answer are the same as those which stand in the way of the customers at every point of the case'.[55] It merits closer attention here, because of the possible impact of his general remarks on the decisions in *Stapylton Fletcher* and, to a lesser extent, *Hunter v Moss*.

He drew the distinction between generic goods and goods ex-bulk already quoted,[56] and then pointed out that in both cases it was necessary to distinguish ascertainment (dealt with in s 16 of the UK Act) from appropriation (dealt with in s 18 of the UK Act):

... a priori common sense dictates that the buyer cannot acquire title until it is known to what goods the title relates. Whether the property then passes will depend upon the intention of the parties and in particular on whether there has been a consensual appropriation of particular goods to the contract. On the latter case the law is not straightforward. ... In fact, however, [this] case turns not on appropriation but on ascertainment, and on the latter the law has never been in doubt. It makes no difference what the parties intended if what they intend is impossible: as is the case with an immediate transfer of title to goods whose identity are not yet known.[57]

He then quoted with approval a statement by Blackburn to the effect that the rule about ascertainment was 'founded on the very nature of things' and necessarily entailed that, even in a sale ex bulk, property is not ascertained until it is ascertained which part of

---

[55] [1994] 2 All ER 813–4.   [56] See text to n 29 above.
[57] Ibid 814.

the stock is to be sold.[58] This is of course strictly obiter, but more importantly it over-simplifies the issue. Necessarily, the rather more complex questions raised by the decisions in *Hunter* v *Moss* and *Stapylton* v *Fletcher* are not addressed, and should properly be regarded as still open. In particular, why is the rule about ascertainment in sales ex bulk in 'the very nature of things' in relation to goods ex bulk when, as demonstrated by *Hunter* v *Moss*, it is not in the nature of things in relation to a choses in action such as shares in a company? In what relevant way do goods behave differently from shares in a company? And even in relation to goods, what is to happen about the situation faced by the judge in *Stapylton Fletcher* in respect of the customers' wine in bond, which had clearly been *appropriated* en masse to customers, and could in no sensible way be regarded as still the property of the company, although the individual customers' entitlements had never been ascertained in the sense demanded by Blackburn? What is the mischief in allowing Judge Paul Baker's analysis to prevail in this situation?

The non-allocated claimants argued in the alternative that they had acquired an equitable interest by virtue of a declaration of trust. As Lord Mustill pointed out, there were only two possibilities here. The company might have declared in favour of each customer that it held its stock on trust for the customer, so that the customer acquired an undivided share—an analysis clearly at odds with the intentions of the parties and with the commercial realities of the situation. He then considered briefly, as an alternative, an analysis resembling the one that succeeded in *Stapylton Fletcher*:

Nor is the [declaration of trust] argument improved by reshaping the trust, so as to contemplate that the property in the res vendita did pass to the customer, albeit in the absence of delivery, and then merged in a general equitable title to the pooled stock of bullion.[59]

This also was obviously not consistent with the reality of the transaction—no purchaser intended to acquire a proportion of a shifting bulk—but again it is very far removed from the *Stapylton Fletcher* situation, where there was a fixed bulk in the sense of fully documented specific customer entitlements completely segregated

[58] Quoted from C. Blackburn, *A Treatise on the Effect of the Contract of Sale* (London, 1845), 122–123 by Lord Mustill at [1994] 2 All ER 814.

[59] Ibid 815.

from the company's assets. Lord Mustill's added comment—'Even if the present contract had been a sale ex-bulk, in the sense that the contractual source was the bulk of bullion in the store, s 18 [ie s 16 of the UK Act] would have prevented the property passing on sale'—must be read in the light of this, especially since the bulk he was considering was throughout treated by the company as (and mixed with) its own property.

The real problem here was that the bulk claimed in this case bore no relation to the subject matter of the customers' contracts. It consisted only of bullion the company had bought for its own purposes, including, but not even confined to, the purpose of keeping enough bullion in stock to meet demands for delivery so that it could keep up the pretence that it had complied with its contractual commitments to buy bullion for customers. The company had never committed itself to fulfilling the contract claims out of *this* bulk, as opposed to from other sources.

The other obvious problem with accepting that the non-allocated claimants had claims to this bulk, was that there was simply not enough of it to go round. This meant that any argument based on anything other than entitlement in undivided shares was unlikely to succeed.[60]

The third point to make about the bulk brings us back to the ascertainment point. The customers' expectation was that they could take or leave 'their' bullion whenever they chose. Lord Mustill said that in law such an expectation could be fulfilled only by a system under which the company obtained bullion and immediately stored it separately in the name of the customer, leaving it untouched until the moment when delivery was required. However, this was not in fact what the company had represented it would do. Even if it had complied with all its commitments these amounted to no more than undertakings that it would maintain bullion, separate from its own stock, which would in some way stand as security or reassurance that bullion would be available when the customer called for delivery. Even if the company had complied with these commitments, no property would have passed to customers until delivery since there would still have been no ascertainment for the purposes of the Sale of Goods Act provisions.

---

[60] Otherwise promising estoppel-based arguments failed on (inter alia) these last two grounds: ibid 816–819.

Interestingly, however, Lord Mustill did here admit the possibility that a *Stapylton Fletcher*—type system might have worked to fulfill the customers' expectations:

> If the scheme had contemplated that, properly performed, it would have brought about a transfer of title to the individual customer before that customer's appropriated bullion was mixed in the undifferentiated bulk, analogies could have been drawn with *Spence* v *Union Marine Insurance Co Ltd* (1868) LR 3 CP 427 [and the other mixing cases] ... Since, however, even if the company had performed its obligations to the full there would have been no transfer of title to the purchaser before admixture, these cases are not in point.[61]

As a route towards claiming the bullion stock, the non-allocated claimants also put forward arguments based on a contention of fiduciary relationship between themselves and the company. None of these arguments succeeded, and consequently it was held that none of the non-allocated claimants had any right to the bullion stock. Since their claims to a proprietary interest over the purchase price and its fruits (their main route to the other assets of the company) also failed in total, they were left with no redress whatsoever.[62]

The Walker & Hall claimants fared little better. It had been held at first instance that there had been a sufficient ascertainment and appropriation of goods to the individual contracts to transfer title to each customer, and that thereafter the customers held undivided shares in the pooled bullion—a decision consistent only with *Stapylton Fletcher* being correctly decided, at least as far as post-1983 customers were concerned. However, the pooled bullion was then wrongly mixed with the Goldcorp trading stock. Applying conventional tracing principles the judge at first instance concluded that their claim was limited by the rule in *James Roscoe (Bolton) Ltd* v *Winder*[63] to the lowest intermediate balance in the mixed fund—in other words, to the value of the lowest balance of metal held by Goldcorp between the date when it took over the Walker & Hall bullion to the date of the receivership. This was a relatively small amount, and consequently the debenture holder did not appeal against the finding of liability on this ground. However, it

[61] [1994] 2 All ER 820.
[62] The amount secured by the debenture holder's floating charge exceeded the total value of the company's assets, and so consequently any non-proprietary claim was worthless.				[63] [1915] 1 Ch 62.

sought to re-open the point after the Court of Appeal judgment re-opened the question of quantum. Eventually, it was agreed between the parties that the bank would accept the first instance decision on liability if the Privy Council also confirmed the first instance decision on the level of recovery. This the Privy Council did (by confirming that *Roscoe* v *Winder* applied to limit recovery to the lowest intermediate balance) and consequently the *Stapylton Fletcher* point was never reopened.

This final skirmish on the Walker & Hall claims also revealed that there are major questions still to be settled on the nature and scope of equitable proprietary relief. The Walker & Hall claimants went on to claim an equitable lien on all the property of the company at the date of the receivership to recover the value of their bullion unlawfully misappropriated by the company. This claim was based on observations of Lord Templeman in *Space Investments Ltd* v *Canadian Imperial Bank of Commerce Trust Co (Bahamas) Ltd*[64] which have attracted a considerable amount of controversy.[65] Whilst declining to enter the fray[66] Lord Mustill nevertheless made it clear which areas he considered worthy of reconsideration, and the directions he thought such reconsideration should go. He described the law relating to the creation and tracing of equitable proprietary interests as 'still in a state of development', and after referring to the Privy Council decision in *A-G for Hong Kong* v *Reid*[67] and the House of Lords decision in *Lord Napier and Ettrick* v *Hunter*[68] he concluded:

When the scope and ambit of these decisions and the observations of the Board in *Space Investments* fall to be considered, it will be necessary for the history and foundations in principle of the creation and tracing of equitable proprietary interests to be the subject of close examination and full

[64] [1986] 1 WLR 1072 PC, 1074.
[65] See for example R. M. Goode (1987) 103 *LQR* 433, 445–447, P. B. H. Birks *An Introduction to the Law of Restitution*, Oxford, 1989, 377–401 and R. Goff and G. Jones, *The Law of Restitution*[4], London, 1993, 73–75.
[66] The Board decided that even if an equitable lien was appropriate and available here, it would, for various reasons, be inequitable to impose one in favour of the Walker & Hall claimants.
[67] [1994] AC 324 (held that money received by an agent as a bribe was held in trust for the principal who is entitled to trace and recover property representing the bribe).
[68] [1993] AC 713 (held that payment of damages in respect of an insured loss created an equitable charge in favour of the subrogated insurers so long only as the damages were traceable as an identifiable fund).

argument and for attention to be paid to the works of Paciocco in (1989) 68 Can Bar Rev 315, Maddaugh and McCamus *The Law of Restitution* (1990), Emily L Sherwin's article 'Constructive Trusts in Bankruptcy' (1989) U Ill L Rev 297 at 335 and other commentators dealing with equitable interests in tracing and referring to concepts such as the position of 'involuntary creditors' and tracing to 'swollen assets'.[69]

Meanwhile, pending the outcome of this wide-ranging academic debate, the Goldcorp customers were to have no redress. It would be interesting to know whether they would have suffered the same fate in the jurisdictions of the writers Lord Mustill referred to.

II Formalities and the nature of equitable interests

Whilst the Law Commission has announced its intention of taking on that stalwart of the undergraduate trusts syllabus—formal requirements for the creation and transfer of an interest under a trust: reform of section 53 of the Law of Property Act 1925[70]—its earlier exercise in reform of formal requirements continues to draw attention. The new rules on formal requirements for the creation of contracts for the disposition of interests in land were introduced by section 2 the Law of Property (Miscellaneous Provisions) Act 1989, implementing Law Commission recommendations made in 1987.[71] The few cases so far decided under the 1989 Act have on the whole demonstrated that the new rules do indeed work more or less as the Law Commission anticipated,[72] a trend now continued by the Court of Appeal decision in *Robert Leonard Developments Ltd* v *Wright*.[73]

This case is the obverse of *Record* v *Bell*[74] discussed in the 1992 *Annual Review*.[75] Both cases concerned agreements for the sale of a house and contents. The problem both cases was concerned with was the requirement in section 2 of the 1989 Act that a valid

[69] [1993] AC 832.
[70] Law Commission Press Release, 11 May 1994, 'What formal requirements are needed to create a trust and to transfer an interest under a trust?'.
[71] Law Commission Report *Contracts for Sale etc of Land 1987* (Law Com. No. 164).
[72] See Alison Clarke (1992) 45 CLP 82–88 on *Spiro* v *Glencrown Properties Ltd* [1991] 2 WLR 931 (options to purchase) and *Record* v *Bell* [1991] 1 WLR 853 (collateral contracts), and also *Tootal Clothing Ltd* v *Guinea Properties Ltd* (1992) 64 P & CR 452 CA (executory and completed contracts).
[73] [1994] EGCS 69 CA.   [74] [1991] 1 WLR 853.   [75] pp 82–88.

contract for the sale or other disposition of an interest in land must incorporate *all* the express terms of the contract. In its Report the Law Commission gave detailed consideration to the question of whether such a requirement would operate unfairly. After pointing out that such a requirement already applied in the then existing law,[76] it concluded that there were sufficient remedies available in the existing law to ensure that this particular recommendation would not cause 'undue injustice', despite the fact that the doctrine of part performance would no longer operate under the new law. In particular, it concluded that the remedies of rectification and enforcement of a collateral contract would be available in appropriate cases where the parties had reached agreement but failed to record all the terms in writing.[77]

The decision in *Record* v *Bell*[78] confirmed that this was indeed the case as far as collateral contracts were concerned. In that case the term omitted from the signed contract was a last-minute warranty of title given in a side letter. The judge concluded that it constituted a separate contract collateral to the sale contract and therefore did not have to be incorporated into the sale contract to satisfy the requirements of section 2 of the 1989 Act.[79] In *Robert Leonard Developments Ltd* v *Wright*[80] the contract was for the sale of a show flat and the term omitted was that the vendor would sell and the purchaser would buy the contents of the flat. There was an agreed schedule of the contents to be included in the price, a copy of which was sent to the vendor by the purchaser with the purchaser's signed part of the contract[81] in anticipation of exchange of contracts. However, no copy accompanied the vendor's part of the contract, and when the purchaser moved in on completion she discovered that all the contents had been removed. As Dillon LJ observed, 'The obvious inference from this underhand removal of the chattels just before completion is that [the vendor] had realised

---

[76] For example under s 40 of the Law of Property Act 1925, which required written evidence not just of the contract but of all its terms: see para 4.7 of Law Com No 164.

[77] Law Com No 164 Part V especially paras 5.1, 5.3, and 5.6–8.

[78] [1991] 1 WLR 853.

[79] See also on this point *Tootal Clothing Ltd* v *Guinea Properties Ltd* (1992) 64 P & CR 452 CA, 456 Scott LJ.

[80] [1994] EGCS 69 CA.

[81] The question of whether it was sufficiently annexed to it to be incorporated into it was not raised.

that the contracts exchanged did not mention the chattels and decided to pull a fast one.'

Given the circumstances, the judge's decision at first instance to award the purchaser damages was unsurprising. However, he was concerned about section 2 of the 1989 Act. It was accepted that agreements for the sale of land and contents could constitute two separate contracts, in which case section 2 would apply only to the land contract and it would be immaterial whether or not this contained reference to the chattels. He decided that this was such a case. The Court of Appeal disagreed, although confirming his decision on damages, taking the view that this was a single arrangement for the sale of a package at a single price, and that therefore section 2 of the 1989 Act required the agreement as to the contents to be included in the written sale contract.

However, they ordered rectification of the contract, satisfied that the requirements for rectification established in *Joscelyne* v *Nissen*[82] were clearly satisfied. Dillon LJ expressed some reservations about using rectification to admit an omitted term, if, as suggested by Hoffmann J in *Spiro* v *Glencrown Properties Ltd*,[83] the objective of section 2 of the 1989 Act was 'to prevent disputes over whether the parties had entered into a binding agreement or over what terms they had agreed'. Nevertheless, he recognised that section 2 of the Act explicitly contemplates rectification,[84] and that it would be unjust if it was not available as a remedy. It was left to Henry LJ to trace the history of section 2 and demonstrate that the Law Commission anticipated the use of rectification in this precise situation to avoid hardship or unfairness. Rectification therefore, in his judgment, achieved the intention of the Act.

SECTION 2: EFFECT ON EQUITABLE INTERESTS

Section 2 was, of course, intended to apply to contracts to dispose of an interest in land at a future date rather than to immediate dispositions. Neverthless a side effect of the section has been to stimulate reconsideration of the nature and rationale of informal equitable interests in land. Before 1989 informally-made grants or

---

[82] [1970] 2 QB 86: 'The requirements are a prior agreement or continuing common intention to contract on certain terms and convincing proof that the written document does not adequately reflect the terms of the agreement.'
[83] [1991] Ch 537, 541.   [84] See s 2(4).

dispositions of interests in land would be effective in equity, despite failure to comply with formalities requirements[85] because of an extension of the doctrine in *Walsh* v *Lonsdale*.[86] Traditionally the rationale given for this long standing recognition of informally created interests was as follows. If the only problem was a failure in formalities, equity would treat a defective grant or transfer as a contract to carry out the transaction in question, and if the circumstances were such that equity would have granted specific performance of that notional contract, it would treat that contract as already performed, on the basis that equity treats as done that which ought to be done; hence equity would treat the grantee/ transferee as already holding the interest purportedly granted or transferrred. In other words, a failed grant of a legal mortgage/ lease/fee simple etc conferred the equivalent equitable interest if the reason for failure was a failure to comply with formal require-ments. The question raised by section 2 of the 1989 Act is this. Does the *Walsh* v *Lonsdale* analysis require that there should *actually be* a valid contract between the parties before equity will treat the failed attempt to create a legal interest as effective to create its equitable equivalent, or will equity simply *assume* a valid contract whenever the only defect in the transaction is a failure to comply with formalities, which it will treat as enforceable (and hence already performed) at the suit of anyone who is not a volunteer? If the former, informally created interests will now be effective only if they comply with the formal requirements of section 2. If the latter, section 2 is irrelevant—if the executory contract is notional, it does not make sense to say that it must satisfy formal requirements.

The latter view has considerable attractions. Historically the contract analysis was the justification used by equity for circum-venting formalities rules. It would be odd if the condition to be satisfied before equity could intervene were to be compliance with a different (and in some cases more stringent) set of formal requirements. Equity needs to be able to glean from the failed attempt to create a legal interest what it is that the parties were

---

[85] For example, s 52 of the Law of Property Act 1925 which provides that legal estates and interests in land must be created and transferred by deed (subject to exceptions set out in that section and in s 55) and s 53 of the 1925 on the circumstances in which writing is required for the creation and disposition of equitable interests.   [86] (1882) 21 Ch D 9.

trying to achieve (ie the agreed terms of the intended transaction) if
it is to treat the transaction as effective in equity, but this is not the
same as saying that it first needs to ensure that there is an actual
valid and enforceable contract. Before 1989 the real issue was not
whether the notional (or inferred) contract was *enforceable* (ie
whether it complied with the requirements of section 40 of the Law
of Property Act 1925) but whether the circumstances were such
that equity would *grant specific performance* of it. The distinction
between the two was blurred before 1989 because part performance was both a way of making an oral contract enforceable, and a
factor in whether or not to grant specific performance. Now after
1989 specific performance remains the only relevant issue: having
inferred from the failed attempt to create a legal interest that the
parties are contractually bound to grant that interest, are the
circumstances such that specific performance would be granted so
that equity is justified in treating the transaction as effective in
equity?

However, until recently there has been no authority on this
problem, although a great deal of academic discussion.[87] Now at
least one aspect of the problem has finally come before the courts in
United Bank of Kuwait Plc v *Sahib*,[88] raising at the same time a
number of difficult issues in mortgages law.

Mr Sahib and his wife were joint registered proprietors of several
properties, including their house in Hampstead, 37C Fitzjohn's
Avenue, which they held on trust for themselves as equitable joint
tenants. Over the years Mr Sahib had financial dealings with
Société General Alsacienne de Banque SA ('Sogenal') and in 1990
his solicitors, acting on his authority but without the knowledge or
consent of his wife, confirmed to Sogenal that they held the land
certificate of 37C to the order of Sogenal to secure Mr Sahib's
indebtedness to Sogenal. In November 1992 the United Bank of
Kuwait ('Kuwait') obtained a charging order absolute over Mr
Sahib's interest in 37C. The issue was whether Sogenal had an

---

[87] See for example *Emmet on Title* 19th edition, Release 10 para 25.116; K.
Gray, *Elements of Land Law²*, 1993, 743–749 and 943–945; E. Burn, *Cheshire and
Burn's Modern Law of Real Property¹⁵*, 1994, 668–670; *Snell's Principles of Equity*
29th ed by P. V. Baker and P. St. J. Langan, 1990, 445; Baughen [1992] *Conv* 330;
Hill (1990) 106 *LQR* 396; Howell [1990] *Conv* 441; Bently and Coughlan (1990)
10 *LS* 341, and see also Law Commission *Report on Land Mortgages* 1991 (Law
Com No 204) para 2.9.   [88] [1994] *The Times*, 7 July.

equitable mortgage or charge over Mr Sahib's interest in 37C, and
if it did, whether it took priority over Kuwait's charging order.

It was accepted that it was the intention of Mr Sahib and Sogenal
that he should charge 37C to them. Equally, it was accepted that
since Mr Sahib's wife knew nothing about it, whatever security had
been created could have had no effect on her interest in 37C. It was
therefore common ground that the purported charge had no effect
on the legal title to 37C, but that it severed their equitable joint
tenancy and took effect, if at all, as an equitable mortgage or
equitable charge over Mr Sahib's equitable interest as a tenant in
common under the trust for sale of 37C.

An expressly created equitable mortgage or charge must be in
writing signed by the mortgagor/chargor in order to comply with
the requirements of section 53 of the Law of Property Act 1925.[89]
No such writing existed here. Could it be said that there was
instead a specifically enforceable contract to grant a mortgage or
charge? On the facts it was certainly plausible that what was
intended was a security taking immediate effect coupled with a
promise to formalise it on request. However, as the judge
(Chadwick J) pointed out, an immediate problem was that the
intention was to charge the whole legal and beneficial interest in
37C, not merely Mr Sahib's half share of the beneficial interest.
Could the attempt to charge the whole take effect as a charge over
the smaller interest held by Mr Sahib alone?

There is in fact substantial authority for the proposition that an
attempt to convey or mortage a greater interest than you hold or
have power to dispose of (for example, by forging a co-owner's
signature) takes effect in respect of the smaller interest you actually
hold. If the attempt culminates in a conveyance (which included a
formal mortgage), this is achieved by section 63 of the Law of
Property Act 1925.[90] If not, it was held in *Thames Guaranty Ltd* v
Campbell[91] that the same would be achieved by the doctrine of
partial performance:

---

[89] Strictly speaking, an equitable charge of an equitable interest in land, being the
creation of an interest, comes within s 53(1)(a), whereas an equitable mortgage of an
equitable interest (which involves a transfer by way of security of the mortgaged
interest) comes within either 53(1)(a) or 53(1)(c). The only difference between (a)
and (c) is that (a) provides for creation to be by operation of law rather than by
writing.
[90] *First National Securities Ltd* v *Hegerty* [1985] QB 850 CA; *Ahmed* v *Kendrick*
(1988) 56 P & CR 120.   [91] [1985] 1 QB 210.

It is a well established principle of equity that where, in the course of concluding a contract, a person has represented that he can grant a certain property, or is entitled to a certain interest in that property, and it later appears that there is a deficiency in his title or interest, the other party can obtain an order compelling him to grant what he has got . . .[92]

Chadwick J accepted that prima facie that applied here, but the question then arose whether section 2 of the 1989 Act altered the position. He concluded that it did. He said that the doctrine of partial performance could only apply where there was a valid enforceable contract, and since in this case there was no writing to satisfy section 2 in respect of an agreement to charge the whole of 37C there was no contract in respect of which partial performance could be ordered. This must be correct. The doctrine of partial performance is not a failed formality rule; it is concerned with real contracts, not inferred or notional ones, and so it must follow that if there is no contract, performance of it cannot be ordered.

However, counsel for Sogenal argued in the alternative that an immediate security interest had been created by the notional deposit of the land certificate which occurred when Mr Sahib's solicitors stated that they held it to Sogenal's order. Before 1989 it had been long established that a deposit of title deeds with intent to create a security constitutes an equitable mortgage or charge, enforceable in equity even if done orally.[93]

There has been considerable speculation over whether this rule has survived section 2 of the 1989 Act.[94] The arguments for saying that it has not survived are essentially those explained above: equity enforced a mortgage by deposit of title deeds because the deposit constituted part performance of an agreement to mortgage, and since specific performance would have been ordered of such an agreement, equity treated the mortgagee as having the mortgage he would have had if specific performance had been ordered.

To counter this, counsel for Sogenal adopted an argument suggested in *Emmet on Title*:[95]

It is open to argument that the charge created by deposit of title documents is more properly regarded as a *sui generis* equitable charge rather than an agreement to create a charge. If this is correct, then its validity is unaffected

---

[92] Ibid 235.
[93] The principle is generally taken to have been established by the decision in *Russel* v *Russel* (1783) 1 Bro CC 269.
[94] See n 87 above.   [95] 19th Edition, Release 10, para 25.116.

by the 1989 Act. The basis of the argument is that deposit of title documents has long been regarded as creating a security valid and enforceable by the mortgagee: this could not be the case if enforcement in the absence of writing satisfying S.40 of the LPA 1925 depended on the doctrine of part performance, because of the general principle that the person seeking to enforce an agreement must rely on his own part performance of it, not that of the other party.

Chadwick J examined the numerous authorities on the origins of the equitable mortgage by deposit and concluded that there was no authority to support any conclusion other than that it was contract based. Because of that, he held, the argument must fail and section 2 of the 1989 Act must now be taken to apply to mortgages by deposit. Therefore, he concluded, Sogenal failed to establish that they had a security interest over Mr Sahib's equitable interest.[96]

Nevertheless, it is doubtful whether this will prove to have finally concluded the matter (although it most certainly reinforces the advice given in *Emmet on Title* and endorsed by Chadwick J, that 'lenders cannot safely assume that any security will be created by mere deposit of title deeds'[97]). No one can deny that a contract analysis was the historical justification for equity intervening to circumvent statutory formalities requirements. The problem is whether the courts were (and are) required to find an actual contract or whether they may infer one. It should also be said that the Court failed to consider an alternative argument which has been put forward, and which deserves judicial consideration. This is that whatever the origins and nature of the mortgage by deposit before 1925, equitable mortgages by deposit are expressly recognised by the 1925 legislation[98] and therefore survive the removal of their original basis.[99]

However, it will be a pity if this issue has to be decided by a minute examination of eighteenth and nineteenth century authorities. Mortgages by deposit are intended to take immediate effect and therefore there is no particular reason why they should

[96] Even if they had succeeded on the s 2 point, they would have still have failed to establish an interest, since the notional deposit of the land certificate was by Mr Sahib only and not by his wife, and Chadwick J confirmed that this could not create an effective security. The same conclusion was reached in *Thames Guaranty Ltd* v *Campbell* [1985] 1 QB 210 CA.

[97] 19th edition, Release 10, para 25.116.

[98] S 97 of the Law of Property Act 1925 and s 66 of the Land Registration Act 1925.   [99] Burn, *Cheshire and Burn*, 670.

be governed by a formalities rule designed for executory contracts. On the other hand, since they can affect third parties even if their existence is not even mentioned on a register,[100] and they are nearly always taken to protect commercial rather than family or personal interests, there seems very little justification for allowing them to be created orally. Perhaps a rather wider review of formal requirements than that proposed by the Law Commission would be appropriate?

III Tenant's Continuing Liability

Meanwhile the Law Commission-inspired Bill to regulate the continuing contractual liabilities of ex-tenants and ex-sureties has failed yet again to reach the statute book,[101] whilst a ceaseless tide of cases testifies to the urgent need for reform.[102]

In an area so thoroughly litigated over recent years it might seem that there is now very little room for development outside Parliament. Certainly, the Courts have made it clear that they do not now consider that it is open to them to challenge the basic rule—that, in the absence of agreement to the contrary, the original landlord and tenant (and their sureties) remain contractually liable for performance of the obligations under the lease throughout the term of the lease, even after assignment of the term to a third party.

---

[100] In this case, for example, if Sogenal had been found to have an equitable mortgage or charge Chadwick J held that it would have taken priority over Kuwait's charging order as a prior equitable interest, since he held that the rule in *Dearle* v *Hall* (1828) 3 Russell 1 did not apply in relation to a non-consensual charge. However, there was no way in which Kuwait or any other subsequent encumbrancer could have discovered the existence of the prior charge unless they had sought the land certificate in order to register their interest or protect it by caution. Whilst a requirement of writing does not necessarily make a prior interest more discoverable, it does at least settle any arguments about its terms once it has been discovered.

[101] A Private Member's Bill, the Landlord and Tenant (Covenants) Bill, had its first reading in the House of Common on May 13 1994, but it had to be withdrawn in the face of lack of time and determined opposition by the British Property Federation. Whether it will be re-submitted in the next session is yet to be announced. For a discussion of the terms of the Bill see Hasselberg and Silverman, 'Privity of Contract: Return of the Abolition Question' [1994] 23 *EG* 116.

[102] Including, amongst many others this year, *Estates Gazette Ltd* v *Benjamin Restaurants Ltd* [1994] 26 EG 140 CA, *Allied Dunbar Assurance plc* v *Fowle* [1994] 25 EG 149, *W H Smith Ltd* v *Wyndham Investments Ltd* [1994] *The Times* 26 May, *Hindcastle Ltd* v *Barbara Attenborough Associates Ltd* [1994] *The Times* 6 July CA.

Nevertheless, whilst avoiding confrontation with the basic rule, the House of Lords has firmly rejected the attempt to allow it to distort fundamental orthodoxy. In *City of London Corporation v Fell*,[103] the House dismissed an appeal against the Court of Appeal decision discussed in last year's *Annual Review*.[104] In what would otherwise seem a remarkably short single judgment decision[105] the House of Lords confined itself to a purely conceptual analysis, scrupulously avoiding all reference to policy or practical implications. The issue was whether the original tenant's liability extends beyond the originally agreed term of the lease into any statutory extension of the term under Part II of the Landlord and Tenant Act 1954, which provides that tenancies of business premises 'shall not come to an end until . . .' terminated by either party serving a statutory notice (which triggers off the tenant's right to apply to the court for a new tenancy on similar terms).[106] The House of Lords affirmed the Court of Appeal's decision that (subject to provision to the contrary in the lease) the original tenant's liability does not continue into the statutory extension of the term but is confined to the contractual term of the lease.

Lord Templeman, giving the main judgment, dealt with only one of the arguments put forward on behalf of the landlord. This was that the 1954 Act required that (and could only work if) the liability under the lease of the person who was the tenant at the expiry of the contractual term continued thereafter. However, it was argued, the current tenant's liability is dependent on the continued enforceability of the original tenant's covenants: the lease must be underpinned by the original tenant's covenants, because the covenants in the lease are the original tenant's covenants, and so if they are no longer enforceable against the original tenant they can no longer be enforced against the current tenant. In order to continue the current tenant's obligations into the statutory extension, therefore, the original tenant's liability must also continue.

If this argument were correct it would mean that the continuing liability under the lease of the original tenant was fundamental to

---

[103] [1993] 3 WLR 1164.

[104] P. Kohler (1994) 47 *CLP Annual Review* 111.

[105] Lord Templeman gave the main judgment in less that four sides of the law reports, with Lords Goff of Chieveley, Jauncey of Tullichettle, Browne-Wilkinson and Mustill agreeing in two to three lines each.

[106] S 24 Landlord and Tenant Act 1954 (as amended).

our leasehold system. In fact, as Lord Templeman pointed out,[107] the argument confuses contract and status. What is fundamental to the leasehold system is privity of estate—that is, that the benefit and burden of the leasehold covenants which touch and concern the land are annexed to the term and reversion, enforceable by and against the holders for the time being of the term and the reversion. The fact that in the English (as opposed to the Scottish) system the original landlord and tenant also remain liable is merely a quirk of contract law—or, as Lord Templeman put it, 'because of the sacred character of covenant in English law'.[108] It can quite easily be reversed without doing any harm to the integrity of the system of leasehold tenure.

The basic premise of the landlord's argument—that if covenants cannot be enforced against the original tenant they cannot be enforced against the current tenant—was therefore wrong in principle, and the landlord's appeal against the Court of Appeal's decision was dismissed.

Whilst the importance of the principle reasserted by the House of Lords here is undoubted, the decision itself has little practical significance to anyone other than the parties. It is standard practice to provide expressly in the lease that the original tenant's liability will continue into any statutory extension of the term, and the decision of the Court of Appeal in *Herbert Duncan Ltd* v *Cluttons*[109] confirming the effectiveness of such a provision remains unaffected by the House of Lords decision in *City of London Corporation* v *Fell.*[110]

Nevertheless, the whole issue of continuing liability will continue to be of immense practical importance for so long as the recession in the property market lasts. Landlords with insolvent tenants holding long leases with rents fixed at a level above current market value will continue to seek to attach liability to long-gone former tenants and their sureties, who will continue to seek grounds for avoiding it or for enforcing indemnities given by their assignees.

---

[107] [1994] 3 WLR 1169.   [108] Ibid 1168.

[109] [1993] 2 WLR 710.

[110] The two cases were heard together in the Court of Appeal: see [1993] 2 WLR 710. For the combined effect of the Court of Appeal Decision in *Herbert Duncan* and the House of Lords decision in *Fell:* see further *Emmet on Title* 19th ed, Release 22 para 26.122.

This has gone as far, in at least two recent cases, as bringing companies back from the grave (or wherever it is that dissolved companies go) in order to revive liabilities. The most interesting of these is *Re Forte's (Manufacturing) Ltd, Stanhope Pension Trust Ltd v Registrar of Companies*.[111] A 42 year lease was granted to Forte's (Manufacturing) Ltd in 1960. Soon afterwards, the lease was assigned to Post Inns Ltd, another company within the Forte group, as part of a group reorganisation. The original company, Forte (Manufacturing), was then put into voluntary liquidation. In 1979 the lease was assigned to BCCI, which went into liquidation in 1992. The landlord therefore sought to fix liability for the rent on to someone else. Of all the companies who had held the lease over the years, the only one still in existence and solvent was Post Inns, but since it had assigned the lease and was not the original tenant it was not liable to the landlord. However, all tenants have a statutory right of indemnity from their assignees.[112] The landlord therefore applied to the court under section 651 of the Companies Act 1985 to have the dissolution of the original tenant made void, so that it could sue it for the rent, thus bringing into existence a new asset of the revived company, namely its right of indemnity against Post Inns. Whilst the landlord would not be able to insist on the revived company assigning this right of indemnity to it, nevertheless the revived company would have only one creditor (the Landlord) and one asset (the right of indemnity from Post Inns) and therefore the landlord's claim against the revived company would be satisfied. The Court of Appeal accepted this argument and ordered Forte (Manufacturing) Ltd to be restored to the companies register.[113]

There are no signs that anything can stop this sort of costly manoeuvring for so long as we continue to regard this particular aspect of the 'sacred character of covenant in English law' as inviolable. Except, perhaps, an up-turn in the property market.

---

[111] [1994] BCC 84 CA.

[112] In these circumstances, under Land Registration Act 1925 s 24(1)(b).

[113] The other revival from the dead case was *Allied Dunbar Assurance Plc v Fowle* [1994] 25 EG 149 QBD where a company struck off the register was revived in order to revive the liabilities of sureties who had guaranteed its liabilities as tenant.

LAW OF THE EUROPEAN UNION

Margot Horspool, Oonagh Buckley, and William Robinson

This survey covers developments in European Community Law, in particular after the ratification of the Treaty on European Union (TEU), the 'Maastricht' Treaty. It treats the European institutions, the external relations of the European Union, and the case law of the European Court and the Court of First Instance.

I The Treaty on European Union

After a series of events had brought the impetus created by the signing of the Maastricht Treaty to an abrupt halt,[1] turning the latter half of 1993 into an *'annus horribilis'*, a period of consolidation, consultation and consideration had to follow.

The ratification of the TEU turned out to be a long and painful process. The second Danish referendum brought a sigh of relief in Europe with a convincing 'yes' vote (56.8%). In the UK, the ratification process dragged on for most of the summer, a number of votes in the House of Commons were very close indeed, the main bone of contention being the Protocol on Social Policy annexed to the TEU which had not been signed by the UK. After having overcome a constitutional challenge,[2] ratification finally took place on 2 August 1993.

There now only remained one country which still had to ratify, Germany. As in most countries, apart from the UK, the debate on 'Maastricht' had been minimal to start with and the German government had had little trouble piloting the Treaty through

---

[1] See annual survey of European Community Law by O'Keeffe (1994) 47 *CLP*, at 74–77.
[2] *Regina v Secretary of State for Foreign and Commonwealth Affairs, ex parte Rees-Mogg*, [1993] 1 All ER 457.

Parliament.[3] Only when it became clear what the TEU would mean in reality, and in particular that the Deutschmark eventually would have to disappear in the Economic and Monetary Union (EMU), did a debate start. This culminated in a number of constitutional complaints (*Verfassungsbeschwerden*) lodged with the Federal Constitutional Court by four Green MEP's and by Manfred Brunner, a former EEC official. The judgment, rendered on 12 October 1993,[4] declared the Greens' complaint inadmissible, but dealt at length with the Brunner application. It concluded that the transfer of powers to the Union, and in particular those concerning the Economic and Monetary Union, fell within the acceptable limits of the democratic principle guaranteed by the Basic Law[5] which precludes such transfer if it leaves the Parliament devoid of sufficient sovereign powers. With what *Die Zeit* called 'judicial self-restraint' (in English)[6] the Court held that the decisive factor was that the democratic foundations of the Union should be extended in step with further integration. The Union remains a Confederation (*Staaten(ver)bund*) rather than a Federation (*Bundesstaat*). It states, however, that the federal government has a constitutional obligation to submit any decision on entry into the third stage of economic and monetary Union to the *Bundestag*[7] and that any decision on a 'softening' of the convergence criteria should be approved by Parliament. The Court clearly restricts integration in its statement on a 'dynamic interpretation of Community law'.[8] The judgment states that if any judgment of the European Court of Justice in its interpretation of Community law 'is tantamount to an extension of the Treaty' such a decision could not be considered as binding and the Constitutional Court reserves the ultimate right of review on the model of its decision in *Solange I*.[9] The Court does,

---

[3] Both *Bundestag* and *Bundesrat* voted for an amendment to the *Grundgesetz*, (Basic Law), inserting a new Article 23, and an addition to Arts. 52 and 88, in order to enable the Federal Republic to cooperate in the development of the European Union, which 'is bound by the principles of the democratic rule of law and federative principles . . '

[4] 2 B v R 2134/92 and 2 B v R 2159/92, [1994] CMLR 57.

[5] Art.38 GG (Basic Law).   [6] 'die Zeit', 15.10.93.

[7] Art. 109j, para.4 TEU.

[8] Bleckmann and Pieper in *Recht der Internationalen Wirtschaft*, Heft 12 Dec. 1993, pp 969–977.

[9] The *Internationale Handelsgesellschaft* case, BVerfG Fn.14 271, Case 11/70 (1970) *ECR* 1125.

however, stress its 'relationship of co-operation' with the European Court of Justice.[10]

Thus, the Treaty on European Union, which was ratified by Germany the next day, finally entered into force on 1 November 1993, 10 months late.

II The Institutions

During this period, attention in the European Community, or the European Union, as it had now become, had already turned to the 1996 intergovernmental conference (IGC) which will deal with institutional reform and any changes in the Treaty in connection with this and any which will have become necessary in the light of the experience of 'Maastricht'. Numbers of proposals and suggestions have already been made in this respect, notably by the European Parliament as early as July 1993[11] and taken up by the German Christian Democrats in their proposals. These proposals concern the Presidency of the Council which should last longer, but should not be necessarily in alphabetical order, in order to avoid a run of presidencies of small countries, changes in the voting system in the Council, with the probable elimination of unanimity voting, and a reduction of the number of Commissioners.

In September 1994, the German Christian Democrats published their strategic programme under the German Presidency, aimed at creating a 'hard core' of European states, which would include Germany and France in particular. This followed similar proposals meade a few days earlier by Edouard Balladur, the French Prime Minister. The concept of 'variable geometry' is preferred to the less subtle commitment to a 'multi-speed Europe'. The proposals include the elimination of qualified majority voting in the Council of Ministers, and new Community structures to cope with the widening and deepening of the European Union.[12]

The Corfu summit on 24 and 25 June 1994 agreed on the establishment of a 'Reflection Group' responsible for the preparing of the IGC, as proposed at the earlier Ioannina summit (see below). The reluctance of certain member States, (France in particular) was

---

[10] See also N. Foster 'The German Constitution and EC Membership', *Public Law* 1994, 392.
[11] *Agence Europe* 1 July 1993.   [12] 'The Times', 2 Sept. 1994.

overcome and it was decided that two MEP's would participate in the Group, which would further consist of representatives of the Foreign Ministers and the President of the Commission. The Spanish Government will select a person to chair the Group and it will begin its work in June 1995.[13]

A number of inter-institutional agreements between the Council, the Commission and the European Parliament were drawn up in order to improve cooperation between them and more clearly to define their respective powers. An example is the interinstitutional agreement on rules for exercising the powers to implement acts adopted jointly by the European Parliament and the Council under Art. 189b TEU, the article introducing the new co-decision procedure between Council and Parliament, whereby Parliament was given the power to reject Community legislation.[14] Given the absence of specific provisions in the TEU, the Commission produced this agreement to take account of the EP's new role as joint legislature by involving it in a review of implementing acts with a legislative content. Such acts would be subject to review by the EP and by the Council. The Commission wishes to reconcile the need for effective decision-making with the need to reinforce democratic legitimacy, avoiding the use of ad-hoc solutions which may lead to difficulties and delays in implementing the legislation.

The Brussels European Council on 29 October 1994[15] which was held in order to celebrate the entry into force of the TEU, but was somewhat subdued as a result of the delay experienced in ratification, laid down guidelines for the implementation of the TEU. It confirmed 1 January 1994 as the start date of the second stage of EU and decided that the European Monetary Institute (EMI)(the precursor of the European Central Bank), which would start operating on that date, was to be headed by Baron Lamfalussy and to be located in Frankfurt. A number of decisions were taken concerning the seat of various Community institutions, the main ones being the EUROPOL drugs unit in The Hague, the Trade Mark Office in Spain, the Environment Agency in Copenhagen, and the Office for the Evaluation of Medicinal Products in London.

---

[13] *Agence Europe*, No. 6260, 26 June 1994.
[14] Adopted by the Commission on 19.4.1994: Bull. EU 4–1994, point 1.7.1.
[15] Bull. EU 4–1994, No.10, Vol 26.

The European Council also welcomed the inter-institutional agreement between the Council of Ministers, the Commission and the European Parliament concluded on 25 October, which lays down procedures governing the exercise of the powers conferred on the Community Institutions without calling into question the *acquis communautaire*.[16] The procedures are designed to ensure that the institutions check at the stage of intitial proposal or of the subsequent amendments that any proposed measure complies with the provisions on subsidiarity, both as regards choice of legal instrument and content. The Agreement also requires the Commission to draw up an annual report on the observance of the principle of subsidiarity, which will be the subject of public debate in the EP, with the participation of Council and Commission.[17]

SUBSIDIARITY

Article 3b of the TEU introduces the principle of subsidiarity into Community law, which should ensure that decisions are taken as close as possible to the citizen, lending it, in the opinion of the Parliament, the status of a constitutional provision.[18] The Commission regards it more as a 'political principle, a sort of rule of reason'.[19] Regardless of this substantial difference of opinion,[20] both are concerned that it should affect neither the distribution of powers among the Institutions nor the *acquis communautaire*. In practice, it will require the Community to demonstrate that there is a legitimate need for each initiative, and that the correct type of instrument is being used in each case. In 1993, the Commission withdrew some 150 proposals, mostly obsolete, and legislative proposals have dropped in numbers from their pre-1992 peak.

---

[16] Bull. EU 4–1994 point 1.6.3.
[17] Bull. EU 4–1994 point 2.2.2.
[18] Resolution on the adaptation of Community legislation to the subsidiarity principle, Bull. EU 2–1994.
[19] Commission report to the European Council on the adaptation of existing legislation to the subsidiarity principle. Com(93) 545 final p.1. Even more generally, it refers to it as 'primarily a state of mind which, to be given substance, presupposes a political answer to the fundamental questions which application of the principle will undoubtedly raise . . .' p 2.
[20] The difference in interpretation could be crucial in the event of a judicial review by the ECJ. See the discussions by Toth, Steiner and Emiliou in O'Keeffe and Twomey (eds), *Legal Issues of the Maastricht Treaty* (1994).

Existing legislation has been reviewed, with a view to simplifying or withdrawing it.[21]

Problems have arisen. The Commission has had to refuse unsuitable Council requests for legislative proposals. National administrations often resist the reviewing process from a mututal lack of confidence. More seriously, it is difficult to decide which rules require action, when no clear definition of subsidiarity yet exists, and the areas of exclusive competence for the Community have yet to be defined. The Commission is pressing for a hierarchy of Community norms to be introduced at the 1996 IGC. In the meantime, it is refusing review of recent legislation, to avoid renewed battles on the substance of the law.

THE COMMISSION

In December 1993, Jacques Delors, the President of the Commission presented to the European Council meeting in Brussels a White Paper entitled: Growth, Competitiveness, Employment. The Challenges and Ways forward into the 21st century.[22] This paper had been requested by the Copenhagen summit in June 1993.[23] It notes that over the past three years unemployment has risen to 17 million or 11% of the work force. This was compared to the 1990 level which, in spite of representing the lowest level for a decade, still had 12 million unemployed, i.e. 3% of the work force. The White Paper wants the Community to set a target of creating at least 15 million jobs by the year 2000, thus halving the level of unemployment. Factors to contribute to such a development are: the increased competitiveness created by the single market, the development of the regions through programmes financed in the context of economic and social cohesion;[24] keeping pace with technological development, creating 'trans-European' road, rail and telecommunications networks within the EC and towards Central and Eastern Europe, creating a favourable world trading

---

[21] Requests by Member States for revision of existing legislation have been favourably received by the Commission. Sixteen of a list of twenty-two, submitted in June 1993 by the UK and France, will be withdrawn or amended. Reform proposed by the Commission includes such diverse areas as the recognition of professional qualifications, VAT legislation and environmental rules. Background Report ISEC/ B3/94.   [22] Bull. EU—supplement 6/93.

[23] See Editorial Comment, 31 *CMLRev* No.1, 1994, 1–6.

[24] Art. 130 TEU.

environment. Five factors are essential to achieve this: a)education and training policies; b) improving the functioning of labour markets including greater deregulation; c) the possibility of job sharing and a reduction in the average working time; d) an active employment policy, promoting jobs to meet new needs; e) a reduction of labour costs. Average social contributions amount to 40% of labour costs, as against 20% in Japan and 30% in the US.

The Brussels summit expressed support for the White Paper, but the question of how to finance the trans-European networks, which would involve borrowing 8 billion Ecu, was referred to the Council of Ministers (of Economic Affairs and Finance, Ecofin). Nevertheless, the other issues in the document were considered positively and the European Council decided that the White Paper would become an annual exercise.

In January 1994, the Commission presented its legislative programme for 1994.[25] This programme was conceived in an environment of co-decision and the inter-institutional agreement on procedures for implementing the subsidiarity principle of 25 October 1993.[26]

Economic growth

The Commission will proceed with the implementation of EMU and the boosting of economic growth. Under Art. 103 TEU the European Council is empowered to establish the broad lines of economic policies of the Member States and to instruct the Council to adopt recommendations on the basis of its conclusions. The Commission hopes thus to restore the dynamism of the period 1985/90. The second stage of EMU is to be consolidated by establishing the EMI and by implementing legislation on public finance. It will follow up the White Paper on Competitiveness and Job Creation (see above). Its cohesion policies under art. 130a TEU are to be strengthened with the establishment of a cohesion fund in 1994. The necessary plans to improve structure are to be agreed as a matter of urgency. Trans-European transport, energy and telecom networks are to be promoted. A fourth framework programme is to be launched for R & D to contribute to restoring growth. Generally, Article 130 TEU is to be used to obtain a sustainable

---

[25] Bull. EU—Supplement 1/94; (Com (93) 0588.
[26] see N 17.

environment-friendly growth, always respecting the 'diversity of national and regional situations.

Democracy and citizenship

The inter-institutional declaration on democracy, transparency and subsidiarity, which incorporates the agreement on subsidiarity which came into force on 1 November 1993 gives effect to the guidelines agreed at the Edinburgh and Birmingham European Councils, bringing the Union closer to its citizens. A first citizenship right is the right to move and reside freely throughout the territory of the Member States 'on the terms set out in the Treaty itself and in secondary legislation'. The first proposals are, therefore, those on the right of residence, a standardisation of EEC cards by amendment of the directives on the rights of residence of the self-employed,[27] students, pensioners, and those of independent means,[28] measures to standardise visas and to introduce the right to vote and stand in local elections. A proposed Council Directive[29] lays down detailed arrangements for the exercise of the right to vote and stand as a candidate in municipal elections by citizens of the Union residing in a Member State of which they are not nationals.

Cooperation in Justice and Home Affairs

Title VI (Articles K and K.1–9), the intergovernmental 'third pillar', 'constitutes progress in itself. Measures will have to be taken quickly, some of them by the Commission.' This part of the TEU is not subject to the jurisdiction of the ECJ, but it contains Article K.9, the so-called *passerelle*, or 'bridge' provision. This provides that Article 100c of the TEU may apply to some of the areas of the Third Pillar, notably asylum and immigration policy.[30] In June 1994, the Council expressed its agreement with the Commission's view that it is not yet time to proceed with such a development.[31] Article 100c(1) provides for visa arrangements for third country

[27] Dir. 73/148 of 21 May 1973 on the abolition of restrictions on movement and residence within the Community for nationals of Member States with regard to establishment and the provision of services; OJ 1973 L 172/14.
[28] Directives 91/364/365/366 of 28 June 1990; OJ 1990 L 180/26/28/30.
[29] Com(94) 38 final, 23.02.1994.
[30] Art. 100c(6) of the EC Treaty (as amended by the TEU) provides: 'This Article shall apply to other areas if so decided pursuant to Article K.9 of the provisions of the TEU which relate to cooperation in the field of justice and home affairs. . . .'
[31] *Agence Europe* No. 6259, 24 June 1994.

nationals to be determined by the Council. These provisions, therefore, form part of the EC Treaty as amended by the TEU and are subject to the jurisdiction of the ECJ and the legislative procedures contained in the EC Treaty.

In the year under review, proposals have been made and co-operation has been strengthened in several fields. A draft Regulation for a uniform format for visas[32] was introduced in July 1994. Ministers of Justice meet regularly to discuss such matters as immigration, drugs, terrorism and extradition. The draft convention for the creation of Europol should be finalised by October 1994.

The social model

The Commission has presented a green paper on the future of social policy which mainly refers to the Protocol on Social Policy annexed to the TEU. In April, the Commission submitted a draft directive to the Council concerning the setting up of works councils.[33] This was the first proposal under the Social Protocol, so that consultations took place without the UK. This led to a realisation in the UK that a matter like this which would have an effect on UK companies with subsidiaries in other Member States was now being negotiated without an input from the UK, so that doubts began to arise in UK industry as to the desirability of the 'opt-out'.

External ambitions

Under the intergovernmental 'second pillar' of the Treaty, the Foreign and Security Policy (CFSP)(Title V, Arts. J and J 1–11) the main reference is to enlargement.

Internal market and common policies

The Commission will continue to improve practical management of the Single Market in partnership with the Member States. The reforms agreed to on the Common Agricultural Policy (CAP) in 1992 must be implemented. Generally the Commission will strive for enhanced openness, accessibility and efficiency.

The Commission reviewed progress on the implementation of the White Paper in April and submitted a report to the Corfu summit

---

[32] Com(94) 287 final, 13.07.94.
[33] *Agence Europe* No. 6209, 13 April 94.

under the Greek Presidency in June 1994. Although the discussion on the White Paper there was overshadowed by the acrimonious debate concerning the appointment of the President of the Commission (see below), Jacques Delors was able to note that progress on the whole had been satisfactory and that the framework provided by the White Paper was still in existence. He particularly singled out the conclusions on the improvement of competitiveness by reforming employment, and the priority attached to small and medium sized businesses (SME's). The Council selected 11 top priorities in the transport infrastructure from the report presented by Transport Commissioner Henning Christophersen.[34]

ELECTION OF THE PRESIDENT OF THE COMMISSION

The Corfu summit on 24 and 25 June was dominated by the election of the new President of the Commission. The proposed candidate, Belgian Prime Minister Jean-Luc Dehaene, was vetoed by John Major. This was perhaps less to do with M Dehaene's reputation as a Federalist than with the fact that France and Germany appeared to have agreed on a candidate beforehand without proper consultation with their partners. At the next summit in Brussels, marking the start of the German Presidency of the Council, a new candidate, Jacques Santer, the Luxembourg Prime Minister, was agreed upon and accepted by all 12 heads of state and government.[35] On 21 July, M Santer addressed the European Parliament before his endorsement as President.[36] The EP voted on this nomination as a political act.[37] In a close vote his nomination was endorsed by 260 votes to 238 with 23 abstentions. M Santer's strong plea for unity and promise to be a strong President may well have swayed some MEP's. The opposition was led by Pauline Green, head of the 198 strong Socialist Group (PES) who objected to the method of appointment and the use of the

---

[34] *Agence Europe* No. 6256, 22 June 1994, p 7.

[35] *Agence Europe* 26 June 94, special edition.

[36] *The Week in the European Parliament*, Final Edition, Strasbourg 19–22 July 1994, doc. PE 182.739.

[37] Art. 158 (2)TEU first para: The EP is to be merely *consulted* on the proposal for a Commission President, whereas it has to give its *consent* to the appointment of the entire Commission. (Art. 158 (2) TEU, third para).

British veto.[38] German Foreign Minister Klaus Kinkel promised to examine Article 158 TEU, which refers to the election of the President 'by common accord', i.e. unanimity with no abstentions and which, therefore, allowed the right of veto. He would seek to remove this.

THE 'IOANNINA COMPROMISE' ON ENLARGEMENT[39]

On 29 and 30 March, 1994, an 'informal' European Council meeting in Ioannina in Greece, under the Greek Presidency of the Council, had been convened to mark the end of the negotiations for accession with four aspirant Member States, Austria, Finland, Norway and Sweden (see below).

An issue which had already arisen at the previous summit meeting in Brussels in December 1993[40] now came to a head and threatened to endanger the accession process. Qualified majority voting is the most common method of adoption of Community legislation, and has been further extended by the TEU, reducing the sphere of unanimity voting. The intergovernmental 'pillars' of the new Treaty, on Common Foreign and Security Policy[41] and on Justice and Home Affairs[42] have unanimous voting in practically all cases. The proposal was that on accession of new Member States[43] the qualified majority should be increased in proportion to the increased number of total votes, which would rise to 90, keeping the same percentage of 71%, or 64 votes. This would mean that the amount of votes required for a 'blocking minority' would rise from 23 votes to 27 votes. This proposal met with opposition by the UK, initially supported by Spain. It advocated the retention of the present system, which would mean that two large Member States could block a decision with the support of just one small Member State. Raising this number, as had been done previously upon the accession of other countries, would mean that at least one other country's votes would be needed to obtain a blocking minority. In Ioannina Spain soon dropped its opposition to the proposal,

[38] This stance was supported by the ELDR, the Liberals, the European Radical Alliance (ERA), the Greens and the European Left.
[39] *Agence Europe*, 14 April 1994—documents section.
[40] *Agence Europe* No. 1625, 10 December 1993.
[41] Title V. Art. J–J.11.   [42] Title VI, Art. K–K.9.
[43] They will have the following number of votes in the Council: Austria and Sweden: 4 votes; Norway and Finland: 3 votes.

leaving the UK exposed. Eventually, a compromise was reached which was acceptable to the UK and negotiations for new membership were concluded with a sigh of relief.

The relevant part of the European Council's *Decision*(para c), was as follows:[44] 'If Members of the Council (of Ministers) representing a total of 23 *to* 26 votes indicate their intention to oppose the adoption by the Council of a decision by qualified majority, the Council will do all in its power to reach, within a reasonable time and without prejudice to obligatory time limits laid down by the Treaties and by secondary legislation, such as in Arts. 189b and 189c of the EC Treaty, a satisfactory solution which could be adopted by at least 68 votes. During this period, and always respecting the Rules of Procedure of the Council, the President takes, with the assistance of the Commission, any initiative necessary to facilitate a wider basis of agreement in the Council.'

This decision was followed by a declaration by the Member States, with which the four applicant countries concurred. They agreed with the third paragraph of the decision, prefacing their agreement by the statement that the necessary threshold for a qualified majority should be established at 64 votes. They further agreed that the whole question should be re-examined by the 1996 Intergovernmental Conference (IGC) and inter-institutional reports are to be prepared, proposing options on the weighting of votes and the threshold of qualified majority decisions, taking into account future enlargement.

The Commission issued a statement indicating that these transitional arrangements should not set a precedent which would influence the 1996 IGC.

Thus, if there is a minority of at least 23 but less than 27, there should be a 'reasonable' lapse of time in which the Council Presidency and the Commission will try to achieve a consensus between Member States. However, under the Council's own Rules of Procedure, any Member State may raise the question as to what constitutes 'reasonable' and the Council will then be able to put this question to the vote by a simple majority. If this vote is carried, the blocking majority will then rise to 27. At the Corfu summit, a 'Reflection Group' of personal representatives of Heads of State and Government was set up to prepare the 1996 IGC and deal with this question.

The precise nature of the compromise has given rise to much debate. The British Prime Minister, John Major, regarded the compromise as legally binding and justiciable before the European Court of Justice.[45] The Commission's view, as communicated to the Committee of Permanent Representatives[46] was that the compromise constituted a political statement with which the twelve Member States must comply 'in all good faith.' This view was confirmed by the Greek Presidency. The statement itself 'is a political document without legal form, which includes a Council decision, which however does not form part of the Accession Treaty of the four new Member States.

Comparisons have been made with the 1966 'Luxembourg Compromise', which was reached in order to put an end to France's 'empty chair' policy.[47] This stated that where, in the case of a decision to be taken by a majority vote 'very important interests' of one or more partners were at stake, the Council would endeavour, *within a reasonable time* to reach solutions which can be adopted by all the Members of the Council. France considered that, where very important interests were at stake, discussions should continue until unanimous agreement was reached. The six delegations noted there was a divergence of view as to what to do in the event of a failure to reach complete agreement, but nevertheless agreed to resume their work.[48] This was, therefore, hardly a compromise, and its precise status has remained unclear to this day. There is even disagreement as to whether it still exists; it has not been used in recent years, although threats have been made to use it from time to time (most notably by France during the recent GATT negotiations).

The Ioannina Agreement does, however, seem to be a genuine agreement. Nevertheless, unlike the Luxembourg Compromise, it is not limited to 'very important interests', so any matter could be used and this makes it potentially worse than the Luxembourg Compromise. Nevertheless, Commission President Delors, in a statement to the European Parliament on 20 April 1994[49] once

---

[44] *Agence Europe* No. 6201, 14 April 1994—documents section.
[45] *Agence Europe* No. 6203, 1 April 1994, 1.
[46] *Agence Europe* No. 6203, 1 April 94, 3.
[47] Editorial Comments (1994) 31 *CMLRev* at 456–457.
[48] Bull. EEC 3–1966, 9.
[49] *Agence Europe* No 6215, 21 April 1994.

again underlined the temporary and political nature of the compromise and expressed the hope that it would not dominate the 1996 IGC.

Whether the Agreement is justiciable would, if it came to that, have to be decided by the ECJ. The Court has held that any Community act which created legal effects, irrespective of its nature, was an act *sui generis* which was subject to the Court's jurisdiction.[50]

II External Relations of the Union

COMMON FOREIGN AND SECURITY POLICY

On November 1st, 1993, the rules on intergovernmental political co-operation between the Member States were replaced by a Common Foreign and Security Policy (CFSP). The Member States will, from now on, be bound by their common decisions under Title V, TEU. For the present, the Western European Union (WEU) will deal with defence matters; it will probably be incorporated into the Union itself before its treaty expires in 1998.[51]

The Union quickly decided on their first 'joint actions', sending humanitarian aid to the former Yugoslavia and observers to the December elections in the Russian Federation.[52] The Brussels European Council also decided that they would jointly promote the creation of a Pact on Stability, as an attempt to deal with nationality tensions in Europe.[53] The inaugural conference in Paris was attended by representatives of the fifty-two contracting parties of the Conference on Security and Co-operation in Europe (CSCE), and of the Council and the Commission.[54] It was decided to concentrate initial efforts on those states, whose future accession to the Union has been agreed.[55] Two round table discussions, for the Baltic region and Central and Eastern Europe respectively, will

[50] Case 22/70 *Commission v Council (ERTA)* [1971] ECR 263.
[51] Art J.4.6, TEU requires that the CFSP be revised as part of the general review in 1996. The de Gucht Report has recommended incorporation, *Agence Europe* No. 6158, 28 January 1994.
[52] *Agence Europe* No. 6102, 6 November 1993.
[53] Bull. EC 12–1993, point 1.16.
[54] Bull. EU 5–1994, point 1.3.2. The concluding document of the conference is printed at point 2.2.1.
[55] Poland, Hungary, the Czech Republic, Slovakia, Bulgaria, Romania, Estonia, Latvia and Lithuania. The European Council meeting in Copenhagen in June 1993 decided that those countries could become members of the Union.

attempt to reach agreement on issues such as minorities and border disputes. Any bilateral agreements reached could also be included in the Pact, at its envisaged adoption in 1995.

The Union showed its political and economic muscle at this conference. It offered its services as a mediator in disputes, and suggested that the existing Community programmes for assistance, PHARE[56] and TACIS,[57] could be used to further the process of reconciliation. However, as a response to the difficulties in its sphere of influence, it could best be described as inadequate. It is a diplomatic measure aimed at conflict prevention, and is not intended to influence those already at war. The Union will not act as the Pact's 'guardian'; that role is left to the unwieldy CSCE.

The combined foreign policy efforts of the Member States have failed to stop the conflict in the former Yugoslavia, despite intensive diplomatic efforts.[58] Frequently, when nominally co-operating, the countries seemed to be acting at cross-purposes, best exemplified by the row over the recognition of Slovenia and Croatia by Germany, said to be one of the root causes of the Serb-Croat conflict. The impression of incoherence in policy towards the conflict was reinforced by the unilateral imposition by Greece of an embargo on Macedonia on the 17th February, 1994. Greece imposed the embargo as a response to the recognition of the Former Yugoslav Republic of Macedonia by six Member States of the Union.[59] The Greek government cited Article 224 EC which permits a unilateral derogation from the Common Commercial Policy by a Member State in exceptional circumstances, in particular 'serious international tension constituting a threat of war'. This provision was maintained despite the new powers under Article 228a EC, to jointly impose sanctions, after a decision by the Council under the CFSP.[60]

---

[56] *Poland and Hungary—Assistance with Restructuring the Economy.* At the 1989 Western Economic Summit in Paris the Commission was given the task of coordinating aid from the 24 OECD countries, the G–24, to Poland and Hungary, later extended to the rest of Central and Eastern Europe.

[57] *Technical Assistance Programme for the former Republics of the Soviet Union.*

[58] Declaration on the Former Yugoslavia, agreed at the Brussels European Council, Bull. EC 12–1993, point 1.17.

[59] Germany, Italy, Denmark, the Netherlands, the United Kingdom and France, *Agence Europe* No. 6131, 17 December, 1993.

[60] See discussion by Kuyper, 'Trade Sanctions, Security and Human Rights and Commercial Policy', in M. Maresceau (ed.), *The European Community's Commercial Policy after 1992: The Legal Dimension* (1993), 387–422.

Despite the disapproval of its fellow Council members, Greece has maintained the embargo, implicitly rejecting the idea of a Common Foreign and Security Policy, and regrettably using its rights under the EC Treaty to do so, rights which remain unaffected by the new rules on foreign policy.[61] The European Commission, concerned about this threat to the Common Commercial Policy, has asked the Court of Justice to rule that it was an incorrect use of the derogation.[62] Greece argues that it is a purely political issue, not one of trade. The Court will have to rule on the difficult question of the real nature of sanctions, in an area where commercial and foreign policies are both at issue.

The Union Treaty obliges the 1996 Intergovernmental Conference to review the CFSP, in particular its security and defence aspects.[63] The review has two major challenges—to create more focus in Union actions, and to make those actions more forceful. One suggestion is to form a Security Council, which could respond quickly to crisis situations.[64] Incorporation of the WEU into the framework of the Union would give the Union the logistical framework to take action, but the means to do so have yet to be developed. The Intergovernmental Conference could consider the creation of a peace-keeping force, so that, in the words of a Commission Vice-President, the Union has the 'means of preventing, intervening in and controlling conflicts, with the blessing of the UN of course.'[65] Clearly any larger security role for the Union will have important implications, for the Member States themselves, and for those security organisations with European Union membership. Different obligations for the Member States in this area seem inevitable; the creation by France, Germany and Belgium of the Eurocorps is the most cogent example of this trend.

[61] Under Art. M, TEU.
[62] C–120/94 *Commission v Greece* (pending). Although the Court of Justice refused to grant interim measures, it will need more time to evaluate the substantive arguments of both sides, which turn on whether the actions of Macedonia amount to a real 'threat of war', *Agence Europe* No. 6269, 8 July 1994, 11.
[63] Under Arts. J.4.6 and J.10, TEU.
[64] Comments by Commissioner van den Broek, *Agence Europe* No.6243, 3 June 1994.
[65] Commission Vice-President Marin, *Agence Europe* No. 6282, 27 July 1994. The acceptance by Austria, Finland and Sweden of all the implications of the development of the CFSP removes the doubt that their traditional neutrality could weaken that development, see below.

RELATIONS WITH THE WIDER EUROPE

The most ambitious foreign relations enterprise of the Union—to expand to a membership of over twenty European states—has begun. This will involve substantial revision of the structure of the Union itself. The Union has however insisted on complete acceptance of the *acquis communautaire*. It has also to prepare the potential Member States for the economic and political burdens of membership.

The first of a series of enlargements of the Union is planned for the 1st January 1995.[66] On that day, Austria, Finland, Norway and Sweden bring Union membership to sixteen. The success of the national ratification procedures[67] depends on the concessions each country may claim they wrested from the Union. Each had their own particular concerns,[68] although the negotiations were held in parallel. Alpine transport, agriculture and the level of payments to the Union budget were particularly contentious. Nevertheless the priority of the Union, to widen without weakening its own structure, was broadly achieved;[69] the applicant states received temporary derogations and limited compromises at best.

Norway refused to sign for two weeks after the other states, in its determination to force concessions from the Community on its fishing industry. It feared destruction of its third-largest industry, in particular if the enormous Spanish fleet could have access to its fishery resources. The Community was willing to make some concessions, as it was partly on this issue that membership was rejected by the Norwegians in 1973. Norway received a derogation

[66] Bull. EU 3–1994. See the commentary on the negotiations in Editorial Comments, (1994) 31 *CMLRev* 453. A full discussion on enlargement of the Union is in last year's survey (1994) 47 *CLP Annual Review* 73 at 80–85. The Commission opinions on the applications for membership are at: Austria Bull. EC-Supp. 3/92; Sweden Bull. EC-Supp. 5/92; Finland Bull. EC-Supp. 6/92; Norway Bull. EC-Supp. 2/93.

[67] Each country must hold a referendum on ratification. The Austrian vote was passed by a large majority on 12 June, 1994. Finland will vote on the 16th October, Sweden on the 13th and Norway the 28th of November. It is hoped that a 'domino' effect of ratification will persuade Norway, the most sceptical applicant, to vote yes.

[68] C. Goybet, 'L'Europe à Seize', *Revue du Marché Commun*, no 378, May 1994, 289.

[69] Commission Report, *Europe and the Challenge of Enlargement*, Bull. EC-Supp. 3/92. For the compromise that had to be reached on voting procedures in the Council, see above.

until 1998 on full access; Spain had to be content with a larger quota now, and a promise to review the restrictions on its fleet in 1996.

A particular concern of the Union prior to the negotiations was the effect of the accession of three traditionally neutral countries on the CFSP.[70] A commitment to full involvement in the policy, including the development of a common defence policy, was needed, even though that might involve peace-making as well as peace-keeping activities. In the event, all four countries accepted the full implications of membership. They will bring useful experience to the diplomatic activities of the Union, acting as a bridge to Eastern Europe in future negotiations.

Negotiations have already begun for the next accessions, of Malta and Cyprus.[71] These can only take place after the 1996 institutional reforms but, once those issues are resolved, those countries will not make a major impact on the working of the Union. Hungary[72] and Poland[73] have formally submitted their requests for accession to the Union; the Commission is now considering their applications under the procedure of Article O of the Treaty. Although the Copenhagen European Council accepted the future accession of these, and all Central and Eastern European States who have signed Association Agreements, it will involve a substantial reform of the policies of the Union, notably agriculture and regional policy.

A lengthy period of preparation will be needed before these new market economies are ready for membership. In response to a request of the Corfu European Council to draft a strategy, designed to prepare the Associated states for membership,[74] the Commission has proposed economic integration by building on the Europe Agreements that each has or will have signed with the Union.[75] Other aspects of the Union will be dealt with in a 'structured relationship' of joint meetings and co-operation. Future Member states can be included in discussions on issues of foreign policy and

---

[70] See the Commission opinions on the countries' applications for accession, supra n 66; Parliament resolution on enlargement and neutrality, OJ C 114/61.
[71] Commission's opinions on their applications: Malta Bull.EC-Supp.4/93, Cyprus Bull. EC–Supp. 5/93.   [72] Bull EU 4–1994 point 1.3.18.
[73] Bull. EU 4–1994 point 1.3.19.
[74] *Agence Europe* No. 6260, 26 June 1994.
[75] Strategy aimed at preparing Central and Eastern European countries for accession to the European Union, *Europe Documents* No. 1893, 21 July 1994.

home affairs that affect them and to which solutions are required at a pan-European level. Unfortunately the political dialogue, announced with such fanfare at the Copenhagen Council in June 1993, has had a limited inception. In twelve months only two ministerial level meetings, and three political dialogue meetings, took place. The German Presidency, in the second half of 1994, is committed to increasing the integration of Central and Eastern European countries into the working of the Union. More regular meetings are likely, and co-operation may extend to include meetings between parliamentarians.

The Union's strategy for integrating the Central and Eastern European States depends upon the completion of far-reaching trade and co-operation agreements with potential member states. Free trade agreements have accordingly been signed with the Baltic States—Latvia, Lithuania[76] and Estonia,[77] and negotiations have begun with these states and Slovenia[78] for full association status with the Union.

The Union has no intention of agreeing to the eventual accession of the larger Eastern European states. Their economic problems are too enormous and diverse to be successfully incorporated into a Union with smaller and far richer states. If Russia were ever to accede, Commissioner van den Broek has asked, 'Who would be joining whom?'[79] The Union has limited relations to partnership and co-operation agreements, which offer a mixture of trade, aid and economic co-operation, based firmly on the principles of human rights and the market economy. They have been signed with Russia,[80] the Ukraine,[81] Kazakhstan,[82] Kyrgyzstan[83] and Moldova.[84] These treaties are a substantial improvement on previous agreements but do not commit the Union to eventual

---

[76] Signed on 20 and 27 June, 1994: *Agence Europe*, No. 6258, 24 June 1994.
[77] *Agence Europe* No. 6274, 14 July, 1994. These agreements will come into force on 1 January, 1995. A free trade area already exists between the three states.
[78] *Agence Europe* No. 6260, 26 June 1994.
[79] *Agence Europe* No. 6194, 19 March 1994.
[80] Bull. EU 4–1994, point 1.3.27. The agreement was signed by President Yeltsin at the Corfu summit, 24/25 June, 1994.
[81] *Agence Europe* No. 6249, 14 June 1994.
[82] Initialled on 20 May 1994, Bull. EU 5–1994 point 1.3.35.
[83] Initialled on 31 May, 1994, Bull. EU 5–1994 point 1.3.36.
[84] Initialled, *Agence Europe* No. 6281, 27 July 1994.

inclusion of those countries in the political and economic processes of integration.

The 'concentric' structure of the new Europe has become clear since the commitment at the Copenhagen Council to the principle of a large future membership. At the centre are the present Member States of the Union, with, probably, the four new members acceding in 1995. Around that are the members of the European Economic Area (EEA), in a wide-ranging free trade area. The third ring is of the Associated states, whose future accession is guaranteed, and who have growing economic and political links to the Union. The outer ring consists of those states with whom more traditional trade and aid links are intended.

Perhaps only one state will be out of place in this structure—Switzerland. Because of the Swiss rejection of membership of the EEA in 1992, their application for future accession to the Union is doubtful, although their government insists that it will continue to work towards that goal. In the meantime, relations will consist of bilateral agreements on selected sectors, such as free movement of persons, research and public procurement.[85] However, a draft agreement on transport[86] received a setback, when the Swiss voted to ban road haulage traffic from 2004, in an effort to prevent deterioration of the Alpine environment.[87] The Swiss tradition of democracy continues to hamper its negotiations with the Union; perhaps the latter could learn a valuable lesson of the need for popular consent in its future relations with third countries.

The Agreement on the EEA, without the Swiss, came into force on the 1st January, 1994.[88] It seems doomed to an unhappy existence. Its ratification was delayed by an unfavourable opinion of the Court of Justice, followed by the Swiss 'No'.[89] No sooner had it come into force than four of its members agreed terms for accession with the Union. This will leave the EEA with only

---

[85] Commission communication of future relations with Switzerland, Com(93) 486; Bull. EC 10–1993 point 1.3.11; Council conclusions, Bull. EC 11–1993 point 1.3.4. An agreement on the free movement of persons has been drafted, Bull EC 12–1993 point 1.2.32.

[86] Bull. EC 9–1993 point 1.2.80.

[87] Bull. EU 5–1994 points 1.2.24–25.

[88] Bull. EU 1/2–1994 point 1.3.27.

[89] For discussion of the development of the EEA see (1993) 46 *CLP Annual Review* 53, 58–60, and (1994) 47 *CLP Annual Review* 73, 81–83.

Iceland, and probably Liechtenstein,[90] as members on the EFTA side, heavily outnumbered by the sixteen Union members and the Community. The EEA will continue to function in this lopsided fashion;[91] its use as a vehicle for integration into the Union for other countries has not been mooted as an option.

THE COMPLETION OF THE URUGUAY ROUND

Although most outside attention on the Union's external relations has concentrated on its new powers under the Maastricht Treaty, the European Community has long held exclusive powers in trade negotiations with third countries and in international organisations. The Community is the largest trader in the world, and its fortunes received a significant boost from the signing of the Final Act of the Uruguay Round at Marrakesh in Morocco on the 15th April, 1994.[92] It played a major role in the protracted and often difficult negotiations in the seven years since the Punta del Este declaration in 1986. At that time the original aims of the contracting parties had been broadly achieved, despite the ambitious inclusion of the most difficult areas of international trade—agriculture and textiles. The GATT regime was extended to services and trade-related aspects of intellectual property and investment. The parties also agreed to the formation of a new multilateral organisation, the World Trade Organisation (WTO), designed to cope with the new requirements of the global market.[93]

The EC Commission has proposed to the Council[94] that the Community, as well as the Member States, become members of the WTO. This is not the situation under the GATT, where the Community, while being a de facto member,[95] has no voting rights; instead the Commission is in the happy position of co-ordinating the votes of the twelve Member States. Membership would formalise Community involvement in the organisation.

---

[90] Liechtenstein ratified membership of the EEA by referendum, but has had to resolve the difficulties caused by its monetary and customs union with Switzerland. It is hoped that it will become a member by the end of 1994 under Art 1(2) of the Protocol adjusting the EEA Agreement. EEA Council Conclusions Bull. EU 5–1994 point 1.3.22.   [91] Bull. EU 5–1994 point 1.3.22.
[92] Bull. EU 4–1994, point 1.3.61.
[93] Leon Brittain, Guest Editorial (1994) 31 *CMLRev* 229–234.
[94] Bull. EU 4–1994, point 1.3.61.
[95] As a customs territory under GATT Art. XXIV.2.

THE PROBLEM OF RATIFICATION

Once the negotiations ended, the institutions turned their attention to the problems associated with ratification of the agreement. The problem is one of competence—does the Community have the power to ratify the agreement by itself, or must the Member States also ratify? The Commission has forced the issue by proposing ratification on the sole legal bases of Articles 113 and 228 EC,[96] thus declaring the European Community alone has competence to ratify the agreement. The Court of Justice has been asked for its opinion under Article 228(6) EC.[97]

The difficulty arises due to the restricted scope of the Community's competence under the commercial policy. Not all measures covered by the ambitious Uruguay Round agreement have previously been dealt with under Community powers. The Court has held that the policy is not limited to traditional trade liberalisation measures,[98] but has never ruled on its expansion to include new areas of the world economy such as services. The need to preserve the proper functioning of the Common Market would suggest that it should be included, by a broad interpretation of the scope of a modern commercial policy.[99] Such a broad approach might include the trade-related aspects of intellectual property and investments. However the exclusive competence of the Community in external commercial policy would sit uneasily with the Member States' competence when trade internal to the EC is involved.[100]

An alternative Community competence to act externally lies in those areas where it is necessary for the attainment of a specific objective for which powers have been granted in the internal system.[101] Thus the power to regulate services would arise from those articles in the Treaty which deal with its internal aspects, and would be dealt with on the same procedural basis. The Community's

[96] Bull. EU 4–1994, point 1.3.61.
[97] Opinion 1/94. Judgment is expected in late 1994.
[98] Opinion 1/78, *International Agreement on Natural Rubber* [1979] ECR 2909.
[99] Mengozzi, 'Trade in Services and Commercial Policy', in Maresceau, *Commercial Policy*, supra n 60, 223–247, 230 *et seq.*
[100] Under Art 36 EC, the Member States may derogate from the principles of free movement of goods to protect industrial and commercial policy. See Govaere, 'Intellectual Property Protection and Commercial Policy', in Maresceau, *Commercial Policy*, 197–222.
[101] Case 22/70 *Commission* v *Council(ERTA)*[1971] ECR 263; Opinion 2/93, *Re ILO Convention No 170* [1993] 3 CMLR 800.

power to negotiate would then depend upon internal developments in the transfer of competence from the Member States to the Community. Problems could arise with regard to intellectual property, and the planned negotiations on environmental matters, both areas where the Member States retain substantial concurrent powers. Any gaps in EC competence would have to be filled on the basis of Article 235 EC, which requires unanimous agreement by the Council members.

The Community and the Member States could jointly ratify the agreement as a 'mixed' agreement, avoiding any difficulties as to competence. Subsequent activities in the WTO might be compromised, if a consensus is resisted by one of the Member States.[102] Although this would be a way to quickly resolve the problem of ratifying the WTO, assuming no national problems of ratification arose, the long-term problem of defining the scope of the Common Commercial Policy would remain.

The issue of ratification has become urgent, as fears are expressed that it will be delayed until next year.[103] The EU would not then be a founder member of the WTO, and might give a reason to others to delay ratification in their turn. The Council has suggested to the Commission that agreement on a Code of Conduct might determine the role of the Community in the WTO.[104] Ratification could then proceed without an opinion of the Court of Justice. However, a judicial declaration of the scope of the Common Commercial Policy would certainly outweigh the 'soft law' value of a code of conduct.

A separate problem was raised by the Parliament, who are insisting on the need for their assent to the agreement before the Council may vote on it.[105] Under Article 228(3) EC, the Parliament must be consulted on agreements, except where they are pure trade agreements. However, they insist that the WTO is an agreement for whose ratification Parliamentary assent is required, under Article 228(2) EC, as it incorporates a stronger dispute resolution system, capable of binding the European Community. The Parliament has

[102] See E. Devuyst, 'The EC's Common Commercial Policy and the Treaty on European Union', (1993) 16 *World Competition* 67, at 77, for the difficulties that can arise in GATT discussions.
[103] Editorial, *Financial Times*, August 11 1994.
[104] *Agence Europe* No. 6312, 10 September 1994.
[105] Parliament resolution on the outcome of the Uruguay Round of the GATT multilateral trade negotiations OJ C 114/27.

already expressed its disquiet about the lack of social and environmental provisions in the agreement. Although it is unlikely to refuse its assent, the final compromise of the Uruguay Round would come under fierce scrutiny.

AN EXTERNAL RELATIONS POLICY?

The Maastricht Treaty significantly expanded the role of the Union in external relations, and yet the present powers of the Union are inadequate, and worse, ill-defined. At Maastricht the Commission proposed a general external relations policy, covering issues of trade, development policy, foreign policy, security and defence. However the Council reacted negatively to this far-reaching suggestion.[106] The Member States are under an obligation to review the CFSP at the 1996 Intergovernmental Conference. It is possible that, with experience of the CFSP, and in light of the difficulties of ratifying the WTO agreement, the proposal may be revived and received with more enthusiasm. Otherwise the Union's potential as a 'world partner' will remain unfulfilled.

III Substantive Community Law

In the year under review, several fundamental principles of Community law have been restructured and re-focused in order to concentrate upon their core elements. The burgeoning caseload of the Luxembourg Courts indicates the practical success of the Single Market and the Union, rather than its failure. However, as the core elements of the Single Market are successfully completed and inconsistencies eradicated, the extremities of Community law have been tested. The Court has noticeably shied away from taking potentially bold steps on the periphery of its existing jurisprudence. Three areas in which there have been significant developments will be considered below; substantive economic law, the judicial protection of the individual and social law. These areas indicate that the conservative trend has not been uniform. Consequently, it is too simplistic to attribute single causes or hypotheses to the variable jurisprudence of the Court in this year. Instead, the

---

[106] See discussion in Maresceau, 'The Concept "Commercial Policy" and the Difficult Road to Maastricht', in Maresceau *Commercial Policy*; and Devuyst (1993) 16 *World Competition* 67.

jurisprudence on principles in the Treaty on European Union may provide an indication of the Court's new approach.

KECK, MENG AND AUDI

The Court of Justice decided three cases in November 1993 which touched upon the existing limits of Community Law. The three judgments were: first, Joined Cases C-267/91 and C/268/91, *Keck and Mithouard*,[107] concerning the free movement of goods; second, Case 2/91, *Meng*,[108] which considered the application of the Community's competition rules to actions of Member States; and lastly Case C-317/91, *Deutsche Renault* v *Audi*,[109] in the field of intellectual property law, as considered under Articles 30 and 36 EEC. The judgments share certain central principles which indicate a re-alignment by the Court from the expansion of Community Law towards a concentration upon the core aspects of the Treaty's rules. The substance of each case is considered briefly below.

In *Keck*, the Court was asked whether the French law prohibiting the re-sale of goods at a price lower than the cost price was compatible with the provisions of the free movement of goods. Keck and Mithouard contended that the prohibition placed them at a competitive disadvantage to those retailers in other Member States, and would hinder trade between Member States. However, the Court ruled that 'contrary to what has previously been decided', national provisions concerning 'certain selling arrangements' do not constitute measures having equivalent effect to quantitative restrictions as prohibited by Article 30. The Court noted the increasing tendency of traders to invoke Article 30 as a means of challenging almost any national rule which limits their commercial freedom.[110] This tendency has its origin in the Court's landmark *Dassonville* formulation of measures having equivalent effect, namely, 'all trading rules enacted by Member States which are capable of hindering, directly or indirectly, actually or potentially,

---

[107] Judgment of 24 November 1993, nyr. See Moore, 'Revisiting the limits of Article 30 EEC', 19 *ELRev*, 195, and Gormley, 'Reasoning Renounced? The Remarkable Judgment in *Keck and Mithouard*' [1994] *EBL Rev* 63.

[108] Judgment of 17 November 1993, nyr. See also the Court's judgments of the same date in C–245/91 *Ohra* and C–185/91 *Reiff*, nyr.

[109] Judgment of 30 November 1993, nyr.

[110] See, for example, the *Sunday Trading* cases (e.g. case C–169/91, *Council of the City of Stoke-on-Trent* v *B & Q plc* [1993] 1 CMLR 426).

intra-Community trade'.[111] In *Keck*, the Court has restricted this previously unlimited formulation by excluding selling arrangements provided that the national provisions apply to all traders in the national territory and that they affect in the same manner the marketing of domestic products and those of other Member States.

In *Meng*, a German regulation prohibited insurance intermediaries from passing to their clients commissions which they receive from the insurance companies. Meng argued that this constituted a State-imposed breach of the Community's competition rules, relying on the operation of Article 85(1) with Articles 3(f) and 5. The Court was asked to consider whether the competition rules could extend to actions of Member States rather than merely to agreements between undertakings. The Court found that national regulations could infringe the competition rules if they required or encouraged the conclusion of agreements restricting competition, reinforced the effects of such agreements or removed the state character of any regulation by delegating enforcement to private parties. However, the Court held that the German prohibition did not fall within these categories and did not therefore breach the competition rules.

In the third case, Audi objected to the use by Renault of the 'Quadra' and 'Espace Quadra' signs in Germany as it had already protection for its 'quattro' sign. Renault submitted that certain generic names should be excluded from monopolisation by trademark law in the interest of the free movement of goods, in this case four-wheeled drive vehicles throughout the Community. The Bundesgerichtshof further asked whether the concept of confusion between marks existed in Community law. The Court held, on a narrow interpretation of the existing caselaw, that Community law was not concerned with the definition of the subject matter of trademarks, but noted the strict standards in German law on the regulation of generic names. Similarly, Member States had exclusive jurisdiction to define the concept of confusion, for which there was no autonomous Community definition.

The judgments are examples of a more restrictive attitude of the Court of Justice.[112] The Court appears to have decided these cases whilst on the back foot. In particular, the Court's formal

---

[111] Case 8/74, *Procureur du Roi* v *Dassonville* [1974] ECR 837 at para 5.

[112] See Reich, 'The "November Revolution" of the European Court of Justice: *Keck, Meng* and *Audi* revisited' (1994) 31 *CMLRev* 459.

interpretation of the Treaties contrasts with its expansive use of the *effet utile* of Community law and allows national law to re-assert its 'sovereignty' in certain areas. However, the reluctance of the Court to expand further Community law also indicates that the central goals of the existing Treaties have been achieved. Whilst the Court has been highly inventive in its treatment of situations which fell outside the anticipation of the founding fathers of the Treaties,[113] on-going legal challenges now seek to advance the Union beyond its textual constitution. The Court's early and extremely generalised formulations have been superseded by the development of Community law. However, the momentum and diversity of that development casts doubt upon the reasoning and legal certainty encapsulated in these judgments. The jurisprudential re-alignment may not therefore be complete prior to the fundamental consideration of the constitution in 1996.

JUDICIAL PROTECTION OF THE INDIVIDUAL

The Court handed down two important judgments in the year under review in the field of the interaction of Community law with national law, and in particular the ability of individuals to claim and fully enforce those rights in national courts.

In the first case, *Dori*,[114] the Giudice Conciliatore di Firenze raised the vexed question of whether directives may have 'horizontal' direct effect, thereby creating rights *and obligations* upon individuals which national courts must protect and enforce.[115] Although the prohibition on the horizontal enforcement of directives was imposed, *obiter dicta*, by the Court of Justice in *Marshall I*,[116] the inability of individuals to rely directly upon the provisions of directives against other individuals in national courts lies at the heart of the inconsistencies and distortions in the judicial protection of the individual.

The Court has minimised these inconsistencies through three devices: first, the expanded concept of vertical direct effect through

---

[113] e.g. environmental protection and consumer protection.

[114] C–91/92 *Paolo Faccini Dori* v *Recreb Srl*, Judgment of 14 July 1994, nyr.

[115] Horizontal direct effect should be contrasted with 'vertical' direct effect, whereby individuals may rely upon clear and precise provisions of directives against the State, or emanations of the State.

[116] Case 152/84 *Marshall I* [1986] ECR 723, at para 48.

a wide interpretation of "State";[117] second, in the case of *Marleasing*,[118] the obligation placed upon national courts to interpret any national law as far as possible in accordance with the wording and purpose of Community directives; and, lastly, the principle of the liability of Member States in damages under certain conditions for failure to implement directives.[119] The Court recognised these principles in order to mitigate the absence of rights as between individuals.

The lacuna which remains between these three principles has been well documented by Members of the Court[120] and academics alike. *Dori* provided the Court with the opportunity to complete the circle of judicial protection of the individual and overrule *Marshall I*. The facts which gave rise to the case were straight-forward.

Ms Dori, an Italian national, had purchased an English language correspondence course whilst at Milan Central Railway Station, away from the language company's place of business. She sought to cancel the course four days later, relying upon Directive 85/577[121] which provides, at Article 5(1), for the renunciation by notice within not less than seven days of such consumer contracts. Unfortunately for Ms Dori, neither the contract nor the Italian Civil Code provided for the renunciation of a consumer contract in this manner. Furthermore, the case arose between the expiry of the period set for transposition of the Directive and the effective date of implementation by the Italian Government.[122]

Despite an Opinion from Advocate General Lenz which provided

---

[117] See Case C–188/89 *Foster* [1990] ECR 1–3313 and Case 31/87 *Beentjes* [1988] ECR 4635.   [118] Case C–106/89, [1990] ECR I–4135.

[119] Joined Cases C–6 & 9/90 *Francovich and Bonifaci* [1991] ECR I–5357, at para 20.

[120] See Advocate General van Gerven's opinion of 26 January 1993, Case C–271/91 *Marshall II* (nyr), at para 12; Advocate General Jacobs' Opinion of 27 January 1994, Case C–316–93 *Vaneetveld* (nyr), at paras 16-35; Judge Schockweiler, 'Effets des directives non-transposées en droit national à l'égard des particuliers', in Díez de Valasco (ed.), *Hacia un nuevo orden internacional y europeo*, Madrid, 1993; van Gerven, 'The Horizontal Effect of Directive Provisions Revisited', Institute of European Public Law, (1993). For a recent contrary assertion see Advocate General Darmon's Opinion in Case C–189/91 *Kirsammer-Hack* [1994] IRLR 185, at para 80.   [121] OJ 1985 L 372/31.

[122] The date for transposition was 23 December 1987; Italy implemented the Directive on 3 March 1992 by Decreto Legislativo No 50 of 15 January 1992 (GURI, ordinary supplement to No. 27 of 3 February 1992, p 24).

for the prospective introduction of horizontal direct effect, the Court of Justice, in a terse and minimalist judgment, did not introduce the principle of horizontal direct effect. It preferred instead to confirm its existing jurisprudence. It relied upon its judgment in *Marshall I*, the nature of directives under Article 189 and the limited power of the Community to enact obligations for individuals with immediate effect only in the form of regulations. Furthermore, it maintained that the principle of the vertical direct effect of directives is based upon *nemo auditor*, thereby seemingly quashing the possibility of future challenges to the horizontal/ vertical divide in direct effect.

The maintenance of the *status quo* will relieve the Member States, initially at least, as seven of them had submitted observations to the Court against the principle of horizontal direct effect. Similarly the Court's limited clarification of the remit of liability under *Francovich*, that liability should be established in accordance with national law, may allow Member States to avoid liability by virtue of their own laws.[123] However, there are implicit suggestions in the judgment that national courts could consider the unimplemented provisions of directives as an element of public policy, which may be enforced 'vertically' and independently of the parties through a *Marleasing* interpretation of national law. This radical and neat solution would remove, if substantiated, the imperfections in the uniformity and efficiency of Community Law. A further implication is that when a *Francovich* remedy is appropriate, i.e. in the absence of direct effect and a *Marleasing* interpretation of national law, the national courts themselves must join the State as co-defendant in order to secure the individual's rights. Such an obligation would increase the Member States' litigious workload and exposure to damages and costs. Two pending cases[124] seeking further clarification of the principle established in *Francovich* will prove critical in determining whether Member States may rue their conservative maintenance of the *status quo*.

The Court has limited the progression of a second line of jurisprudence on the judicial protection of the individual. In the

[123] See L. N. Brown and F. Jacobs, *The Court of Justice of the European Communities*[3], 1989, 137: 'There does not exist within the 12 countries of the Communities a common *corpus* of legal principles governing State liability in tort.'

[124] Case C–48/93 *Factortame III* (OJ 1993 C 94/16) and Case C–46/93 *Brasserie du Pêcheur* (OJ 1993 C92/5).

landmark case *Emmott*[125] the Court of Justice held that prescrip-
tion or limitation periods under national law cannot begin to run
until the directive, which founds directly effective rights, has been
properly implemented. An individual may therefore claim directly
effective and unimplemented Community rights for periods from
the date for transposition of the directive. The principle is based
upon the presumption that an individual does not know his or her
Community law rights until they are implemented into national
law. It logically exposes Member States to extensive financial
liability for unimplemented rights, particularly in fields such as
social security, but is consistent with both the endorsement of *nemo
auditor* and the implicit acceptance that individuals cannot know
their rights until implementation, in the Court's judgment in *Dori*.
Furthermore, the Court of Justice held in *Marshall II* that national
procedures, in that case a maximum limit on financial compensation for discrimination on the grounds of sex, cannot compromise
the full and effective protection of Community rights.[126]

However, in a recent case the Court has distinguished *Emmott*
and interpreted narrowly the requirement for full and effective
protection.[127] In *Steenhorst–Neering* a Dutch law limited payment
of incapacity benefits to not earlier than one year prior to the date
of claim. The Court was asked to consider whether this law was
consistent with Council Directive 79/7 on the equal treatment for
men and women in the field of social security.[128] The Court first
recited its caselaw specifying the conditions under which national
rules of procedure must exist; namely, that they are no less
favourable than those relating to domestic actions and they are not
framed so as to render virtually impossible the exercise of
Community rights.[129] The Court bluntly held that the Dutch rule
satisfied these conditions. Founded upon this assertion, the Court
held that, unlike in *Emmott*, the Dutch law did not affect the right

---

[125] Case C–208/90 [1991] ECR I–4869.

[126] See D. Curtin's casenote on *Marshall II*, (1994) 31 *CMLRev*, 631.

[127] Case C–338/91 *Steenhorst-Neering v Bestuur van de Bedrijfsvereniging voor
Detailhandel, Ambachten en Huisvrouwen* [1994] IRLR 316; and see Advocate
General Gulmann's Opinion of 1 June 1994 in Case C–410/92 *Elsie Rita Johnson* v
Chief Adjudication Officer, pending before the Court.

[128] OJ 1979 L 6/24.

[129] See Case 45/76 *Comet v Produktschap* [1976] ECR 2043 and Case 33/76
Rewe-Zentralfinanz v Landwirtschaftskammer [1976] ECR 1989.

of individuals to rely upon Directive 79/7; it merely imposed a restriction on the retroactive effect of claims for the attainment of sound administration. The Dutch rule of procedure was not therefore contrary to Community law.

At first glance, this judgment is striking in its conservatism. The line drawn by the Court between the inability to bring proceedings and the inability to claim a full and effective remedy is not easy to sustain in the light of the principles underlying cases such as *Emmott*, *Factortame*[130] and *Francovich*. Indeed, the rejection of national restrictions in favour of the complete protection of Community rights lies at the heart of *Marshall II*. However, although, as has been noted, the principle exposed in *Emmott* is in accordance with the underlying tenets of *Dori*, a retreat would appear necessary in the light of the potential interrelationship and joint consequences of *Francovich* and *Emmott*.[131] Without a limit on the liability of, for example, the United Kingdom in damages for breaches of social law dating back until 1972,[132] such exposure would potentially be financially ruinous. The retreat from *Emmott* in *Steenhorst–Neering* may therefore be a necessary prerequisite to the expansion of the principle of State liability in *Francovich*.

It is to be hoped that the apparent conservatism of the Court of Justice in the *Dori* and *Steenhorst–Neering* cases signals a movement away from direct effect towards the liability of Member States in damages and not a retreat by the Court from the full and effective protection of Community rights in national courts, which has contributed so significantly to the practical development of the Union. The issues raised in these cases are likely to be addressed before the English courts following two cases decided by the Court of Justice in the social law field; namely, *Webb v. EMO*[133] and *Commission of the European Communities v. United Kingdom*.[134]

---

[130] Case C–213/89 *R v Secretary of State for Transport, ex parte Factortame* [1990] ECR I–2433.

[131] See further, Carmen Plaza Martin, 'Furthering the Effectiveness of EC Directives', (1994) 43 *ICLQ* 26.

[132] See below on the developments in the social field.

[133] Case C–32/93 *Webb v EMO Air Cargo (UK) Ltd.* [1994] 4 All ER 115.

[134] Cases 382 and 383/92 *Commission of the European Communities v United Kingdom*, judgment of 8 June 1994, *The Times* 27 June 1994, *Financial Times* 14 June 1994.

SOCIAL LAW

The judgment of the Court in *Webb* v *EMO* has settled beyond doubt the rights attributed to pregnant women. Ms Webb was engaged by EMO to cover for a pregnant employee. Upon later discovering that she too was pregnant, Ms Webb was dismissed. She brought a claim for unlawful discrimination on the grounds of her sex before an Industrial Tribunal based upon ss1(1)(a) and 6(2) of the Sex Discrimination Act 1975. The case hinged upon the interpretation of the test for direct discrimination laid down in section 1(1)(a), that the defendant had 'on the ground of her sex treated her less favourably than he . . . would [have treated] a man.' The interpretation of this definition of direct discrimination had also to be considered in the light of the caselaw of the Court of Justice on Directive 76/207 on the implementation of the principle of equal treatment for men and women.[135]

The Court of Appeal held unanimously that EMO would have dismissed a male employee in the nearest comparable situation (a temporary illness)[136] and that the Court of Justice did not intend its formulation in *Dekker*[137] to apply universally. The House of Lords sought a preliminary ruling from the Court of Justice. The Court emphatically and unconditionally held that the dismissal of a female worker on account of pregnancy constitutes direct discrimination on grounds of sex, referring to its previous caselaw and its recent judgment in *Habermann–Beltermann*. Furthermore, there could be 'no question' of comparing the situation of a pregnant woman with that of a man incapacitated for medical or other reasons. As Ms Webb had a contract for an unlimited period, her dismissal constituted unlawful discrimination on the grounds of sex. The clarity of the Court's decision must be welcomed and represents a significant advance in equal treatment.

Despite the clarity of the judgment, Ms Webb is likely to face further hurdles to obtaining her rights on returning to the House of

---

[135] OJ 1976 L 39/40.

[136] See the development of English law through *Turley* v *Alders Stores* [1980] *ICR* 66 and *Hayes* v *Malleable Working Men's Club* [1985] *IRLR* 367.

[137] Case C-177/88 *Dekker* v *VJV Centrum* [1990] ECR I–3841 and see Case 179/88 *Hertz* v *ALDI* [1990] ECR I–3879; a refusal to employ a woman on grounds of pregnancy constituted direct discrimination.

Lords. The Court of Appeal had pointed out, again unanimously, that should these circumstances arise, the Sex Discrimination Act could not be interpreted within the meaning of *Marleasing* to give effect to such a judgment of the Court of Justice. The Court of Justice did not consider this problem. *Webb* v *EMO* was delivered on the same day as *Dori*, clearly indicating that the national court should rely upon *Marleasing* and *Francovich* in the absence of horizontal direct effect. If the House of Lords is not prepared to reformulate the Sex Discrimination Act in order to give effect to the judgment of the Court of Justice, an option beyond its obligation in *Marleasing*,[138] but prefers to rely upon *Duke* v *GEC Reliance Systems*,[139] then the issues of the practical application of *Francovich* and the joinder of the State will become directly relevant to Ms Webb.

The second case of considerable significance in the social field is *Commission of the European Communities* v *United Kingdom*. The United Kingdom was found in breach of its duty to implement two directives, namely those on the safeguarding of employees' rights in the event of transfer of undertakings[140] and on collective redundancies.[141] The Court of Justice found that their implementation in the Transfer of Undertakings (Protection of Employment) Regulations 1981[142] and the Employment Protection Act 1975 was defective.

First, the Court held that the United Kingdom must take all appropriate measures to ensure the fulfilment of employees' rights of information and consultation in the specified circumstances of the directives. The UK Government had argued that as English law did not require the designation of trade unions' or workers' representatives, the directives could not impose such a condition. The Court reformulated this contention; whilst the directives did not compel the recognition or designation of such organisations, the complete absence of a representative would constitute such limited harmonisation that the directives would be deprived of effect. The UK Government was therefore obliged to ensure that national legislation must take appropriate measures to ensure that

---

[138] See for example *Litster* v *Forth Dry Dock and Engineering* [1990] 1 AC 546.
[139] [1988] 1 CMLR 733.　　　[140] Directive 77/187, OJ 1977 L61/26.
[141] Directive 75/129, OJ 1975 L49/29.
[142] SI 1981 No 1974, as amended after the initiation of the proceedings by the Trade Union Reform and Employment Rights Act 1993.

the protection unconditionally guaranteed by the directives was given effect. The Court therefore utilised the principle of full effectiveness of Community law, which had been interpreted so restrictively in *Steenhorst–Neering*. The principle was again at the heart of the second finding that the sanctions provided against employees for failure to respect employees' rights did not constitute a real and effective sanction. The limited sanctions were thus contrary to Community law.

Lastly, the exclusion of undertakings 'not of a commercial venture' in the UK Regulations, a restriction which does not appear in the directive, was found to be an incorrect implementation, and a breach of Community law. It is noteworthy that this same provision had previously been subject to the House of Lords' 'blue pencil' as incompatible with the directive in its *communautaire* judgment in *Litster*, noted above.

The case may illustrate one further point. It has been estimated that the judgment could found a cause of action in damages under *Francovich* for over a million civil servants who lost their jobs following the Government's privatisation programme. However, the United Kingdom signalled almost immediately after the ruling that it would oppose such claims for indemnification.[143] The Court's judgments may therefore provide further fuel for the smouldering fire that is the extent of *Francovich* liability.

DEVELOPING PRINCIPLES OF COMMUNITY LAW

In contrast to the boundaries of existing highly developed principles described above, the Court's approach to the new principles of the TEU may provide unencumbered guidance as to the future development of Community law. Amongst these principles, the concept of citizenship is of particular importance to the Union.[144] Two approaches may be taken to the rights listed in Articles 8 to 8E. This catalogue may constitute either a restatement of existing rights, packaged as those of a Union citizen, or more boldly it may represent an unexhaustive list of rights belonging to a more fundamental principle of citizenship. Two cases have recently been

---

[143] See *Agence Europe* No.6248, June 1994 at p. 10.
[144] See D. O'Keeffe, 'Union Citizenship' in O'Keeffe & Twomey, *supra* n 20, 87.

lodged before the Luxembourg Courts which are likely to indicate the development of citizenship and intrinsically the wider approach of the present Court.

Firstly, the English High Court has referred question to the Court of Justice in *R* v *Secretary of State for the Home Department, ex parte Adams*[145] in order to determine whether the right of free movement granted to Union citizens in Article 8A (1), 'within the territory of the Member States', merely consolidates the existing right to free movement of workers or whether it constitutes a new (more extensive) fundamental right. The case arises from the Home Secretary's exclusion of Gerry Adams, the President of Sinn Fein, from Great Britain, thereby preventing him from addressing Parliamentarians within the House of Commons at the invitation of Tony Benn MP. Secondly, *The Guardian* newspaper has challenged a decision by the Council to deny it access to documents and minutes of the Agriculture and Social Affairs Councils in November 1993 and January 1994.[146] The case raises wider issues of fundamental rights and citizenship, whether access to public documents constitutes either a third generation human right and/or an unenumerated right of Union citizens.

CONCLUSION

The caselaw of the Court of Justice in the year under review has been a mixed blessing. Its judgments in *Keck*, *Meng* and *Audi* in the substantive field and *Dori* and *Steenhorst–Neering* on the relationship of national law to Community law have sought to concentrate upon the existing fundamental tenets of Community law and appear conservative in the extreme. The apparent withdrawal from the progression through law towards an ever closer union may be merely an implicit recognition of the difficulties which the Union has recently faced, and is likely to face in the near future. As such, a period of consolidation can be expected.

However, the boldness of the Court's judgments in *Webb* v *EMO* and *Commission* v *United Kingdom* militate against such a conclusion. As has been indicated, the judicial protection of the individual may be undergoing a realignment towards *Francovich*

---

[145] Judgment of Steyn LJ and Kay J, 29 July 1994, nyr.
[146] See *Agence Europe*, No. 6275, 16 July 1994, 14.

liability, the transition to which necessitates caution. It is to be hoped that the existing fundamental principles of Community law are restructuring, rather than centering upon, core elements. However, it may not be possible to evaluate the full consequences of this caselaw until further cases are decided.

PUBLIC LAW

Jeffery Jowell, Rodney Austin, Helen Reece, and Susan Hall

Introduction

This section begins with a report of another case brought by the well-known and successful prisoner litigant Mark Leech.[1] It is an important (and somewhat neglected) decision, establishing fundamental rights as implied in our common law and employing a test in effect similar to proportionality to determine its scope. Another vexed question in public law is then examined, namely, the extent to which substantive expectations will be protected by the courts. The *Matrix-Securities* case suggests they may well be in appropriate circumstances.[2]

The right to hunt deer may not seem as high on the list of fundamental rights as other rights, but that issue, and the statutory right to ban hunting, is next considered.

In the *Equal Opportunities* case[3], the House of Lords dealt with a number of cases of public law, including bodies susceptible to judicial review, matters of Community law, and locus standi. The susceptibility to judicial review is considered again in connection with the insurance ombudsman.

Finally, we consider how the exercise of perogative powers have been recently reviewed, and the new law in relation to the suspect's right to silence.

I Fundamental Human Rights

PROPORTIONALITY

Leech, an important decision in the Court of Appeal raised again the question whether fundamental human rights are recognised by

---

[1] R v Secretary of State for the Home Department, ex p Leech (No 2) [1994] QB 198; [1993] 4 All ER 539.

[2] *Matrix-Securities Ltd* v *Inland Revenue Commissioners* [1994] 1 All ER 769 HL.

[3] *Equal Opportunities Commission and another* v *Secretary of State for Employment* [1994] 1 All ER 910.

our common law and the extent to which the concept of proportionality plays any part in determining the extent to which such rights may be infringed.

The applicant prisoner applied for judicial review by way of a declaration that rule 33(3) of the Prison Rules 1964 was ultra vires section 47(1) of the Prison Act 1952. Section 47(1) confers power on the Secretary of State to make rules for the 'regulation and management' of prisons and for the 'classification, treatment, employment, discipline and control of persons required to be detained therein'. The material part of the Rule 33(3) provided that a prison governor could read every letter to or from a prisoner and stop any letter that was 'objectionable or of inordinate length'. A further rule, Rule 37A, provided that the governor was not entitled to read or stop correspondence between a prisoner who was party to proceedings in which a writ had been issued and his legal adviser.

The applicant contended that Rule 33(3) enabled the governor to read and stop correspondence with his legal adviser if no legal proceeding were pending, whereas nothing in the 1952 Act authorised interference with the solicitor/client relationship and its attendant privilege. The question before the court was thus whether section 47(1) of the Act by necessary implication authorised the making of rule 33(3).

Steyn LJ, for the Court, answered the question by addressing the following issues of basic principle: first, that a convicted prisoner retains all civil rights which are not taken away expressly or by necessary implication. Second, a prisoner's unimpeded right of access to a solicitor is an inseparable part of the right of access to courts themselves.[4] Lord Wilberforce in *Raymond* v *Honey*[5] called such a right a 'basic right'. Steyn LJ preferred to call it a 'constitutional right'. Third, there is a presumption against statutory interference with vested common law rights and that such a presumption includes a presumption against a statute authorising interference with those rights by subordinate legislation.

The expression of these principles in such categorical terms by such a powerful court[6] emphasises that our law is prepared explicitly to recognise fundamental rights, deriving from our unwritten constitution, even in the absence of assistance from our

---

[4] Cf *Golder* v *UK* (1975) 1 EHRR 524.   [5] [1982] 1 AC 1 at 10.
[6] Neil, Steyn and Rose LJJ.

treaty obligations under the European Convention of Human Rights.[7]

It will be recalled that in the case of *Brind*[8] the House of Lords acknowledged, albeit less emphatically than in *Leech*, the existence of a common law right—in that case the right to free expression. It was held there however that the conferral of wide discretionary power effectively rebutted the presumption in favour of the maintenance of free expression. Their Lordships were not willing in that case to apply the principle of proportionality to determine whether the interference with free expression was 'necessary', in the interest of a 'pressing social need'.[9]

In *Leech* the governing statute did not confer wide discretionary power. The question was therefore whether section 47(1) was broad enough to permit interference with the fundamental right of access to the courts. The test adopted by the Court of Appeal to decide that question was as follows: was there a 'self-evident and pressing need for an unrestricted power to read letters between a prisoner and a solicitor and a power to stop such letters on the ground of prolixity and objectionability'?[10] Elsewhere the test was phrased as requiring 'objective need' for a rule such as Rule 33(3) in the interests of regulation of the prisons;[11] and 'demonstrable need' for an unrestricted power to read and examine letters.[12] It was held that since no objective or pressing need was demonstrated, the rule was ultra vires the statute.

Finally, the Court of Appeal extended its consideration of 'settled principles of our domestic law'[13] to consider also the jurisprudence of the European Court of Justice[14] which, although not directly binding, 'reinforces a conclusion that we have arrived at in the light of the principles of our domestic jurisprudence'.[15]

Leech is an important case. While still leaving open the situation when wide discretionary powers are conferred, it confidently accepts the existence of home-grown domestic rights derived by

---

[7] See e.g. *Derbyshire CC v Times Newspapers Ltd* [1992] QB 770, CA; discussed in (1993) 47 CLP Annual Review, 104 et seq.

[8] *R v Secretary of State for Home Affairs, ex p. Brind* [1991] A.C. 696.

[9] Although the majority (Lords Bridge, Roskill and Templeman) were not willing to exclude proportionality as a test for the future. *Contra* Lords Ackner and Lowry.

[10] [1993] 4 All ER 539 at 550 Steyn LJ.

[11] Ibid at 550–1.   [12] Ibid at 551.   [13] Ibid at 554.

[14] The case referred to was *Campbell v UK* (1993) 15 EHRR 137.

[15] Supra, n 1, at 555.

implication from our unwritten constitution. Perhaps more significantly, it employs the test of proportionality without using the term. Substitutes such as 'pressing' or 'demonstrable' need, however, serve the same ends as proportionality, and indeed are more specific enunciations of its intent. Finally, the Court of Appeal had no qualms about having regard to the European Convention on Human Rights by reference to the case law of the European Court of Human Rights, in order at least to 'reinforce' its conclusion.

SUBSTANTIVE LEGITIMATE EXPECTATIONS

It is clearly established that the actual or potential disappointment of a legitimate expectation gives rise to a right to a fair hearing. But does our law now require the actual substantive expectation to be fulfilled?

This question arose in *Matrix-Securities Ltd* v *Inland Revenue Commissioners*.[16] The applicants were involved in a sophisticated scheme designed to obtain capital allowances of £38 million when only £7.2 million were available. The applicant sent a letter approved by leading counsel to the local inspector of taxes, seeking the Revenue's assurance whether the capital allowances would be available. The inspector wrote back granting the assurances without qualification. The Financial Division of the Revenue then wrote to the applicant effectively revoking the tax clearance given by the inspector.

In the House of Lords it was unanimously held that the scheme was a manifestly impermissible tax avoidance scheme. It was also held that in these circumstances the scheme should have been put to the specialist Financial Division of the Revenue and not to the local inspector, on whose advice therefore the applicant was not entitled to rely. It was also held that in this case there was not full disclosure to the inspector; the applicant did not 'put all his cards face upwards on the table'.[17] In the event, remarks on whether it is an abuse of power for the Revenue to go back on its assurances were strictly obiter. Lord Browne-Wilkinson, with whom Lord Griffiths agreed, had no doubt that disappointing an expectation based on

---

[16] [1994] 1 All ER 769 HL.
[17] *R* v *Board of Inland Revenue, ex p. MFK Underwriting Agencies Ltd* [1990] 1 WLR 1545 at 1569 Bingham LJ.

an assurance would be an abuse of power when it would be unfair to contend for a different tax consequence.[18] Lord Griffiths however raised also the more complex question that has not yet received judicial consideration, namely, under what circumstances may an assurance giving rise to a substantive legitimate expectation be revoked (he was referring here to the assurance of the local tax inspector, assuming it was authorised in an appropriate case, being revoked by the Financial Division)?

In the present case the Financial Division had revoked the inspector's decision before any money had been invested by the public in the scheme. However, if the applicant had, in legitimate reliance on the inpector's clearance, spent money promoting the scheme, 'then it seems to me that fairness demands that the applicant should be reimbursed for this out-of-pocket expense and it could be regarded as an abuse of power for the Revenue to refuse to do so'.

Matrix-Securities, like *Preston* before it, was dismissed on the facts of the applicant's claim. The strong dicta however leave little doubt that in a suitable case the courts would hold that the disppointment of a legitimate expectation of a substantive benefit may amount to an abuse of power. Would such an abuse of power then entitle the applicant to the full benefit of the expectation (in this case the full value of the scheme)? If Lord Griffiths is followed, a half-way house may be the appropriate solution where the representation has sought to be revoked. In such a case the applicant may only be entitled to be reimbursed for out-of-pocket expenses, but not to the full benefits that had previously been promised.

HUNTING AND MORALITY

In August 1993 the Somerset County Council passed a resolution to ban the hunting of deer with hounds on land owned by the Council in the Quantock Hills. The resolution was debated at a full meeting of the Council at which the majority decided in favour of the motion to ban hunting for two principal reasons. First, that it is for every landholder to decide (within the general framework of the

---

[18]   As had been said by Lord Templeman in *Preston* v *IRC* [1985] AC 835 at 864.

law) what activities to permit on his or her land, and second, that
for reasons primarily of moral repugnance the Council did not wish
to allow deer hunting on this piece of their land. The result of the
ban was in effect to make it impossible for the hunt to continue on
the Quantocks and an application for judicial review was made to
challenge the ban.[19]

The single issue of principle running through *Fewings* was
whether the subjective opinion of the majority of the councillors
voting for the resolution, that deer hunting is morally repulsive, is a
consideration which at law the Council was entitled to regard as
relevant. As Laws J pointed out, if that consideration were indeed
relevant, and the ban therefore lawful, it was so more by good luck
than judgement, as the County Solicitor failed to draw the
members' attention to the statutes under which the Council
acquired the relevant land.

Laws J made it clear that public bodies such as local authorities
do not possess unfettered discretion and must justify their every
action by positive law. Where a statute does not by express words
define the purposes for which the powers it confers are to be
exercised, the decision maker is bound to apply the aims of the
statute, since 'no statute can be purposeless'. In this case the
governing statute was the Local Government Act 1972 section
120(1)(b) which authorises local authorities to acquire land which
conduces to 'the benefit, improvement or development of their
area'. Did the authority transgress the limit to their powers
contained in that provision?

Laws J entertained no doubt that there may be circumstances in
which a prohibition on hunting could be said to promote such a
statutory purpose as is contained in section 120. This would be so if
the ban were introduced, for example, to protect rare flora
damaged by the hunt, or to eliminate physical interference with the
enjoyment of others of the amenities offered on the land. These
objectives however are not fuelled by 'the ethical perceptions of the
Councillors about the rights and wrongs of hunting'. That is not to
say that moral or ethical considerations could not be relevant to
some of the Council's functions. The power for example to control
Sunday trading could be said to 'engage a moral element'. In such a

---

[19] *R v Somerset County Council ex p. Fewings and Ors., The Times* 10 February
1994. Transcript C/O 93 February 1994.

case however the moral element in the decision is 'itself part and parcel of the purposes for which the power in question is conferred'; part of the councillors' 'compulsory terms of reference'. In this case however the language of the statute was held not to be wide enough to permit decisions based upon 'free-standing moral perceptions'. The statute was instead about matters that would 'conduce to the better management of the estate'. The ban was therefore outwith the powers of the statute, or, in the words of the moment, *Padfield* illegal rather than *Wednesbury* unreasonable.

Two further points arising in *Fewings* are worthy of attention. Firstly, it should be observed that the language, even in a case of this kind, is of rights and proportionality. Laws J said:

A prohibition on hunting, which manifestly interferes with the *lawful freedom* of those who take part in the sport, could only be justified under the subsection if the Council reasonably concluded that the prohibition was *objectively necessary* as the best means of managing the deer herd, or was otherwise required, on objective grounds, for the preservation or enhancement of the amenity of their area (emphases added).

Later he said that the court will presume against this 'particular encroachment upon personal liberty' unless the empowering statute 'positively requires the authority in question to bring its moral views to bear upon the subject in hand'.

Secondly, it was made clear that the fact that the local authority were an elected body would not influence the court to interpret 'benevolently' the particular decision's confluence with the statute's permissible scope, as may be the approach in the case of an assessment of the reasonableness of the exercise of a discretionary power.

Does this judgment leave any scope for other councils to ban the hunt? It all depends upon the statute under which they acquired the land. If the operative statute is the 1972 Act, then indeed there is some scope, provided that management of the herd, amenity and environmental considerations are the genuine and primary motives of the ban, and that ethical and moral considerations are put aside.

II Judicial Review

EQUAL OPPORTUNITIES

In the widely reported and celebrated decision of *Equal Opportunities Commission and another* v *Secretary of State for Employment*[20] the House of Lords held that the differential treatment of part-time and full-time employees under the Employment Protection (Consolidation) Act 1978 constituted unlawful sexual discrimination, contrary to Article 119 of the EEC Treaty.

The Employment Protection (Consolidation) Act 1978 provides protection from unfair dismissal, compensation for unfair dismissal and the right to statutory redundancy pay. These provisions come into operation only when the employee has worked continuously for a qualifying period. The qualifying period is two years for employees who have worked for at least sixteen hours per week but five years for employees who have worked between eight and sixteen hours per week. Workers employed for less than eight hours per week are afforded no protection. The Equal Opportunities Commission argued that this amounted to indirect discrimination because the vast majority (87%) of part-time employees are women. The Secretary of State accepted this but responded that the provisions were objectively justified. The House of Lords was unanimous in rejecting this defence, with Lord Jauncey (who dissented on the preliminary question of whether the Equal Opportunities Commission had locus standi) making it clear that he would have reached the same decision as the other Lords on the substantive issue.

The substantive decision will have wide ramifications in Employment Law, but it is the House of Lords' decisions on the procedural questions which are of direct relevance to Public Law and which will arguably have the greatest long-term impact. Indeed it has been suggested that this aspect of the case is symptomatic of a constitutional and political shift in favour of a national judiciary which has been empowered by European Community law.[21]

The first question to be determined was, was there a decision susceptible to judicial review? Under Order 53, Rule 1 of the Rules

[20] [1994] 1 All ER 910.
[21] See Malcolm Ross, 'The British EOC Case—A Model of Compliance?' [1994] *Int. J. Comp. Labour Law and Indus. Relns.* 139.

of the Supreme Court Act, an application for mandamus, prohibition or certiorari[22] may be made by way of an application for judicial review. In addition, an application for a declaration or an injunction may be granted in judicial review if the Court considers that it would be just and convenient for them to be granted by way of judicial review, having regard to the nature of the matters in respect of which relief may be granted by way of an order of mandamus, prohibition or certiorari. The relevant issue to which these provisions give rise is whether a declaration can be granted despite the unavailability of the prerogative orders.

In order to side-step this issue, the Chief Executive of the Equal Opportunities Commission attempted to elicit a 'decision' from the Secretary of State, by writing to him to ask whether he would be prepared to introduce legislation to remove the allegedly discriminatory provisions in the Act. The Secretary of State wrote back, expressing his belief that the provisions were justified by the need to strike a fair balance between the interests of employees and employers. The Commission seized on this reply as the reviewable 'decision' which would then have been liable to have been quashed, by way of an order of certiorari. The House of Lords held, however, that the letter merely expressed the Secretary of State's view and that the real object of the Commission's attack was not the letter but the legislation itself. Once the legislation has been recognised as the subject of the application for judicial review, it becomes difficult to see how any of the prerogative orders could be granted. The court cannot quash primary legislation, nor can it order the Secretary of State to repeal it. This was in effect the Secretary of State's argument. He contended that a declaration could be granted in proceedings for judicial review only if one of the prerogative orders was available, and that in this case, since there was no 'decision' in relation to which an order could be granted, a declaration was not permissible.

The House of Lords rejected this restriction on its powers. Although the House agreed that none of the prerogative orders was available, it interpreted Order 53 as allowing declarations to be made even in those cases in which no order could be granted; Lord Browne-Wilkinson in particular took the view that since *O'Reilly* v

---

[22] Or an injunction restraining a person from acting in any office in which he is not entitled to act.

Mackman[23] any declaration as to public rights which could
formerly have been obtained in civil proceedings in the High Court
could also be obtained in judicial review proceedings.[24] The House
of Lords regarded the *Factortame* series of cases[25] as a precedent
for the availability of judicial review in these circumstances. The
application in *Factortame* was brought by the owners of fishing
vessels denied registration under Part II of the Merchant Shipping
Act 1988, which sought to prevent Spanish fishing vessels from
registering and thereby from obtaining a licence to fish. In
Factortame, according to the House of Lords in the *Equal
Opportunities* case, the courts had judicially reviewed the Merchant
Shipping Act and had granted interim relief to the applicants
through the suspension of the operation of the 1988 Act, on the
basis that the Act was contrary to Community law.[26] The *Equal
Opportunities* case does however represent an extension rather
than an application of *Factortame*. In the latter, an injunction was
obtained against the Crown to prevent the Secretary of State from
implementing the registration system. In the *Equal Opportunities*
case, no remedy whatsoever was granted. The House of Lords
simply declared that the Employment Protection (Consolidation)
Act 1978 was incompatible with European Community Law.

INTERNATIONAL TREATY OBLIGATIONS

The question may be asked whether the Divisional Court had
jurisdiction to declare the United Kingdom in breach of obligations
under Community law? The decision that judicial review was
available to declare that United Kingdom legislation was incompatible with Community law led directly to the question of

---

[23] [1982] 3 All ER 1124 (the dicta in *IRC* v *National Federation of Self-
Employed and Small Businesses Ltd* [1981] 2 All ER 93 notwithstanding).

[24] Otherwise, he argued, the requirement in *O' Reilly* that public law cases be
brought by way of judicial review would have had the effect of preventing plaintiffs
from obtaining declarations. See also Richard Gordon, 'Judicial Review and Equal
Opportunities' (1994) *Public Law* 217, arguing that this was not the effect of
O'Reilly.

[25] *Factortame Ltd* v *Secretary of State for Transport* [1989] 2 All ER 692;
Factortame Ltd v *Secretary of State for Transport (No 2) Case C–213/89* [1991] 1
All ER 70; *R* v *Secretary of State for Transport, ex p Factortame Ltd Case C–221/89*
[1991] 3 All ER 769.

[26] In particular Article 7, which prohibits discrimination on grounds of
nationality, and Article 58, which provides for freedom of establishment.

whether it was also available to declare that the United Kingdom was in breach of its obligations under Community law. The House of Lords did not answer this question, on the basis that the former declaration was sufficient for the purposes of the Equal Opportunities Commission and was all that was consistent with precedent. The difficult issue of whether the Equal Opportunities Commission was attempting to enforce the international treaty obligations of the United Kingdom was thereby avoided.

The importance of a declaration that the United Kingdom was in breach of its international obligations, in this case by having failed to repeal discriminatory laws in breach of Article 119 of the EEC Treaty, was of course that such a declaration would have facilitated actions against the United Kingdom for compensation. These could have been brought, on the principles set out in the *Francovich* case,[27] by workers deprived of the opportunity to obtain compensation from their private employers because they had not worked for the period necessary to qualify for protection under the Employment Protection (Consolidation) Act. The House of Lords felt that such actions should be dealt with as and when they arose since the issues in compensation actions would not be identical to those raised in the case before them. This seems correct. For example, under *Francovich*, it was held to be a defence for the Member State to show that at the date of enacting the relevant legislation it had an honest and reasonable belief that it was implementing the relevant directive properly, a point not in issue in the *Equal Opportunities* case.

It remains to be seen how the courts will respond to such claims for compensation. One issue which will have to be resolved is that of limitation periods. In *Emmott* v *Minister for Social Welfare and another*[28] the Court of Justice observed that time could not begin to run against an individual until a directive had been properly transposed. The question will be therefore whether time runs from the date of the House of Lords judgment or, more plausibly, only from formal revocation of the discriminatory legislation. The spectre of *Francovich* claims is in any case likely to result in little difference between these dates.

The House of Lords unequivocally held that the Divisional Court, the only English forum in which the issues could have been

[27] *Francovich* v *Italian State* C–6/90 and *Bonifaci* v *Italian State* C–9/90 [1991] ECR I–5357.   [28] Case C–208/90 [1991] ECR I–4269.

adjudicated, was an appropriate forum. The only alternative would have been proceedings before the European Court instituted by the European Commission against the United Kingdom under Article 169 of the EEC Treaty. The House of Lords took the view that this alternative did not detract from the suitability of the Divisional Court and that the Divisional Court might well be more appropriate since the Court of Justice of the European Communities had held that it was for the national court to determine whether there was objective justification for indirectly discriminatory pay practice.[29] This aspect of the decision is to be welcomed if only because judicial review can, in appropriate cases, be obtained in a matter of days whereas it can be years before a case reaches the European Court.

At a late stage Mrs Day, a cleaner who had been made redundant after having been employed by Hertfordshire Area Health Authority for eleven hours per week for just under five years, was joined as a second applicant. The House of Lords held that Mrs Day's claim was essentially a private law claim for redundancy pay which would prevail over the allegedly discriminatory provisions of the Act.[30] Industrial tribunals had been entrusted with the task of deciding this type of case and they were fully competent to deal with them.

LOCUS STANDI

The House of Lords' decision on Mrs Day's claim made it all the more crucial to determine the more interesting question of whether the Equal Opportunities Commission itself had locus standi, especially since the public impact of the decision of an industrial

[29] *Bilka-Kaufhaus GmbH* v *Weber von Hartz* Case 170/84 [1986] ECR 1607 at 1628.

[30] Redundancy pay is 'pay' within the meaning of Article 119 of the Treaty (see Case C–262/88 *Barber* v *Guardian Royal Exchange Assurance Group* [1990] 2 All ER 660) and so, if the provisions of the Employment Protection (Consolidation) Act 1978 were not objectively justified, Mrs Day would have a good claim against her employers under Article 119, which would prevail over the discriminatory provisions by virtue of s 2(1) of the European Communities Act 1972. Moreover she would have an additional action under the equal pay directive and the equal treatment directive which were directly applicable against her employers because her employers were an emanation of the state (see Case 152/84 *Marshall* v *Southampton and South West Hampshire Area Health Authority (Teaching)* [1986] 2 All ER 584).

tribunal in relation to an individual complainant is clearly much less significant than a ruling under Order 53.[31]

Overturning the Court of Appeal's judgment on this point, the House of Lords held that the Equal Opportunities Commission did have sufficient interest in the matter to which the action related. Citing the Commission's duties under section 53(1) of the Sex Discrimination Act 1975 to work towards the elimination of discrimination and to promote equality of opportunity between men and women generally, duties which in his view the Commission was fulfilling in bringing the action, Lord Keith said:

In my opinion it would be a very retrograde step now to hold that the EOC has no locus standi to agitate in judicial review proceedings questions related to sex discrimination which are of public importance and affect a large section of the population.[32]

It remains to be seen whether this decision will lead to a more relaxed approach to locus standi, opening the door to pressure groups and trade unions seeking to establish a point of public interest, or whether its impact will be confined to the special statutory duties of the Equal Opportunities Commission.[33] Certainly the decision should extend as far as local authorities given the wide ambit of section 222 of the Local Government Act 1972.[34]

In *R v HM Inspectorate of Pollution and Ministry of Agriculture, Fisheries and Food, ex p. Greenpeace Ltd*,[35] Otton J held that Greenpeace had locus standi to challenge the Inspectorate's decision to vary authorisations for the discharge of radioactive

---

[31] See Simon Deakin, 'Part Time Employment, Qualifying Thresholds and Economic Justification' [1994] *Indus. LJ* 151.

[32] *Equal Opportunities Commission* v *Secretary of State for Employment* [1994] 1 All ER 919.

[33] It has been predicted that the Lords' decision will henceforth expose government actions to more challenges by pressure groups seeking to pursue test cases under European Union law. The Joint Council for Welfare of Immigrants has already received leave to review the Home Office's failure to provide an appeals procedure against deportation of European Union nationals on the ground that this is contrary to European law (see Jonathan McLeod, 'Part-timers' win bolsters EU law', *Law Society Gazette*, 9th March 1994). Locus standi for pressure groups is obviously particularly important in immigration cases, in which the individual applicant will often be unable to bring the case.

[34] This provides that a local authority may appear in any legal proceedings and, in the case of civil proceedings, may institute them in their own name, where they consider it expedient for the promotion or protection of the inhabitants of their area.

[35] [1994] Env LR 76.

waste from Sellafield, warning however that his decision did not
imply that interest groups would automatically be afforded
standing as this would depend on the individual circumstances of
each case. The circumstances which led Otton J to grant standing in
this case were as follows: Greenpeace had a number of supporters
in the Sellafield area who were inevitably personally concerned
about the potential discharge of nuclear waste; the issues raised
were serious[36] and Greenpeace was the most appropriate and
effective applicant, since it had the resources and expertise to
mount a relevant and well-argued challenge. Otton J further
regarded the nature of relief sought, in this case certiorari, relevant
to the decision on standing. These two cases seem to imply that the
courts are now prepared to relax the more restrictive approach to
standing adopted in the *Rose Theatre* case.[37] However the *Equal
Opportunities* case by no means gives the green light to each and
every pressure group seeking to challenge a public decision. The
reasoning of the majority of the Lords was based very much upon
the EOC's statutory duties and public law role. It is one thing to
allow a challenge to Parliament by a publicly funded statutory body
set up by Parliament, and quite another to allow them to ad hoc
oppositional pressure groups.

'PRIVATE' OMBUDSMEN

Previous Public Law surveys in the *Annual Review* have examined
the susceptibility to judicial review of bodies apparently exercising
'public functions' whose powers are not derived from statute. On
the whole the courts have been reluctant to extend judicial review
to these bodies, particularly when their jurisdiction derives from
contract between them and their members. This trend has
continued in the most recent case.

In *R v Insurance Ombudsman Bureau ex parte Aegon Life
Assurance Ltd*[38] it was held that decisions of the Insurance
Ombudsman were not subject to judicial review. The powers of the
Insurance Ombudsman were held to be derived from contracts

---

[36] It is interesting to note that the 'public importance' of the action also played a
part in determining the question of standing in the *Equal Opportunities* case.
[37] See *R v Secretary of State for the Environment ex p Rose Theatre Trust Co*
[1990] 1 QB 504; Konrad Schiemann, 'Locus Standi' [1990] *Public Law* 342.
[38] *The Times*, 7 February 1994, Div Ct.

between the Insurance Ombudsman Bureau (IOB) and member companies. The IOB was established in 1981 by the insurance industry at its own expense. Although in some ways an offshoot of another 'self- regulated' industry, its existence has some statutory underpinning. It is recognised by the Life Assurance Unit Trust Regulatory Organisation (LAUTRO), which is itself established under the Financial Services Act 1986,[39] as performing functions under that Act[40].

The court focused in *Aegon* upon the derivation of the powers of the IOB. Since the government played no part in its formation, and neither funds nor monitors its activities, and since its relationship with its members is strictly contractual, judicial review was held not to lie. This follows the approach of other recent cases.[41] Nor would the court exercise its powers under Order 53 rule 9[42] to enable proceedings to continue as if begun by writ, as private law remedies were available to be pursued.

The Divisional Court in *Aegon* has continued to shy away from the test of 'public function' suggested as a basis for judicial review in *Datafin*, and has preferred to look at the derivation of power, even in this case where the body concerned has a clear statutory underpinning. Apart from the merits of such a test, it will lead to inconsistency: some of the new commercial ombudsmen are creatures of statute (e.g. The Building Societies' Ombudsman),[43] while others (such as the Banking Ombudsman) are not. Should member banks and building societies who wish to question identical decisions made by their respective Ombudsman have to continue to do so by different procedures?

III The Royal Prerogative

The decision in *R v Secretary of State for the Home Department, Ex parte Bentley*[44] appears to have widened even further the scope for judicial review of the royal prerogative. The prerogative of

---

[39] s.10.
[40] Under Schedule 2. About 6% of the IOB's work concerns cases under the Financial Services Act.
[41] *R v Jockey Club ex p. Aga Khan* [1993] 1 WLR 909; *R v Lloyds of London ex p. Briggs* [1993] 1 Lloyds Reports 176.
[42] *R v Panel on Takeovers & Mergers ex p. Datafin* [1987] QB 815.
[43] Created under the Building Societies Act 1986.
[44] [1993] 4 All ER 442.

mercy, expressly reserved by Lord Roskill in *Council of Civil Service Unions* v *Minister for the Civil Service*[45], (the GCHQ Case), as one of the unreviewable prerogative powers, 'because their nature and subject matter are such as not to be amenable to the judicial process',[46] is now subject to judicial review on grounds of error of law. The decision deserves attention not least for the fact that it enabled the Home Secretary publicly to acknowledge that his predecessor in 1953 had erred in not commuting the death sentence passed on Derek Bentley upon his conviction of conspiracy to murder, thus bringing to an end the extraordinary campaign waged by Bentley's sister for nearly 40 years.

The decision is notable in a number of ways. First, leave to apply for judicial review was granted by a two-judge Divisional Court and the decision on the application for review was given by a three-judge Divisional Court, including two Lords Justice of Appeal.

Secondly, the applicant, the sister of the late Derek Bentley, had alleged that the Home Secretary had erred in law in not granting a posthumous free pardon. But it became clear during the hearing that the Home Secretary had acted lawfully and properly in declining to grant a free pardon, since free pardons were not granted unless the Home Secretary was satisfied of the moral and technical innocence of the convicted person. What the Home Secretary failed to do was to consider what other appropriate forms of pardon there might be in all the circumstances of the case. By not considering the possibility of a conditional posthumous pardon the Home Secretary had failed to recognise that the prerogative of mercy was capable of being exercised in many different circumstances and over a wide range, and had failed to consider the form of pardon which might be appropriate.

Thirdly, no order of the court was made against the Home Secretary and no grounds were given for declining to make an order, other than that in the circumstances their Lordships did 'not think it would be right to make any formal order nor [was] this an appropriate case for the grant of a declaration'.[47] Instead, their Lordships 'would invite the Home Secretary to look at the matter again and to examine whether it would be just to exercise the prerogative of mercy in such a way as to give full recognition to the

---

[45] [1985] AC 374.   [46] Ibid at 418.
[47] [1993] 4 All ER 442, 455 Watkins LJ.

now generally accepted view that this young man should have been reprieved.'[48]

However interesting these features of the *Bentley* decision may be, it is the substantive ruling on the jurisdiction of the court to entertain an application for judicial review of the direct exercise of the prerogative of mercy by one of Her Majesty's Secretaries of State that is of the greatest import. The apparently explicit exclusion of such a jurisdiction by Lord Roskill in the *GCHQ Case* seemed a formidable obstacle to the exercise of judicial review in this case, yet closer examination of the passage in Lord Roskill's speech revealed that the reason for his exclusion of the prerogative of mercy was 'because [its] nature and subject matter are such as not to be amenable to the judicial process'.[49] Lord Roskill did not elaborate on the causes of this unsuitability for judicial treatment, other than to assert that 'the Courts are not the place wherein to determine whether a treaty should be concluded or the armed forces disposed in a particular manner or Parliament dissolved on one date rather than another.'[50] But Lord Diplock did expand on this issue and in particular distinguished legal issues from government policy, holding that the latter does

not normally involve questions to which, if disputed, the judicial process is adapted to provide the right answer, by which I mean that the kind of evidence that is admissible under judicial procedures and the way in which it has to be adduced tend to exclude from the attention of the court competing policy considerations which, if the executive discretion is to be wisely exercised, need to be weighed against one another, a balancing exercise which judges by their upbringing and experience are ill-qualified to perform.[51]

It is clear from these passages that while disputes over matters of policy arising for decision under the prerogative will not be reviewable, errors in determining questions of law may be. Lord Roskill's exclusion of the prerogative of mercy from judicial review must therefore, in the view of the Divisional Court in *Bentley*, be interpreted as qualified by that distinction between policy and law. Similarly the *Hanratty*[52] and *de Freitas*[53] cases, which held the

---

[48] Ibid.   [49] [1984] 3 All ER 935, 956 d–e, Lord Roskill.
[50] Ibid.   [51] [1984] 3 All ER 935, 951 Lord Diplock.
[52] *Hanratty* v *Butler* [1971] CA Transcript 171.
[53] *de Freitas* v *Benny* [1976] AC 239 PC.

prerogative of mercy to be unreviewable, were not only decided before the *GCHQ Case* but did not concern judicial review of error of law. As if that were not enough to free the Divisional Court from the shackles of authority, 'Lord Roskill's passing reference to the prerogative of mercy in the *CCSU* case was obiter.'[54] Having thus demolished or side-stepped the obstacles of precedent, the Divisional Court then proceeded to justify the jurisdiction to review the prerogative of mercy by reference to its role in the criminal justice system, accepting counsel's arguments that the prerogative was exercised by the Home Secretary on behalf of us all, that it was an important feature of our criminal justice system, and a constitutional safeguard against mistakes.

It would be surprising and regrettable in our developed state of public law were the decision of the Home Secretary to be immune from legal challenge irrespective of the gravity of the legal errors which infected such a decision.[55]

Having thus justified its intervention the court proceeded to identify the error of law upon which it could exercise the review jurisdiction, namely the failure of the Home Secretary to consider that which he had not been asked to consider, a posthumous conditional pardon.

The applicant had sought a declaration that the Home Secretary had erred in law in declining to recommend a posthumous *free* pardon for Bentley and mandamus requiring the Home Secretary to reconsider his decision not to recommend a posthumous *free* pardon for Bentley.[56] The applicant had sought from the Home Secretary a posthumous *free* pardon for Bentley, not a conditional pardon. The Divisional Court explicitly held that the Home Secretary had *not* erred in law in reaching his decision not to recommend a *free* pardon.[57] It is therefore difficult to understand the Court's finding that the Home Secretary erred in law by misconceiving the scope of the prerogative of mercy and thus failed to consider the grant of a conditional pardon, when he had not been asked to do so by the applicant, a fact made abundantly clear by the application for review itself.

As an historical observation, it should be pointed out that if the Home Secretary did err in law as to the existence and extent of the

---

[54] [1993] 4 All ER 442, 453.   [55] Ibid at 452.   [56] Ibid 444.
[57] Ibid 453, 454 and 455.

prerogative of mercy his decision would have been reviewable long before the *GCHQ Case*. Even under the absolutism of the Stuart monarchy, the Courts claimed the jurisdiction to determine the existence and extent of the King's prerogative,[58] though not to question the exercise of the power once recognised. This jurisdiction was acknowledged in the *GCHQ Case*[59] and has not been challenged this century since *A-G v De Keyser's Royal Hotel Ltd.*[60]

The decision in *Bentley* is thus unremarkable in so far as it claims a jurisdiction to review an error in law as to the scope of the prerogative of mercy. In so far as it suggests that on the merits of the case, the Home Secretary ought to have granted a posthumous conditional pardon because his predecessor was wrong not to have granted Bentley a reprieve and commuted his sentence from hanging to imprisonment, the decision is an unjustifiable encroachment on the substantive exercise of a discretionary power by a government minister who is a democratically elected member of the legislature to which he is accountable for the exercise of this power. In so far as the decision indicates a jurisdiction to review errors of law in the exercise of the hitherto highly discretionary prerogative power to pardon convicted criminals it is a welcome extension of the Courts' power to review the prerogative where its exercise affects individual citizens, comparable to the extension of the review power to the issue of passports in *R v Secretary of State for Foreign and Commonwealth Affairs, Ex parte Everett*.[61] It is also indicative that the Courts appear to be willing to continue with their extension of the powers of review of the prerogative in appropriate cases. The initial trickle of legal challenges to the prerogative may well become a flood. Government may eventually decide to abandon use of the prerogative in favour of statutory provisions replacing the prerogative powers.

IV The Suspect's Right to Silence

The Home Secretary may ultimately look back ruefully on his efforts to close off that alleged bolt-hole of the guilty professional

---

[58] E.g. *Case of Proclamations* (1611) 12 Co. Rep.74; *The Case of Ship-Money, R v Hampden* (1637) 3 St. Tr. 825; *The Case of the King's Prerogative in Saltpetre* (1607) 12 Co. Rep. 12.

[59] *CCSU v Minister for Civil Service* [1984] 3 All ER 935, 942, 948.

[60] [1920] AC 508.   [61] [1989] 1 All ER 655.

criminal, the suspect's right to silence. The Criminal Justice and Public Order Bill 1993, Clauses 27–31 inclusive embody the Home Secretary's proposals.[62] The Bill met considerable criticism from a wide spectrum of commentators and opponents, both from within Parliament and from outside interest and pressure groups, while the judiciary showed hostility to some of its provisions. The passage of these provisions of the Bill has been difficult and the Home Secretary withdrew one major clause after it became apparent that it was unacceptable to the Lord Chief Justice, whose views found strong support in the House of Lords.

But these difficulties pale into insignificance in comparison with the looming European challenge to the Home Secretary's measures. The European Court of Human Rights has already held that the compulsory production of documents under customs and exchange control legislation was contrary to Article 6 of the European Convention, because it infringed the privilege against self-incrimination.[63] The European Commission on Human Rights has ruled admissible a complaint that UK legislation compelling persons under investigation in fraud cases to answer questions is contrary to Article 6.[64] A complaint that the modification of the suspect's right to silence in Northern Ireland infringes Article 6 is pending before the European Commission of Human Rights. It is possible that the proposed modification to the right to silence would be held to infringe Article 6 of the European Convention on Human Rights, either on the basis of the privilege against self-incrimination or the presumption of innocence or both.[65]

The previous history of attempts to abolish or modify the suspect's right to silence should also have given the Home Secretary pause for thought and encouraged a degree of caution. The

---

[62] The Bill's clauses concerning the right to silence, as amended on Report and as expected to be passed into law, are significantly different from the original Clauses 27–31 and are now numbered 34–39. This review will consider both the original and the amended versions of these clauses. It is expected that the Bill will receive the Royal assent in early November 1994.

[63] Case of *Funke* v *France* [1993] 1 CMLR 897.

[64] Case of *Saunders* v *UK*, ECHR Application 19187/91, judgment delivered 10 May 1994, not yet reported.

[65] Article 6.1 guarantees everyone a fair trial of any criminal charge against him, and *Funke* implied the right not to be compelled to incriminate oneself, i.e. the right to silence. Article 6.2 expressly guarantees to the accused the presumption of innocence until proven guilty according to law.

Criminal Law Revision Committee in 1972[66] recommended modifying the right by permitting inferences to be drawn by a court or jury from an accused's failure to mention, during police questioning, an exculpatory fact which he later relies upon at trial. But this proposal was so poorly justified by the Committee, and so universally criticised by the legal professional bodies that its implementation was never seriously put forward by the government of the day. The Royal Commission on Criminal Procedure in 1981[67] expressly rejected the Criminal Law Revision Committee's proposal, as did the subsequent Royal Commission on Criminal Justice in 1993.[68] The only other body to support modifying the right to silence was the Home Office Working Group on the Right to Silence in 1989.[69]

The provisions of the Criminal Justice and Public Order Bill not only implement the Criminal Law Revision Committee's proposals, but go significantly further. Clause 27 originally provided that if an accused person, either when being questioned before being charged or cautioned, or on being charged with or officially informed that he might be prosecuted for an offence, fails to mention a fact which he subsequently relies upon in his defence, the court or jury as the case may be, may draw such inferences from that failure as may appear proper, in determining whether there is a case to answer, whether to commit the accused to trial or whether the accused is guilty of the offence charged.

This provision as it first appeared would have applied to police questioning of a person even before he was a suspect or in police custody. At this stage, the person being questioned may not even know that he is under suspicion, may not know what offence is suspected, probably would not know what information or evidence the police have, and in many cases would not at that stage have access to legal advice. The accused would therefore not know what facts were relevant to his defence, and in some cases, only a legal

---

[66] *Criminal Law Revision Committee, 11th Report, Evidence (General)*, Cmnd 4991, (1972), pp 8–34.

[67] *Report of the Royal Commission on Criminal Procedure*, Cmnd 8092, (1981), Ch.4 esp pp 80–91.

[68] *Report of the Royal Commission on Criminal Justice*, Cm. 2263 (1993), Ch. 4, pp 49–56.

[69] *Report of the Home Office Working Group on the Right to Silence*, (Home Office, 1989).

adviser would be able to determine what facts might be pertinent to a defence based on a point of law.

These problems may be alleviated by the provision that the fact must be one which in the circumstances existing at the time the accused could reasonably have been expected to mention when questioned, charged or informed, but this is far from certain. Nor will all of these problems be solved by the amended version of the clause (34), which restricts its application to questioning under caution. Even if the suspect has been cautioned and thus knows he is under suspicion for an offence, he may still not know the precise offence or the evidence held by the police as he may not necessarily be in police custody and may very well not have access to legal advice.

Furthermore, such questioning will in many cases not take place in a police station, because the original clause 27 referred to questioning 'at any time before he was charged with an offence . . . by a police constable trying to discover whether or by whom the offence had been committed', while the amended version (34) merely inserts the words 'under caution' without amending the remainder of the clause. A caution must be administered once the police have grounds to suspect a person of an offence;[70] this can and often will be elsewhere than at a police station and before arrest, which requires reasonable grounds for suspicion of an arrestable offence.

Therefore, not only will the safeguards of the Police and Criminal Evidence Act 1984 and the Codes of Practice not be operative at this stage, but in particular the questioning under caution will not be tape-recorded. As a consequence there may be disputes, incapable of satisfactory and reliable resolution, over precisely what was said by the suspect, i.e. whether or not he did mention the fact which is subsequently relied upon in his defence. The old problem of police 'verbals' will once again bedevil criminal justice, this time in a negative form. Given the progress made since 1984 in reducing and largely eliminating this problem, it seems a highly retrograde step to create the opportunity for its re-emergence. This is especially so in light of the empirical evidence before the Royal Commission on Criminal Justice which demonstrated that, contrary

---

[70] *Code of Practice for the Detention, Treatment and Questioning of Persons by Police Officers*; Code C, para. 10.1.

to anecdotal folklore, there is no evidence which shows conclusively that silence is used by professional criminals; and there is no evidence to support the belief that silence in the police station leads to improved chances of an acquittal.

The most the Royal Commission was able to concede was that 'it is possible that some defendants who are silent and who are now acquitted might rightly or wrongly be convicted if the prosecution and the judge were permitted to suggest to the jury that silence can amount to supporting evidence of guilt.'[71]

Even where suspects are questioned in police custody and are thus protected by the safeguards of the Police and Criminal Evidence Act 1984 and of the Codes of Practice, including access to legal advice, difficulties remain. First, vulnerable suspects may be improperly pressured into making damaging but unreliable admissions for fear of adverse inferences being taken at their subsequent trial. Second, both at this stage and at the later stage of being charged with or officially informed that he may be prosecuted for an offence, it is highly unlikely that the suspect will be fully informed as to the evidence held by the police. Nor will the precise offence for which the suspect may eventually be prosecuted necessarily be known, especially given the role of the Crown Prosecution Service in making prosecution decisions. It is thus difficult for the suspect to make an informed and rational decision as to what facts are likely to be relevant to his future defence and unreasonable to expect him to make disclosure of those facts at that time. Thirdly, as both empirical research[72] and at least one major miscarriage of justice[73] have shown, the quality of legal advice available to suspects in police custody is questionable, so that a suspect's legal adviser may be unaware of what facts are legally pertinent to a possible defence or which facts may be prejudicial to the accused. The combined weight of these criticisms leads to the conclusion that even if there were no objections in principle, Clause 27 (now 34) would be an unworkable and dangerous change in the criminal justice system.

[71] Cm 2263, Ch.4, para.19, pp 53–54.

[72] *The Role of Legal Representatives at the Police Station*, Royal Commission on Criminal Justice Research Study No.3, (HMSO, 1992).

[73] *R v Paris, Miller and Abdullahi* (1993) 97 Cr App Rep 99; this was the case of 'the Cardiff Three' in which convictions were set aside on the basis that confessions had been obtained by oppressive questioning. A solicitor was present throughout the questioning and raised no objection.

At the more general level of principle, the ability to take adverse inferences of guilt from an accused's silence is contrary to the basic principles of English criminal justice that the accused is innocent until proven guilty, that the burden of proving the guilt of the accused beyond reasonable doubt rests on the prosecution and that no person should be compelled to incriminate himself. To make such a fundamental attack on the foundations of the criminal justice system could only be justified by cogent and compelling evidence that adherence to those principles resulted in substantial numbers of criminals going unpunished for serious crimes. As the Royal Commission found,[74] no such evidence exists. These principled objections apply equally to Clauses 28, 29 and 30, (now 35, 36 & 37) which will now be considered.

Clause 28 (now substantially amended and re-numbered 35) attracted the immediate hostility of the judges and the Lord Chief Justice in particular because it required the judge to call upon the accused to be sworn and to give testimony, and if the accused refused to be sworn or to give evidence, permitted the court or jury to draw such inferences from the refusal as appear proper. This was objected to by Lord Taylor on the grounds that the accused would appear to the jury to be defying the judge and flouting the authority of the court, which would unduly prejudice the accused in the eyes of the jury. But his Lordship was not opposed to judges having discretionary power to comment upon the accused's failure to testify or to answer questions. This is what the clause now achieves, permitting a court or jury, in determining whether the accused is guilty of the offence charged, to take such inferences as appear proper from the failure of the accused to give evidence or his refusal to answer questions.

While the amended clause does not expressly directly compel the accused to testify or answer questions and refusal is not therefore contempt of court,[75] the potentially adverse effect of the inference being taken from the accused's refusal is likely to be a highly persuasive factor in discouraging the exercise of the right of silence. Indirectly, the accused is compelled to testify for fear of the adverse inference. Since the European Court of Human Rights in *Funke*[76] and the Commission in *Saunders*[77] have recognised and upheld the

---

[74] See n 72, supra.
[75] Clause 35(4), Criminal Justice and Public Order Bill, Report Stage, July 1994.
[76] Supra, n 63. [77] Supra, n 64.

right not to be compelled to incriminate oneself and Article 6(2) of the Convention expressly guarantees the presumption of innocence until proven guilty, it is highly questionable whether the provisions of even the amended clauses 34 and 35 would survive scrutiny if a case were to be taken to Strasbourg.

Clauses 29 and 30 (now re-numbered 36 and 37) permit adverse inferences to be drawn from the failure of an arrested accused to account for any object, substance or mark on his person, in or on his clothing or otherwise in his possession or in the place where he was when arrested, or his failure to account for his presence in any place, where the constable reasonably believes that the object, substance or mark, or the accused's presence, is attributable to the accused's participation in the commission of the offence. In other words, if a suspect fails at the time of his arrest to explain suspicious physical evidence or his presence in a particular location, the jury may infer guilt. These provisions are subject to the objections raised against Clause 27 (34). At this stage the accused may have no idea of the significance or otherwise of such physical evidence or his presence in a particular place and in the stressful circumstances of an arrest, may well be unable to account for such matters. It is unreasonable to permit an adverse inference to be made from this understandable failure at that stage. Furthermore, at this point the constable need only have reasonable belief, which is a far lower standard than proof beyond reasonable doubt and may be based on inadmissible evidence. Thus a court or jury will be entitled to take an adverse inference of guilt from the accused's inability or refusal to explain some piece of physical evidence, the probative value of which may depend on other information which may not itself be admissible.

Neither Clause 29 or 30 (now 36 or 37) require that the allegedly suspicious mark, substance, object or presence be proven by admissible evidence at trial to be of probative value in relation to the accused's guilt. It is simply his failure at the time of his arrest to account for what the constable at that time believes to be attributable to the accused's guilt from which at trial the court or jury may draw an adverse inference. This in effect reverses the burden of proof and throws on to the accused the burden of establishing that the constable's belief, however reasonable it may have been at the time of the arrest, was in fact ill-founded and that therefore no adverse inference can logically be taken from the accused's failure at that time to account for a substance, mark, object or presence which was in fact not attributable to the accused's guilt.

Furthermore, whereas Clause 27 (now 34) requires reliance at trial upon a fact not mentioned during police questioning, neither Clause 29 or 30 (now 36 or 37) requires any such reliance, merely the failure or refusal to account for the mark, object, substance or presence at the time of the arrest. It is also not entirely clear what constitutes a 'failure' to account for a substance, mark, object or presence—does an explanation which the constable does not believe or is unable to verify constitute a 'failure'? If the arrested person is unable to account for the substance, etc, because he genuinely does not know how it came to be on his clothing or person, and says so in terms, does that constitute a 'failure' to account for the substance, etc?

It will clearly be seen from the foregoing that the clauses of the Criminal Justice and Public Order Bill authorising the taking of adverse inferences from the exercise of the right to silence, even as amended, are poorly drafted, inadequately thought through and likely to lead to a significant number of cases being taken to appeal on points of interpretation and application. Even if these provisions did not offend against principle, which, as is argued above, they manifestly and unjustifiably do, they would be objectionable on the grounds that they are ill-considered. The cynical explanation for such poor legislation is that it is intended to prove the Home Secretary's law and order credentials and to restore the morale and political fortunes of the party in government. To ignore the recommendations of two successive Royal Commissions and to legislate against long-standing and considered opposition from the legal professions and most academic commentators is a recipe for bad law-making. Not only may our courts become embroiled in controversial disputes over the application of the 'right to silence' provisions of the Criminal Justice and Public Order Bill, when it is enacted, but almost inevitably, the United Kingdom will suffer yet again the very public international ignominy of being held to be in breach of its obligations under the European Convention of Human Rights. This is too high a price to pay for short-lived political gain.

INDEX